FRANK STITT'S
BOTTEGA FAVORITA

FRANK STITT'S
BOTTEGA
FAVORITA

FRANK STITT

WITH KATHERINE COBBS

FOREWORD BY WARREN ST. JOHN
PHOTOGRAPHY BY CHRISTOPHER HIRSHEIMER

ARTISAN
NEW YORK

ALSO BY FRANK STITT

Frank Stitt's Southern Table

Frontispiece: Ravioli with Pumkin and Sage Butter (page 114)
Page vi: Bottega Salad Niçoise (page 127)

First published by Artisan in January 2009
A Division of Workman Publishing Company, Inc.
225 Varick Street
New York, NY 10014-4381
www.artisanbooks.com

Library of Congress Cataloging-in-Publication Data
Stitt, Frank, 1954-
Frank Stitt's Bottega Favorita / by Frank Stitt ; photographs by Christopher Hirsheimer.
p. cm.
Includes bibliographical references and index.
ISBN 978-1-57965-302-6 (alk. paper)
1. Cookery, Italian. 2. Bottega Restaurant and Café. I. Title. II. Title: Bottega Favorita.

TX723.S7984 2008
641.5945—dc22   200801536

Designed by Jan Derevjanik

Printed in Singapore
First printing, November 2008

1 3 5 7 9 10 8 6 4 2

To my mother, Marie

CONTENTS

Foreword BY WARREN ST. JOHN

Even though it was twenty years ago, I have vivid memories of the opening of Frank Stitt's restaurant Bottega in my hometown of Birmingham. The event qualified at the time as a full-scale happening. In a city where restaurant debuts were more commonly announced by large tasseled banners on the roadside "Grand Opening, All You Can Eat!" the appearance of a high-end Italian restaurant stood out. The location of this new restaurant—in the Bottega Favorita building, a grand Beaux Arts palazzo with a green terra cotta tiled roof, Corinthian columns, and a façade of gaping stone arches—implied the chef was going for broke. The building's prominent location meant he would succeed or fail in full view.

And then there was Frank Stitt himself. To people my age—I was eighteen at the time—his restaurant Highlands Bar & Grill was chiefly known as the place our parents went to eat without the kids. Or else, it was where you were taken after graduation or some other spectacular achievement, an honor doled out to local youth the way a quarter glass of wine was given to a teenager at a holiday meal. But the young people of Birmingham were indoctrinated enough in civic pride to know that Frank Stitt was a local hero, even if the reason for this acclaim remained at a mysterious remove. He had made his name at Highlands by incorporating the staples of traditional southern fare into haute cuisine and, in the process, had elevated the status of our common food as well as—and this is what we particularly appreciated—the common folk who ate it. But what sort of Italian restaurant would Frank Stitt create? What, after all, did southern food have in common with the cuisine of Italy?

I had a more than passing interest in the outcome of whatever Frank planned at the time, because the opening of Bottega coincided with my developing a bizarre but by no means rare disorder. The symptoms included a sudden interest in opera (where once Led Zeppelin had sufficed) a fascination with high-end, if temperamental, machinery (including cars, bicycles, motorcycles), a compulsion to drink espresso instead of American coffee (and to order said espresso loudly, so that everyone around knew of my coffee expertise), a sudden snobbery regarding the color, texture, and flavor of tomatoes (again, loudly proclaimed) and, perhaps above all, a craven obsession with thin-crust pizza cooked in a wood-burning oven. ("Light on the cheese, burned on the edges, and with extra basil. Per favore.")

The diagnosis was clear: acute Italophilia. It would get worse. I enrolled in Italian classes in college, started dating an Italian girl, and planned a backpack tour of Italy for that very summer. I bought a Pavoni espresso machine that cost a significant portion of my net worth. I drove around Birmingham—and this really says it all—in a Fiat.

As soon as Bottega opened, I went there with friends for dinner. We couldn't afford the white-tablecloth dining room of the formal restaurant, so we made plans to eat in the café next door. We walked in, and then I saw it: Frank Stitt's new restaurant had a proper wood-burning oven.

I camped out at Bottega Café. It was a deeply validating experience, and one I stood to learn from. The place was run by someone who seemed to share my obsession with things Italian, but who was also pulling it off with élan, and without any of the insufferability I had cultivated myself. I ate pizza there, drank espresso by the bucket, downed arugula by the bushel, and became the restaurant's youngest regular. And yet despite all my time at Bottega, I never actually met Frank Stitt. He remained a far-away enabler who had no idea how his culinary vision was affecting the psyche (and bank account) of the teenager out front.

My Italophilia peaked after a summer working at the Guggenheim Museum in Venice, and another summer in Rome and Tuscany. I started drinking American coffee. I wrecked the Fiat. I fell for and married an American. But to this day, though I live in New York, I remain a regular at Frank Stitt's Birmingham restaurants. I've developed a routine for reentry to the town where I grew up that goes like this: I fly from LaGuardia to Birmingham frequently on Friday evenings in order to catch a football game on Saturday. I pick up my rental car and drive straight to Bottega or Highlands, depending on my mood. Twice I've even called from the tarmac to beg the management of Highlands not to send the oyster shucker home—I was on my way, I said, and needed a fix. The request was taken in stride and honored. I got the sense it wasn't the first time a far-flung Frank Stitt junkie had called in with a case of the shakes.

Eventually, I met the man himself—not at one of his restaurants, the farmers' market on Finley Avenue, or any other regular haunt, but in a cavernous convention hall in Atlanta, at a book fair for Southern writers. We were both there to promote our first books, and we connected over the shared excitement and anxiety of first-time authors. We made another connection: Frank was originally from Cullman, a town about 60 miles north of Birmingham, where my father had grown up and where I spent much of my childhood. Our grandfathers, we figured out, had been friends.

Frank and I have since followed their example, and during that time I've come to realize a few things about him that might help put the pages before you in context. The first is that to understand Frank, it's useful to know a thing or two about Cullman. When you hear that Frank Stitt—the renowned southern chef—was raised in a small town in Alabama, you're likely to get the wrong idea. The phrase "small-town Alabama" likely invokes an image of pokiness and languor, of rocking chairs on front porches shaded by big oak trees. There's nothing languorous about Cullman, a town settled in the late 1800s by a German refugee, who then recruited over 100,000 displaced countrymen to join him. Together they created a serious, austere community that has more the temperament of a Bavarian farming village than it does the lazy charm of southern towns like Savannah, Oxford, or Selma. Cullman County is dry to this day (even the city's annual Oktoberfest celebration is alcohol-free). People there get up early, and they work. When it gets hot, they

just wake up earlier. This is the atmosphere in which Frank Stitt grew up. He once confided that his grandfather and father—both good Cullmanites—thought that working less than fourteen hours a day amounted to slacking off. Pokey, they knew, didn't cut it in Cullman.

Frank's career shows a lot of evidence of his Cullman upbringing. As a young man, he sought his culinary education in kitchens in California and Europe with a sense of duty and urgency. Those qualities characterize his restaurants to this day and have a lot to do, I believe, with how they have maintained their pulse and freshness over their remarkable life spans. Bottega and Highlands are high-energy experiences. The waitstaff and the bartenders flit by—they don't saunter. The menus change by the day or week, not the season, to reflect the freshest foods available. Because of that freshness, the dishes themselves crackle with flavor. In this environment, patrons get excited; the bars at Bottega and Highlands buzz on weeknights in Birmingham, when few other venues in town draw a crowd. More than anything else, the signature quality of Frank's restaurants and dishes is this vitality.

When it comes to Bottega specifically, it's worth keeping something else mind: Alabama and Italy have a lot more in common than you might think. They both have sun and heat that in the summer gives way to nourishing afternoon thunderstorms. They have fecund soil. Not coincidentally, in both Italy and Alabama, a perfect vine-ripened tomato—bursting with the earthy sweetness of summertime—is held in near holy reverence. Southerners, like Italians, like to cook with fire, a wood-burning oven being a kind of barbecue pit with a lid. Alabama has a coastline on a warm body of water that generously gives up a bounty of fish and shellfish; here and in Italy, a fresh catch can reach a table in hours, without the need for flash-freezing, cargo jets, or any other modern methods of transportation that leech flavor from fresh food second by precious second. And more broadly, Southerners, like Italians, enjoy in their

LEFT: *At Bottega—from the outside looking in;* **RIGHT:** *Frank Stitt with his wife, Pardis*

food a certain primal simplicity that respects ingredients for what they are more than what they might be. There's a shared respect for the natural rightness of things, and the common food—the food of the people—is eaten by all, regardless of their social status or worldliness.

I asked Frank once about this connection between Southern and Italian food. The image, he said, of an Italian farmer tasting a grape in a vineyard had always reminded him of something he'd seen countless times in Alabama: a country farmer in a place like Chilton County leaning against the opened gate of his pickup truck, pulling out his pocketknife, and carving a slice from a peach he'd grown himself. The images might seem archetypal, but if you've spent time in the country, you'll know they are real.

When I myself was young, I spent weekends and summers working in my father's absurdly oversized vegetable garden at our cattle farm in Cullman. My job was to bust the earth with a front-tined gas-powered tiller that bounced and bucked and vibrated with a violence that left my hands and forearms buzzing for days after I'd put the tiller back in the barn. The work could be miserable, but eventually, the rich, cinnamon-colored soil of north Alabama rewarded us with squash, beans, sweet corn, tomatoes, asparagus, cucumbers, and watermelons of extraordinary intensity. The popcorn we grew produced white puffs the size of cotton balls, and the sweet corn was good enough to eat raw on the cob, just plucked from the stalk. My father and grandfather would oversee the harvest, directing me to pick the produce when they sensed the time was right. Both carried pocketknives for the exact sort of field testing Frank had described, and I'm fairly certain my father was not the only Alabamian whose gardening tray contained a shaker of salt for the purpose.

It's sometimes hard for Birminghamians to separate Frank Stitt the chef from Frank Stitt the cultural force, our town's bulwark against the great creeping sameness that has overrun regional identity in America. When you sit down for a meal at Bottega as a local, you sometimes have to fight through your gratitude to actually taste the food. That's unfair to the food. Likewise, people who come from farther away to eat at Bottega or who are experiencing Frank's vision for the first time through these pages may have to consciously think past his reputation as "the southern chef" to fully appreciate the dishes before them. There's no doubt that Frank's decision to come back to Birmingham, rather than follow the well-trod path of staying in one of the big culinary centers, has benefited the city and region, and given rise to a vital food culture and many other excellent restaurants opened by his protégés. And there is no question that Frank Stitt has been at the vanguard of mining the flavorful seam of southern folk food to surprising and exciting ends, and for an audience that reaches far beyond the region itself. But you can overthink food and get distracted by our natural impulse to categorize.

Instead, I encourage you to approach these pages the way Frank, and all the best Italian chefs, approach their food: with a sense of obligation to the bare ingredients themselves. Local zucchini blossoms, grouper hauled in by a trawler captain down the road, or the eight "very fresh organic eggs" Frank suggests for his farm egg tapenade don't have to be prepared by the town savior or a celebrated chef to be enjoyed. Likewise, when Frank describes the "transparent love that goes into the cooking of a broth," it doesn't matter, as he writes, whether that soup is prepared in Nonna's kitchen in Italy or Grandma's farmhouse in Alabama—so long as care is given to the aromatics, the scrap of cured pork or neck bones, shanks, and ribs that go into the pot. If you keep this in mind, you'll not only enjoy some excellent meals, but you'll also be working in the mode of the chef himself. Do this and you'd be well served to apply Frank's advice from the end of his broth recipe to all your other dishes too: Make extra.

Chef Stitt with David Wright of Wright Dairy, whose natural unhomogenized milk is the next best thing to bringing a cow to Bottega

Introduction

The words "Bottega Favorita" are chiseled into the limestone facade of a solid, elegant Palladian-style building on Highland Avenue in Birmingham, Alabama. It was built in the mid-1920s by the Tutwiler family to house Gus Mayer, the South's finest department store of the day, and designed by the same architects who built the New York Public Library. ("Bottega" is Italian for an artisan's workshop where one's craft is displayed and offered for sale.) When I first noticed this monumental building overlooking the cut through Red Mountain, its former glory had dimmed and a consignment shop in the space was slowly going out of business.

I passed this building almost daily on my way to work at Highlands Bar and Grill just three blocks away, and I'd dream of creating a patio front with a wall of tall banksia roses that would lead into the high-ceilinged dining room. I could transform the dark walnut-paneled dressing rooms and gorgeous antique jewelry cases into waiters' stations and prepare my take on the regional flavors and traditions of Italy. And so it became Bottega Italian Restaurant in 1988. My dream of sharing my love of the seafood risottos of the Veneto, the charcoal grilled steaks and wood oven–roasted pork of Tuscany, the veal and rabbit braises from the Piedmont, the simple grilled fish and seafood stews of Naples, the exotic couscous from Sicily, and the lush and hearty pastas found in Roman trattorias came to fruition.

Cooking from an Italian point of view is a little like going back to a more ancient style of cooking—elemental in its purity and simplicity, primal, where an unadorned slice of rosy prosciutto is savored with a meltingly tender ripe purple fig.

Lawrence Durrell, the author whose writing inspired me to first visit the Mediterranean, captures the essence of this sense of ancient simple flavors. In *Prospero's Cell* (1945) he writes: "The whole Mediterranean . . . seems to rise in the sour, pungent taste of these black olives between the teeth. A taste older than meat, older than wine. A taste as old as cold water."

Bottega has a multifaceted personality. The slightly dressy main dining room is balanced by the slightly raucous café, the other half of the building, with its Pompeii red walls, huge brick wood-fired oven, long bar, and communal table, open from 11:00 A.M. to 11:00 P.M.—it is hard not to feel festive here. The café's patio is *the* destination for an aperitivo on a pretty day or evening. People come here to meet, mingle, see and be seen, and the incredible food and drinks don't hurt.

Bustling, packed, filled with the young and the restless as well as our hard-core regulars, the energy of the café revitalizes. The pizzas, salads, pastas, and simple wood-oven roasts keep them coming back.

Bottega's main dining room is a bit more refined and the menu is slightly more ambitious—grilled squid on polenta squares, roast lobster with basil and bread crumbs, veal scaloppini with asparagus and sweet peas, ravioli with crawfish. The spirit is the same as that of the café, and our Southern ingredients and soul combine to create a restaurant where guests return time and time again.

Like Highlands, Bottega has become an institution in Birmingham, a culture devoted to the best in Italian traditions enriched with the finest ingredients and served with a sense of graciousness, respect, and humor. Here are the stories, the recipes, and the philosophies of Bottega, my Italian table.

Buon appetito!

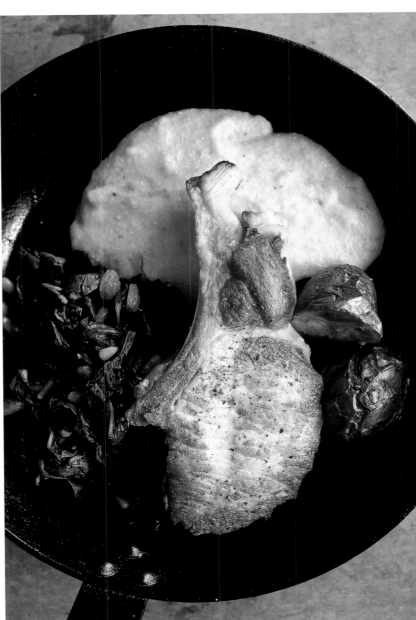

Roast Pork with Venetian Spinach and Tomato Chutney Aïoli (page 165)

The Italian Café

Bottega's Limoncello

Cellotini

Sparkling Limoncello

Harry's Bar

Bellini

Mixing It Up Bottega-Style

Classic Negroni

Dry Vodka Negroni

Mirtillo (Blueberry) Martini

Tegatini

Lemonade

Strawberry Fields

Grappa and Moonshine

Pink Magnolia

Southside

the italian café

In Italy, a café is like a public salon. Mornings start with a coffee, sipped at the bar, and a chat with the owner and other patrons. Afternoon is the time for a pick-me-up espresso, and the early evening for an *aperitivo* to toast the end of the workday—maybe a glass of bubbly prosecco, a Campari-soda, a dry vermouth, or a Bellini. By this time, the long bar is stocked with snacks like olives, almonds, and crispy chips—salty nibbles that are a perfect match for *aperitivi*.

ABOVE: *A café in Turin, Italy;* OPPOSITE: *An aromatic and refreshing Moscato*

BOTTEGA'S LIMONCELLO
Makes about 2 quarts

Our bartenders have perfected the blending and steeping of a few humble ingredients to create this age-old Italian elixir. Limoncello, made by steeping citrus zest in alcohol to extract the aromatic and flavorful oils in the citrus peel, can be chilled and sipped straight as an aperitif or blended into cocktails like our Sparkling Limoncello and Cellotini.

Grated zest of 20 lemons
Grated zest of 2 oranges
1 bottle (750 ml) 190-proof clear grain alcohol
6 ounces Grey Goose orange vodka
4 cups Simple Syrup (page 251)

Combine the citrus zests, grain alcohol, and vodka in a large glass jar. Cover and set the jar in a cool, dark place for 7 to 10 days to infuse the alcohol with the flavorful citrus oils.

Strain the alcohol into a large glass jar. Mix in the simple syrup, stirring to combine. Store the limoncello tightly sealed in the refrigerator, where it will keep for weeks.

CELLOTINI
Makes 1 cocktail

For Bottega's signature cocktail, I brighten our house-made limoncello with fresh sour mix or lemonade and serve it martini-style.

1 ounce Bottega's Limoncello (opposite)
1 ounce lemon or citron vodka, such as Grey Goose, Ketel One, or Absolut
½ ounce sour mix (see Note) or Lemonade (page 14)
Twist of lemon peel

Fill a cocktail shaker half full with ice cubes. Add the limoncello, vodka, and sour mix or lemonade and muddle vigorously with a long spoon for 10 to 15 seconds. Strain into a chilled martini glass and garnish with the lemon twist.

NOTE: To make sour mix, blend equal amounts of fresh lemon and lime juices together, then add an equal measure of Simple Syrup (page 249). Sour mix keeps in the refrigerator for 3 to 5 days.

SPARKLING LIMONCELLO
Makes 1 cocktail

Bottega's bartenders lighten up limoncello with a splash of bubbly white wine for this great predinner cocktail.

1 ounce Bottega's Limoncello
4 to 5 ounces prosecco

Pour the limoncello into a champagne flute and top off with the prosecco.

VARIATION: For a sweeter cocktail, substitute Moscato d'Asti, Italian dessert wine, for the prosecco.

OPPOSITE: *(left to right) Bottega's Limoncello, Sparkling Limoncello, Cellotini*

ABOVE: *(left) Upstairs at Harry's Bar, Venice;* **OPPOSITE:** *A Bellini at Harry's Bar*

harry's bar

I hope our Bottega guests feel a certain sense of anticipation and excitement upon entering our doors as they head for the bar and an aperitif and a warm sincere welcome. A little plate of chips and a few olives are set before them while cocktails are carefully prepared and wine is poured. The aroma of citrus being squeezed to order piques the senses. The vigorous shaking or muddling of a well-iced cocktail provides subtle entertainment. There's a playfulness—a wink from a bartender, a bit of humor—a manner that the Ciprianis have perfected at their quintessential Harry's Bar.

To my mind's eye, Harry's Bar in Venice is a paradigm for all bars. Bartenders blend drinks with style and skill, juicing blood oranges for cocktails and blending the most alluring pale pink Bellinis. Even the simplest carafe of prosecco is served in Venetian cut crystal, gracefully presented by a movie-star-handsome waiter.

As a restaurateur, I marvel at the philosophy of service at Harry's Bar. A pasta order is served at table in a gratin dish—clearly enough for two. It is spooned onto your plate by a waiter who later implores you to "have seconds"—who can refuse?!

BELLINI

Makes 1 cocktail

I had the good fortune some years ago to spend a morning in the kitchen at Harry's Bar. Then I peeked into a room behind the bar and saw a boy seated with a strainer set over a bucket between his legs. He was squeezing fresh, ripe peaches. Back then bellinis were served only when aromatic white peaches were in season. In the fall, grapes are substituted and the cocktail becomes a Tinzano.

1½ ounces chilled peach juice (see Note)
4 ounces prosecco

Fill a champagne flute with the chilled peach juice. Top off with the prosecco, and serve.

NOTE: To make fresh peach juice, use your hands to squeeze 10 to 12 ripe, juicy peaches (preferably white peaches) into a strainer set over a bowl. Taste the juice and add up to 2 tablespoons sugar or the juice of ½ lemon to suit your taste.

MIXING IT UP BOTTEGA-STYLE

A well-stocked bar is not unlike a well-stocked pantry. It gives you the flexibility to be creative and allows you to make your guests' preferred cocktails. This list includes all the spirits required to make the cocktails in this chapter. Start with a few basics, listed here with our personal preferences, then build your inventory to suit your needs.

Angostura bitters (Peychaud)
Bourbon (Maker's Mark)
Brandy (Courvoisier)
Campari
Cointreau
Gin (Bombay, Hendrick's)
Moscato (Marcarini, La Spinetta)
Prosecco (Nino Franco, Bisol)
Vermouth, sweet and dry (Martini & Rossi, Cinzano)
Vodka (Grey Goose, Ketel One, Absolut)
Mixers: club soda, lemonade, cranberry juice, apple juice
Simple syrup
Freshly squeezed citrus juices

The fresh (or marinated or pickled) ingredients we keep on hand at the bar include the following:

Olives stuffed with Gorgonzola
(requested by some for martinis)

Caper berries

Brandied cherries (for Manhattans)

Marinated olives

Fruits macerated in grappa

Pickled onions

Citrus wedges and twists of peel

Pickled okra (for Bloody Marys)

CLASSIC NEGRONI

Makes 1 cocktail

In the 1920s, Gasparé Campari invented a cocktail of sweet vermouth, soda, and Campari—his own trademarked alcoholic blend of sixty-plus bitter herbs and aromatics. It was so popular with American patrons that it became known as an Americano. Legend has it that a few years later an Italian count named Camillo Negroni asked a Florentine bartender to substitute a splash of gin for the soda in his Americano, and, with that, the Negroni was born.

1 ounce Campari
1 ounce gin
1 ounce sweet vermouth
Twist of orange peel

Fill an old-fashioned glass with ice. Add all ingredients except the orange peel. Give a stir. Garnish with the orange twist.

MIRTILLO (BLUEBERRY) MARTINI

Makes 1 cocktail

With all the antioxidant and beneficial properties of blueberries, you could call this a healthy cocktail. Moscato d'Asti is a light, slightly effervescent, aromatic white wine from the muscat grape produced near the town of Asti in Italy's Piedmont region. It has a jasmine-meets-orange-blossom scent and is one of the world's most refreshingly delightful white wines. The amethyst hue of this sparkling cocktail always impresses.

2 ounces blueberry vodka, such as Stolichnaya Blueberi
1 ounce Lemonade (page 14)
1 ounce Moscato d'Asti
3 frozen blueberries for garnish (optional)

Fill a cocktail shaker halfway with ice cubes. Pour in the vodka and lemonade and muddle vigorously—think churn—for 10 to 15 seconds. Add the Moscato and strain into a chilled martini glass. Garnish with the frozen blueberries, if desired.

DRY VODKA NEGRONI

Makes 1 cocktail

In today's cocktail era, vodka reigns supreme, and in our updated Negroni, it replaces the usual gin. The combination of bitters and Campari makes this a cocktail to drink in small, not copious, amounts.

2 ounces Grey Goose, Ketel One, or Absolut vodka
½ ounce dry vermouth
½ ounce Campari
3 dashes Angostura bitters
1 ounce club soda
Twist of orange peel

Fill a cocktail shaker halfway with ice. Add the vodka, vermouth, Campari, and bitters, cover, and give it a good shake. Uncover and add the soda, then strain into a cocktail glass. Garnish with the orange twist.

TEGATINI

Makes 1 cocktail

Not long after Bottega opened, Wayne Russell (known by his Italian nickname, Russelli) came up with this strong and refreshing concoction. Campari and the similar but less potent Aperol belong to the family of Italian elixirs known as "bitters," believed to have restorative properties. Their secret formulas include spices, herbs, barks, and other botanicals, combined almost like a perfume to cure whatever ails you. For a lighter refresher, combine equal parts Campari, fresh orange juice, and soda and serve with an orange twist.

3 ounces Bombay gin
¾ ounce Aperol or Campari
Twist of lemon peel

Fill a cocktail shaker halfway with ice cubes, add the gin and Aperol or Campari, and muddle with a long spoon. Strain into a chilled martini glass and garnish with the lemon twist.

LEMONADE

Makes about 1 quart

Served on its own over ice or blended into many of our cocktails, such as the Mirtillo Martini (page 13) or Cellotini (page 8), homemade lemonade can't be beat. A Southern habit is to combine half lemonade and half iced tea for a summer refresher.

    4 cups spring water
    ¾ cup sugar
    1 tablespoon honey
    ¼ vanilla bean, split
    Juice of 4 lemons

In a large saucepan, combine the water, sugar, honey, and vanilla bean and bring to a simmer, stirring to dissolve the sugar. Remove the pan from the heat and let cool.

Stir in the lemon juice until thoroughly combined, then transfer to a pitcher and chill thoroughly. Lemonade will keep for 1 week in the refrigerator.

GRAPPA AND MOONSHINE Grappa (Italian "firewater") is made from the solid residue—skins, pulp, and pits—left behind after pressing grapes for wine. This distilled spirit has a Deep South bootleg cousin in moonshine. Bootleggers in dry counties throughout the South have long produced crude whiskey from corn mash (derived from the distillation of corn), which was rarely aged for long. They had more thirst for its immediate effects than for a sophisticated whiskey, which calls for patient aging.

But the best of these spirits are oak-barrel-aged Kentucky corn whiskey and grappa made from the sweet, aromatic grapes of the Veneto, which are left with more of their pulp and juice and so result in finer products. Many farmers in both the South and Italy enjoy having a little of their own firewater stashed at home for medicinal purposes, if not for its intoxicating properties.

STRAWBERRY FIELDS

Makes 1 cocktail • Pictured on page 15

Seasonality is just as important with cocktails as it is with food. In this Bottega creation, we have the flavor of spring in a martini glass, to be made only when aromatic strawberries are at their sweet prime.

    2½ ounces strawberry-infused vodka (see Note)
    1½ ounces Lemonade (opposite)
    A strawberry half

Pour the vodka and lemonade into a cocktail shaker half filled with ice. Shake and strain into a chilled martini glass. Garnish with the strawberry.

NOTE: To make strawberry-infused vodka, combine a bottle (750 ml) of vodka with 4 pounds stemmed ripe strawberries and let sit in a cool, dark place for 2 weeks. Strain and sweeten with Simple Syrup (page 251), if desired. You can use the same technique to infuse vodka with other fruits.

PINK MAGNOLIA

Makes 1 cocktail

This cocktail is based on an old-fashioned nonalcoholic fruit punch sipped by Southern ladies on porches during the heat of summer. Patrick Kemmesat, our café manager, retooled it with a shot of gin. The result is a fragrant pink drink, garnished with a handful of raspberries.

    1½ ounces gin, preferably Tanqueray 10
    1½ ounces cranberry juice
    1½ ounces apple juice or cider
    Lime wedge
    5 to 7 raspberries

Combine the gin, cranberry juice, and apple juice or cider in an ice-filled cocktail shaker. Shake well and strain into a chilled martini glass. Garnish with the lime wedge and raspberries.

SOUTHSIDE

Makes 1 cocktail

The house cocktail of New York's 21 Club, this has quite a following at the Bottega bar as well. Think of it as a gin mojito. "Rolling" a drink means to gently pour it from the shaker into a glass in order to mix it.

2 lime wedges
1 ounce Simple Syrup (page 251)
¾ ounce fresh lime juice
2 mint sprigs
2 ounces gin
Splash of club soda

Squeeze the lime wedges into a cocktail shaker and drop them into the shaker. Add the simple syrup and mint. Muddle with a long spoon to bruise the mint and extract some of the oils from the lime peel. Add the gin and enough ice to fill the shaker halfway. Cover and shake. Add a big splash of soda, roll into a highball glass, and serve.

ROOM-TEMPERATURE OR CHILLED

Marinated Olives

Fennel and Parmigiano

Vegetables à la Grecque

Charred Onion Dip

Sardines with Skordalia and Arugula

Day-Boat Fish with Caper Berries and Olive Oil

Antipasto for Two

Grandfather Stitt's Hors d'Oeuvres

Prosciutto di Parma

Beef Carpaccio

Tuna Carpaccio

STUFFED, ROLLED, OR BAKED

Grilled Mozzarella Wrapped in a Lemon Leaf

Farm Eggs with Tapenade

Figs and Prosciutto

Roasted Peppers Stuffed with Goat Cheese

Mapping Italian Cheeses

Baked Feta with Focaccia

Parmigiano-Reggiano

Parmesan Soufflés

CROSTINI AND BRUSCHETTA

Roasted Beet Crostini

Tomato Tapenade Crostini

Crostini

Cauliflower Crostini

Scallop Crostini with Tapenade and Basil

Scallop Crostini with Salsa Verde

Tuna Crostini

Chicken Liver Crostini

Crushed Sweet Pea and Ricotta Bruschetta

Bruschetta

Crabmeat and Avocado Bruschetta

Snow's Bend Farm

OVERLEAF LEFT: *Antipasto for Two (page 25);* **OPPOSITE:** *At Bottega—setting the café for lunch*

MARINATED OLIVES

Makes about 4 cups

We go through these delectable little olives very quickly, so we keep them in the infused oil at room temperature, where they stay fresh for up to a week. If you're planning to make a batch to keep for a longer period, leave out the garlic, rosemary, and chile pepper until you're ready to serve. Long strands of orange and lemon zest are pretty and flavorful options. To keep things interesting, try to include a combination of brine- and oil-cured olives.

1 teaspoon fennel seeds
1 teaspoon coriander seeds (optional)
1 teaspoon cumin seeds
½ cup extra virgin olive oil
4 garlic cloves
6 thyme sprigs
6 marjoram sprigs
6 rosemary sprigs
4 to 5 bay leaves
1 dried red chile pepper crushed for more
   heat or left whole
2 cups Niçoise olives
2 cups Picholine or Cerignola olives
1 cup Kalamata olives
1 cup oil-cured olives (optional)

Combine the fennel, coriander, and cumin seeds in a skillet and toast over medium heat until they are fragrant and beginning to pop. Transfer the spices to a plate to cool.

Heat the oil in a medium saucepan over medium-high heat until hot. Add the toasted spices, the garlic cloves, herbs, bay leaves, and and chile pepper and cook until the garlic turns golden, about 5 minutes. Remove from the heat.

Combine the olives in a bowl and pour the oil and flavorings over them. Let cool.

FENNEL AND PARMIGIANO

Serves 4 to 6

When I traveled through southern Italy with a group of wine buyers, we toured Apulia and the golden town of Lecce. The winter fennel harvest was in full swing as we made our way to town to greet our bigger-than-life host, Cosimo Taurino, who had orchestrated a grand dinner for our group. As the meal was coming to an end, with boisterous enthusiasm he touted the wondrous properties of the raw fennel slices and dry, salty cheese we were served to cleanse the body and refresh the soul. Some might enjoy a bit of crusty multigrain bread . . . and more red wine.

½ fennel bulb, trimmed, cored, and cut lengthwise into
   ½-inch-thick slices
¼ pound Parmigiano-Reggiano or pecorino romano

Serve the fennel slices as you would crudités next to the wedge of Parmigiano or pecorino with a knife for breaking or slicing the cheese into little chunks.

To Drink: Salice Salentino (Taurino)

VEGETABLES À LA GRECQUE

Serves 4 to 6

This is really a combination of two techniques: marinating and pickling. Aromatic spices, champagne vinegar, and olive oil marry in a warm bath for a quintet of vegetables. This mellows and improves with time—over a day or two—and keeps well for a week. We use it as a condiment for grilled fish, as a component of an antipasti platter, and as a garnish for roasted meats or fish.

FOR THE MARINADE

1½ cups champagne vinegar
½ cup extra virgin olive oil
Juice of 1 lemon
20 coriander seeds
10 fennel seeds
2 medium white onions, quartered
4 garlic cloves, crushed
2 bay leaves
A parsley sprig
A thyme sprig

FOR THE VEGETABLES

1 cup small mushrooms, such as brown beech
2 fennel bulbs, trimmed, cored, and cut into julienne
    strips
3 carrots, peeled and cut into julienne strips
2 red bell peppers, cored, seeded, and cut into
    julienne strips
2 yellow bell peppers, cored, seeded, and cut into
    julienne strips
2 baby artichokes, trimmed (see page 254), cooked in
    boiling water until tender, and cut into ½-inch-thick
    wedges (optional)

Combine all of the marinade ingredients in a medium saucepan and heat over low heat until just simmering.

Combine the vegetables in a large bowl and pour the warm marinade over them. Cover with plastic wrap and refrigerate for at least 4 to 6 hours, or overnight, before serving.

CHARRED ONION DIP

Makes 2½ cups

On Sunday afternoons (when Bottega is closed), I often check on things at the restaurant and take stock of what's in the cooler. I reice the seafood, and make plans for the coming week. I usually find it impossible to resist raiding the huge bin of crisp homemade potato chips, for a midafternoon snack, along with our signature charred onion dip. The dip is a bit spicy and hard to pass up. Serve it on game day for a crowd or with drinks before dinner. Don't be afraid of really blackening the onion slices—the deeper the char, the more flavorful and smoky the dip.

2 cups sour cream
1 tablespoon mascarpone
1 scant tablespoon whole-grain mustard
4 dashes Tabasco sauce, or more to taste
1 tablespoon thinly sliced chives
Juice of ½ lemon
2 dashes Worcestershire sauce
Two ½-inch-thick slices Charred Red Onion (page 238),
    1 outer ring reserved for garnish, remaining onions
    finely chopped
Kosher salt and freshly ground black pepper

Combine the sour cream, mascarpone, mustard, Tabasco, chives, lemon juice, and Worcestershire in a medium bowl. Fold in the chopped onions, then taste and season with salt, pepper, and more Tabasco if necessary. The dip is great right away but the flavors are even better the next day.

To serve, put the reserved grilled onion ring on a plate and spoon the dip inside it. Serve with potato chips.

SARDINES WITH SKORDALIA
AND ARUGULA
Serves 4

This little snack makes me smile—and I'm sure my Grandaddy Stitt would shake his head in disbelief that a fancy restaurant would serve canned sardines! But, in combination with garlic, almonds, potatoes, and mayonnaise on a bed of arugula, they can hardly be categorized as plain fare. If you don't have time to whip up our mayonnaise from scratch, grab a jar of a good commercial brand. Good-quality canned tuna, such as Ortiz brand, can be substituted for the sardines.

½ cup Homemade Mayonnaise (page 245) or
    high-quality commercial mayonnaise
2 new potatoes, cooked in boiling salted water until tender,
    about 10 minutes, drained, and diced (about ¼ cup)
2 tablespoons sliced almonds, toasted
1 teaspoon thinly sliced chives
1 garlic clove, crushed and chopped to a paste
Pinch of red pepper flakes
1 teaspoon sherry vinegar
Kosher salt and freshly ground black pepper
2 cups arugula
1 teaspoon fresh lemon juice
¼ cup extra virgin olive oil
Two 4¾-ounce cans oil-packed boneless sardines

Combine the mayonnaise, potatoes, almonds, chives, garlic, red pepper flakes, and sherry vinegar in a bowl, mixing well. Season with salt and pepper to taste. Place a spoonful of skordalia on each serving plate.

Toss the arugula with the lemon juice, olive oil, and salt and pepper to taste. Mound the arugula to one side of the sauce on each plate, arrange the sardines next to the greens, and serve.

To Drink: A dry white, unoaked wine such as Vermentino from Sardinia or Cinque Terre

DAY-BOAT FISH WITH CAPER BERRIES
AND OLIVE OIL
Serves 4

Picture the freshest fish fillet, sliced as thin as possible, quickly grilled and then bathed in a lemon-, marjoram-, or thyme-infused olive oil tub: your own version of cured fish. Prepare this only when you have access to fish that is fresh from the water—as the term "day-boat fish" suggests. Use a very sharp thin knife to slice the flesh, or have your fish-monger slice it into very thin medallions.

This makes a wonderful hors d'oeuvre served in beautiful shallow gratin dishes. Olives, some breadsticks perhaps, and a sliced roasted pepper or two are accompaniments that would turn this into a healthy lunch.

½ pound firm fish, such as mackerel or triggerfish,
    wahoo, or tuna, cut into 4 very thin slices
    (see headnote)
⅓ to ½ cup fruity but delicate extra virgin olive oil
Maldon sea salt and freshly ground black pepper
Grated zest of 1 lemon
¼ cup caper berries, rinsed
1 tablespoon salt-packed capers, rinsed (optional)
2 to 3 marjoram or thyme sprigs, leaves only
1 jalapeño, seeds and membranes removed, thinly sliced
    (optional)
1 garlic clove, thinly sliced (optional)
A handful of arugula leaves
Lemon wedges

Prepare a hot fire in a grill. Bring the fish to room temperature.

Rub the grill grate with a little oil. Season the fish with salt and pepper, drizzle with a little olive oil, and place on the hottest part of the grill. Cook just until the edges begin to turn opaque, about 1 minute. Turn and cook for about 30 seconds more, or until just cooked through (or, if using tuna, just until cooked to rare).

Remove the fish from the grill and place in a gratin dish. Add the lemon zest, caper berries, capers, if using, marjoram or thyme, and jalapeño, and garlic, if using. Add enough olive oil to almost cover the fish. Allow the flavors to come together for at least 20 minutes, or up to 24 hours in the refrigerator (bring just to room temperature before serving). Serve directly from the gratin dish, with a garnish of the arugula and lemon wedges.

To Drink: Something light, crisp, and dry such as Tocai, Soave, or Arneis

ANTIPASTO FOR TWO

Pictured on page 18

This antipasto is ideal for sharing, especially when sitting outside on Bottega's patio or in your own backyard. Think of this as a rough outline and embellish with what you have on hand—some grilled eggplant or zucchini, cured fish, boiled little shrimp, or even leftover roast chicken.

FOR THE MARINATED CHICKPEAS
½ cup cooked or canned chickpeas, rinsed if canned

1 scallion, thinly sliced

1 teaspoon extra virgin olive oil

½ teaspoon red wine vinegar

Kosher salt and freshly ground black pepper to taste

FOR THE MARINATED MOZZARELLA
¼ pound fresh whole-milk mozzarella, cut into 1-inch slices

2 tablespoons extra virgin olive oil

4 fresh basil leaves, cut into chiffonade or torn into little pieces

Kosher salt and freshly ground black pepper to taste

1 very fresh organic egg

1½ cups Marinated Olives (page 22)

2 ounces thinly sliced prosciutto di Parma

2 ounces thinly sliced soppresata

2 ounces thinly sliced mortadella

2 ounces thinly sliced Tuscan salami

½ cup jarred peperoncini

1 red bell pepper, roasted (see page 254), peeled, seeded, and cut into wide strips

Cubed cucumber (optional)

1 scant cup arugula

2 ripe tomatoes, cut into wedges

1 tablespoon extra virgin olive oil

Kosher salt and freshly ground black pepper to taste

4 squares Focaccia (page 82) or 8 to 12 breadsticks

To prepare the chickpeas, combine all the ingredients in a medium bowl and let marinate for 1 to 2 hours at room temperature, or overnight in the refrigerator (bring to room temperature before serving).

To prepare the mozzarella, in a small bowl, toss the mozzarella with the olive oil, basil, and salt and pepper. Marinate for just a few minutes, or for up to a few hours.

To prepare the egg, set up an ice bath. Fill a medium saucepan halfway with water and bring to a boil. Add the egg, and when the water returns to a boil, adjust the heat to a simmer. Cook for 7 to 8 minutes for a soft yolk; for a firmer yolk, cook for 9 to 10 minutes. Transfer the egg to the ice bath to cool, then peel and cut it into quarters.

To serve, choose a large oval platter and make an attractive, rustic, loose arrangement of the various components: Leaving the center of the platter open, arrange the olives, chickpeas, mozzarella, and egg quarters next to each other, keeping them separate so that each stands out. Drape the cured meats in a slightly overlapping fashion to one side. Continue composing the platter with an artful arrangement of the peperoncini, roasted bell pepper, and cucumber, if using. At the last moment, toss the arugula and tomatoes with the olive oil and salt and pepper, and mound in the center of the platter. Serve with the focaccia or breadsticks.

To Drink: Prosecco or a crisp dry white, rosé, or light red

GRANDFATHER STITT'S HORS D'OEUVRES There is something Old Worldly about our Southern fondness for salted and cured fish. Sardines, salted and canned, have been a treat for poor Southerners since the days of the Depression, and my Grandfather Stitt's favorite snack was a smoked canned oyster on a saltine cracker with a dash of Tabasco sauce.

Similar simple snacks abound in Italy. Italians and Southerners share an appreciation for cured seafood (sardines, anchovies, shellfish), as well as for cured, smoked, and dried meats—especially pork. Our country ham on crackers mirrors the prosciutto of Italy, and our salted peanuts find common ground with Italian toasted almonds.

LEFT: *Italian Cobb Salad (page 65)*; RIGHT: *Farm Eggs with Tapenade (page 31)*

prosciutto di parma

Many years ago, as I was preparing to open Bottega, I visited a dairy producing Parmigiano-Reggiano and a prosciutto maker in the hills above Parma. The pigs raised above Parma are fed whey, a by-product of the nearby dairy and a great source of nutrition for them. The hams or hind legs are salted and placed on racks to facilitate drying, and air cured in special buildings with louvered shutters. Depending on the breeze, humidity, and temperature, the shutters are either opened or closed to maintain the drying conditions required to produce what is one of the world's greatest meats. Within nine to eleven months, the hams are ready for sale, though some artisans age their prosciutto for up to twenty-four months to further concentrate the flavor and refine the texture.

Here are some key points to keep in mind when buying prosciutto:

- To be sublime, prosciutto must be sliced as close as possible to serving time. A good butcher will slice prosciutto and arrange a few delicate slices in an overlapping fashion, place a sheet of waxed paper over them, and carefully continue adding layers.

- Different portions of the ham are best suited for specific uses. The shank end is good for flavoring soup or broth and can even be used more than once. The first few slices from the opposite end will be a little dry but are perfect in a duxelles or stuffing. The middle section is best for slicing and eating with little, if any, adornment. When serving prosciutto, don't be tempted to trim away the luscious white fat—that's where a lot of the flavor is.

Beef Carpaccio at Harry's Bar

BEEF CARPACCIO

Serves 4

I love carpaccio's clean vibrant flavors: the sharp tang of grated fresh horseradish, the mellowness of shaved Parmigiano, and the palate-cleansing quality of arugula. We use naturally raised Meyer Ranch or Painted Hills beef eye of round that we trim, wrap, and freeze briefly to facilitate slicing. A trusty old Berkel slicer (a deli-type meat slicer) gives us extra-thin slices. At home, chill the beef for no more than an hour in your freezer (too long, and it will become hard and difficult to slice), then slice it as thin as possible with a long thin-bladed knife.

- 1 pound beef eye of round, trimmed of all fat
- 1 cup sour cream
- ⅓ cup finely grated peeled horseradish, or more to taste
- 1 tablespoon fresh lemon juice
- Dash of Tabasco
- Maldon sea salt and freshly ground black pepper
- Generous cup arugula
- 2 tablespoons extra virgin olive oil
- A ¼-pound chunk of Parmigiano-Reggiano or grana padano
- Cracked black pepper

Wrap the meat in plastic wrap and place it in the freezer for 45 minutes to 1 hour. Chill four large serving plates.

In a medium bowl, whisk together the sour cream, horse-radish, 2 teaspoons of the lemon juice, Tabasco, and sea salt and pepper to taste. If necessary, adjust the amount of horseradish to your liking. Cover and refrigerate. (The horseradish sauce can be made up to a day in advance.)

Slice the beef into very thin (about ⅛-inch) slices, cutting across the grain. Place the slices between sheets of plastic wrap and pound with the smooth side of a meat mallet to uniformly thin slices.

Using the back of a spoon, spread a tablespoon of the horseradish sauce to cover the bottom of each chilled plate. Arrange the carpaccio over the horseradish sauce, overlapping the slices slightly so each plate is covered.

In a medium bowl, toss the arugula with the remaining 1 teaspoon lemon juice, the olive oil, and salt and pepper to taste. Mound equal portions of the greens in the center of the plates. Shave the cheese over the top and sprinkle with a little cracked black pepper.

To Drink: Tocai (Doro Princic)

Beef Carpaccio at Bottega

TUNA CARPACCIO

Serves 4

Spanking-fresh seafood—in this case sushi-grade tuna—is something I adore. But no wasabi, ginger, or soy here: I feel more at ease with the flavors of southern Italian embellishments like herbs and capers. Contemporary Italian cooks have outdone themselves with these *crudi*, versions of sushi or sashimi, served with a sophisticated aesthetic. Sun-dried tomatoes, preserved lemon, caper berries, and tangerine oil are a few options; toasted cubes of bread lend a Sicilian twist and additional texture, but are optional. Jump-start the preparation by slicing and pounding the tuna ahead of time, then cover tightly with plastic wrap and refrigerate. Prep all the other components in advance as well so that assembly, just before serving, is a breeze.

1 pound sushi-grade center-cut ahi or yellowfin tuna, trimmed of sinew

½ cup diced (⅛-inch cubes) baguette or Focaccia (page 82) (optional)

1 lemon

1 fennel bulb, trimmed, halved lengthwise, cored, and very thinly sliced (use a mandoline if you have one)

½ cup celery leaves

⅓ cup flat-leaf parsley leaves

1 tablespoon thinly sliced chives

4 dill sprigs, leaves only

1 teaspoon extra virgin olive oil, plus more for sprinkling

2 tablespoons capers, rinsed

Fleur de sel or other sea salt and freshly ground black pepper

Chill four 6-inch plates. If making the toasted croutons, preheat the oven to 350°F.

Using a very sharp knife, slice the tuna as thin as possible (you can *lightly* pound the slices between plastic wrap if they are uneven or seem too thick). Arrange the slices on the chilled plates, covering the entire surface of each one without overlapping the slices. Refrigerate until ready to serve.

Toast the bread cubes, if using, on a baking sheet in the oven for 8 to 10 minutes, until crispy and golden brown. Set aside to cool.

Cut a ½-inch slice off the top and bottom of the lemon. Stand the fruit on a cutting board and cut away the skin and pith in strips, slicing from top to bottom and working your way around the fruit. Holding the fruit over a bowl to collect the juices, slice along each membrane to release the segments. Remove any seeds, and cut each segment into ⅛-inch dice.

Combine the fennel, celery leaves, parsley, chives, and dill in a small bowl and toss with the reserved lemon juice and the extra virgin olive oil. Mound a portion of the salad in the center of each plate of carpaccio, being careful not to completely hide the brilliant red tuna. Sprinkle some capers, toasted bread cubes, if using, and lemon segments over each serving. Season the carpaccio judiciously with sea salt and black pepper. Finish each plate with a few drops of olive oil.

To Drink: A minerally, earthy white such as Greco di Tufo (Feudi di San Gregorio)

GRILLED MOZZARELLA WRAPPED IN A LEMON LEAF

Serves 4

A single ingredient—a few fresh sardines, juicy melon slices, a round of hand-kneaded mozzarella—is often served in Italy with little embellishment other than a sprinkling of sea salt and a few drops of a green olive oil. Such culinary simplicity may not be a typical American practice, but it's one to consider whenever an ingredient is at its pristine best.

The idea of grilling cheese wrapped in a citrus leaf was exotic to me when I discovered it in restaurants all along the Amalfi Coast, especially Sorrento, a place blessed with some of the world's most perfumed lemons. This makes an impressive and unusual appetizer for an outdoor barbecue. I love using leaves as wrappers for food—the smoky grill imbues the filling with the flavor of the aromatic leaf. A few other leaves to try:

Fig leaves—fantastic aroma

Grape leaves—great for sardines; use leaves that have been cured

Chestnut leaves—perfect for aged goat cheese

We also use certain leaves as garnishes. Tomato leaves make a lovely garnish for a tomato gratin, and peach or pear leaves are an uncommon garnish for desserts.

4 large organic lemon leaves
Four ⅓-inch-thick slices fresh mozzarella
Kosher salt and freshly ground black pepper
Extra virgin olive oil
Agrumato lemon oil (see Sources, page 260; optional)
Grated lemon zest
Crusty bread

Prepare a fire for indirect grilling in a charcoal or gas grill.

Arrange the leaves shiny side down on a work surface and top each with a mozzarella slice. Season the cheese with a sprinkling of salt and pepper and a drizzle of extra virgin olive oil. Fold the leaves over the cheese and secure with kitchen twine or toothpicks.

Oil the grill rack and place the stuffed leaves over indirect heat so the smoky heat warms the leaves and the mozzarella. When the cheese is hot and just oozing, transfer the packets to serving plates. Remove and discard the twine or toothpicks. Open the packets and drizzle a bit more extra virgin olive oil or a few drops of Agrumato oil over the cheese and sprinkle with a little lemon zest. Serve with crusty bread for scooping up the cheese.

To Drink: An aromatic white whine from Campania such as Fiano di Avellino or Falanghina

FARM EGGS WITH TAPENADE

Makes 16 stuffed egg halves • Pictured on Page 26

This may be far removed from anyone's expectations of stellar food, but give me a few of these on a picnic with a crackling cold Tocai Friuliano and a chunk of country bread, and I'm happy. I prefer our homemade tapenade, with a minimum of garlic.

8 very fresh organic eggs
¼ cup Tapenade (page 250)
¼ cup Homemade Mayonnaise (page 245) or high-quality commercial mayonnaise

Put the eggs in a large saucepan, add water to cover and bring to a boil. Reduce to a simmer and cook for 9 minutes. Transfer the eggs to a bowl of ice water.

When the eggs are cool, peel and halve. Scoop out the egg yolks and mash them in a bowl with the tapenade and mayonnaise until thoroughly combined. Spoon or pipe this mixture into the egg halves. Arrange on a plate and serve.

To Drink: A full-flavored white wine such as Tocai (Livio Felluga)

FIGS AND PROSCIUTTO

Serves 6

One of the greatest first courses in summertime—ideally enjoyed on a shaded patio—is a plate of ripe, never-refrigerated figs, halved or quartered, cloaked with prosciutto di Parma, and finished with a few torn mint leaves and a generous drizzle of fruity olive oil, to be sopped up with some crusty bread.

8 slices prosciutto di Parma,
    each sliced lengthwise into 3 strips
12 ripe figs, halved lengthwise
A few mint leaves
Extra virgin olive oil
1 loaf crusty bread

Loosely wrap a piece of prosciutto around each fig half and arrange on a platter. Tear a few mint leaves over the top and drizzle with olive oil. Serve with crusty bread.

To Drink: A lively, fresh white wine such as Arneis (Ceretto)

ROASTED PEPPERS STUFFED WITH GOAT CHEESE

Serves 4

Never absent from the Bottega Café menu are these roasted red and gold bell peppers, split and filled with soft, mild goat cheese, pine nuts, sweet golden raisins, and lots of fresh basil. The stuffed peppers are baked in our extremely hot wood-fired pizza oven and come out bubbly and aromatic—it's a great combination that seems to hit every note just right. This is also a great vegetarian first course.

4 large red or yellow bell peppers, roasted (see page
    254), peeled, slit open down one side, cored, and
    seeded
Maldon sea salt and freshly ground black pepper
¼ pound mild soft goat cheese, such as Coach Farm
    (see Sources, page 260)
6 basil leaves, 4 leaves cut into chiffonade, 2 leaves
    reserved for garnish
2 tablespoons pine nuts, toasted (see page 255)
Scant ¼ cup sultanas (golden raisins), plumped in hot
    water for 10 minutes and drained
2 tablespoons Bread Crumbs (page 239)
About 2 tablespoons extra virgin olive oil
Pinch of cayenne (optional)

Position a rack in the upper third of the oven and preheat the oven to 475°F.

Place the peppers peeled side down on a cutting board and flatten them slightly. Sprinkle with sea salt and pepper. Spread one-quarter of the goat cheese down the center of each pepper, shaping it into an oval. Scatter the basil chiffonade evenly over the goat cheese, and follow with the pine nuts and sultanas. Fold each pepper over to create a package (like a canoe on its side). Press down gently to flatten slightly.

Place the stuffed peppers on a baking sheet. Sprinkle with the bread crumbs and drizzle a little olive oil over each one. Sprinkle with cayenne, if using.

Bake for about 10 minutes, until the bread crumbs turn golden and the goat cheese is bubbly.

Arrange the peppers on small plates and tear the remaining basil leaves over for garnish. Drizzle with a bit more olive oil, if desired.

To Drink: Any light, unoaked, simple white wine, such as a Soave (Pieropan), Sauvignon Friuli, or Vernaccia

mapping italian cheeses

Italy is a nation of regions and this regionalism is reflected in its cheeses. The Piemontese will serve their local cheese and, just maybe, one of the cheeses of a bordering region. Those in Tuscany or the south of Italy remain equally dedicated to their local cheeses. And stores in Napoli carry that area's finest mozzarella, provolone, or pecorino, but you won't find the wonderful northern cheeses there. Along with Parmigiano-Reggiano—the king of all cheese and profoundly good—here are some others that I enjoy:

- Sheep's-milk pecorinos from Tuscany and Sardinia whose flavors range from delicate and fresh to aged and intense, with the best examples not nearly as salty as those from large commercial producers

- A sharp Gorgonzola, whether young and creamy (Gorgonzola dolce) or aged and sharper (piccante)

- The Robiolas of Lombardy and Piedmont are uncommonly luxurious cheeses, often made from a combination of cow's, sheep's, and goat's milks, resulting in a fresh, pure "milkiness" that makes them a creamy after-dinner indulgence

- Fontina can be a bland factory-made product or a delicious raw-cow's-milk cheese with hints of grass and the aroma of rich pastureland. A true Fontina d'Aosta is one of the most versatile cheeses there is—great in sandwiches, with ham or fruit, on crusty bread, or with any red wine

- Taleggio (when very ripe) is like the soft, rich, pungent cow's milk cheeses of France—complex and delicious

BAKED FETA WITH FOCACCIA
Serves 4

This recipe is a throwback to old-fashioned Italian-American restaurants of the 1960s, when a bubbling bowl of marinara sauce was served as a dip for garlic bread. It's a homey, approachable concoction that is easy to prepare. Our twist is the addition of feta, which turns basic marinara into a wonderful cheesey mess. Toasted focaccia is ideal for dunking into the steamy, aromatic sauce.

> **2 cups Marinara Sauce (page 246)**
> **1 cup crumbled feta (about 4 ounces)**
> **Four 4-by-2-inch rectangles Focaccia (page 82)**
> **1 tablespoon olive oil**
> **Pinch of cayenne (optional)**
> **A few basil leaves**

Preheat the oven to 450°F.

Spoon the marinara into a medium gratin dish (approximately 8 inches long) or divide it among four individual gratin dishes or ramekins. Scatter the cheese over the center.

Bake until the sauce is bubbling hot, 8 to 10 minutes.

Meanwhile, cut the focaccia into strips or triangles (large bite-sized pieces) and brush with the olive oil. Arrange on a baking sheet and toast in the oven until golden brown, 5 to 6 minutes.

Sprinkle the sauce with a little cayenne, if desired, and put the gratin dish on a large platter and surround with the focaccia, or put the individual dishes on serving plates and serve the focaccia on the side. Tear the basil leaves over the top. Dig in, or lose out.

To Drink: Rosé or a rustic red from the South, such as Sicily's Regaleali Rosso

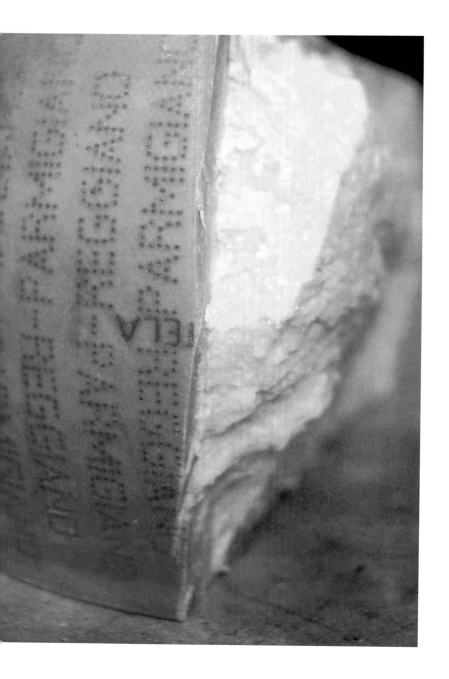

parmigiano-reggiano

Parmigiano is one of my favorite cheeses—and perhaps the world's too—and a great one to enjoy with big red wines. The wonderfully rich and flavorful milk used to make it is one of the keys to its magic.

In Parma, the producers of Parmigiano-Reggiano heat milk and rennet in huge copper cauldrons, stirring with enormous whisks to get the process going. Then they pour the hot milk into huge round bamboo molds in the signature shape of a Parmigiano wheel; each round of cheese weighs about 66 pounds (or 30 kilos). Once in the molds, the cheese is aged in vats of saltwater before being transferred to mammoth shelves and aged for an additional twelve to twenty-four months. Then they get stamped with "Parmigiano-Reggiano," the official appellation of the region.

Grana padano is a slightly less expensive and less profound cheese than Parmigiano, but it's good when you require a grating cheese that does not need the sublime complexity of a true Parmigiano-Reggiano. Both varieties have a wonderful milky, concentrated intensity. Keep both on hand for grating over pizzas, shaving into salads, and incorporating into lasagne, baked shells, and other pasta dishes—or for enjoying after dinner with a glass of bold red wine.

Parmesan Soufflés (page 40)

PARMESAN SOUFFLÉS

Serves 6 • Pictured on page 39

This popular Bottega appetizer is a cloudlike pudding of parmesan, farm eggs, and cream baked in a mold like a soufflé, then unmolded and served with little mushrooms, slivers of prosciutto and a shower of more parmesan. This ultra-rich indulgence may not be spa food, but don't we all deserve a bit of indulgence? (Perhaps follow with a lighter simple grilled entrée.)

FOR THE SOUFFLÉS

8 large eggs

3 cups heavy cream

½ teaspoon roasted garlic puree (see page 254)

Pinch of freshly grated nutmeg

¾ cup freshly grated Parmigiano-Reggiano

½ teaspoon kosher salt, or to taste

¼ teaspoon white pepper, or to taste

Dash of Tabasco or pinch of cayenne

½ recipe White Wine Butter Sauce (page 244)

1 tablespoon unsalted butter

2 cups quartered or thickly sliced cremini, oyster, or button mushrooms or a mix of chanterelles, brown beech, and porcini

1 shallot, minced

2 thyme sprigs, leaves only

Kosher salt and freshly ground black pepper to taste

4 very thin slices prosciutto di Parma, cut into ¼-inch-by-2-inch julienne

Preheat the oven to 300°F. Butter six 6-ounce ramekins (or cups) and place them in a large shallow baking dish or pan.

Combine all the soufflé ingredients in a bowl and whisk until combined. Fill the ramekins almost to the top (use 5½ ounces of the mixture per ramekin). Pour enough hot water into the baking dish to come three-quarters of the way up the sides of the molds.

Cover the pan with foil and bake for 1 hour. Uncover and bake until the soufflés are slightly puffed, set, and golden, about 15 minutes more.

Meanwhile, shortly before the soufflés are done, prepare the butter sauce. Keep the sauce warm while you sauté the mushrooms.

Heat a large sauté pan over medium-high heat, and add the butter. When it is melted, add the mushrooms and sauté until the edges are golden, about 3 minutes. Add the shallot and sauté for 1 minute. Season with the thyme leaves and the salt and pepper and toss for about 30 seconds more. Set aside, covered to keep warm.

Unmold the soufflés onto warm plates, and ladle the butter sauce around. Scatter some of the sautéed mushrooms and sliced prosciutto around each one and serve.

To Drink: A simple, medium-bodied white, such as Vernaccia di San Gimignano (Terruzi & Puthod)

ROASTED BEET CROSTINI
Makes 8 crostini

8 slices (about ½ inch thick and 2 inches long) Focaccia
    (page 82), baguette, or other crusty bread
About 2 tablespoons fruity extra virgin olive oil
½ cup whole-milk ricotta, preferably fresh
Grated zest and juice of 1 lemon
Kosher salt and freshly ground black pepper
2 large beets, cooked and diced (½-inch) (see Note)
2 tablespoons chopped toasted walnuts
Maldon sea salt
Cracked black pepper

Preheat the oven to 450°F.

Brush the bread with about 1 tablespoon of the olive oil. Arrange on a baking sheet and toast in the oven until crisp, 8 to 10 minutes. Set aside.

Mix the ricotta with the lemon zest and juice in a small bowl and season with a little salt and pepper. Spread the mixture on the toasts. Top each with 1 tablespoon diced beets and a sprinkling of chopped walnuts. Garnish each with a few drops of fruity extra virgin olive oil and a sprinkling of sea salt and cracked black pepper.

NOTE: To cook the beets, trim them and wrap in foil. Bake at 350°F for 1 hour, or until tender. Peel when cool enough to handle.

To Drink: Sauvignon Blanc (Villa Russiz)

TOMATO TAPENADE CROSTINI
Makes 8 crostini

8 slices (about ½ inch thick by 2 inches long) Focaccia
    (page 82), baguette, or other crusty bread
About 5 tablespoons extra virgin olive oil
2 cups halved (or quartered) cherry tomatoes
2 tablespoons chopped mint
2 tablespoons L'Estornell Spanish garnacha vinegar (see
    Sources, page 260) or other red wine vinegar
Kosher salt and freshly ground black pepper
4 ounces mild fresh goat cheese, softened
Scant 3 tablespoons Tapenade (page 250)

Preheat the oven to 450°F.

Brush the slices of bread with about 1 tablespoon of the olive oil. Arrange on a baking sheet and toast in the oven until crisp, 8 to 10 minutes. Set aside.

Combine the tomatoes, mint, vinegar, and the remaining ¼ cup olive oil in a small bowl. Season with salt and pepper.

Spread 1 tablespoon goat cheese on each toast, and spoon ¼ cup of the tomato mixture on top of each one. Garnish each with 1 teaspoon of the tapenade and a little black pepper.

CROSTINI—thin slices of toasted bread topped with any variety of goodies, from chopped tomato and basil to a coarse chicken liver puree to simply some of the finest olive oil and a slice of mozzarella—are the "chips of Italy." At Bottega, we serve three different types of crostini on a plate, to be shared before a meal with an aperitif. Good combinations include our roasted beet, scallop with salsa verde, and chicken liver crostini, but the options are endless.

CAULIFLOWER CROSTINI

Makes 8 crostini

8 slices (about ½ inch thick by 2 inches long) Focaccia
(page 82), baguette, or other crusty bread
About 5 tablespoons extra virgin olive oil
½ head cauliflower
2 cloves roasted garlic (see page 254)
Kosher salt and freshly ground white pepper
Dash of Tabasco or other hot sauce
4 sun-dried tomatoes, reconstituted in 1 cup hot water,
drained, and finely julienned
2 tablespoons capers, rinsed
Tiny flat-leaf parsley sprigs
Agrumato lemon oil (see Sources, page 260; optional)

Preheat the oven to 450°F.

Brush the slices of bread with about 1 tablespoon of the olive oil. Arrange on a baking sheet and toast in the oven until crisp, 8 to 10 minutes. Set aside.

Trim the cauliflower and separate it into large florets. Slice one-quarter of the florets into thin slices and set aside.

Steam the remaining florets in a steamer basket over boiling water until soft, 12 to 15 minutes.

Transfer the steamed cauliflower to a food processor, add the roasted garlic and salt and pepper to taste, and puree until smooth. With the processor running, pour in the remaining ¼ cup olive oil. Add a dash or two of hot pepper sauce, then taste and adjust the seasonings.

Spoon a layer of the cauliflower puree on each toast. Top with the sun-dried tomatoes, capers, and raw cauliflower slices. Garnish with tiny parsley sprigs and drizzle with a little Agrumato lemon oil or extra virgin olive oil.

To Drink: A crisp, light white wine, such as Bianco di Custoza

SCALLOP CROSTINI WITH TAPENADE AND BASIL

Makes 8 crostini

Fresh sweet sea scallops have a luxurious texture that is a perfect foil for crisp crostini. We sear them and slice to serve with a little tapenade on our crusty focaccia toasts. Other times we slather a spoonful of white bean puree on the bread first and substitute thin slivers of sun-dried tomato for the tapenade. Our Salsa Verde makes another explosively flavorful garnish for these delicious bites. Be sure to ask your fish merchant for scallops that are dry-packed, without any preservatives.

8 slices (about ½ inch thick and 2 inches long) Focaccia
(page 82), baguette, or other crusty bread
About 2 tablespoons extra virgin olive oil
4 medium dry-packed sea scallops, patted dry
Maldon sea salt and freshly ground black pepper
2 scant tablespoons Tapenade (page 250)
Agrumato lemon oil (see Sources, page 260) or Basil Oil
(page 250) (optional)
8 small basil leaves
Finely grated zest of 1 lemon

Preheat the oven to 450°F.

Brush the slices of bread with about 1 tablespoon of the olive oil. Arrange on a baking sheet and toast in the oven until crisp, 8 to 10 minutes. Set aside.

Heat a small heavy sauté pan over high heat, and add the remaining 1 tablespoon olive oil. When the oil begins to shimmer, season the scallops with sea salt and pepper and sear quickly on both sides, just until golden brown, but not cooked through, about 1 minute per side.

Slice the scallops crosswise into thin rounds. Spread about ¼ teaspoon of the tapenade on each crostini and top with a slightly overlapping layer of sliced scallop. Drizzle with a little lemon oil or basil oil, or extra virgin olive oil. Garnish each with a small basil leaf and finely grated lemon zest. Serve immediately.

To Drink: A dry rosé

SCALLOP CROSTINI WITH
SALSA VERDE

Makes 8 crostini

8 slices (about ½ inch thick and 2 inches long) Focaccia
    (page 82), baguette, or other crusty bread
About 2 tablespoons olive oil
4 large dry-packed sea scallops, tough muscles removed,
    and patted dry
Maldon sea salt and freshly ground black pepper
½ cup Salsa Verde (page 248)

Preheat the oven to 450°F.

Brush the slices of bread with about 1 tablespoon of the olive oil. Arrange on a baking sheet and toast in the oven until crisp, 8 to 10 minutes. Set aside.

Heat a small heavy sauté pan over high heat. Add the remaining 1 tablespoon olive oil to the pan and when the oil begins to shimmer, add the scallops and quickly sear on both sides just until golden brown, but not cooked through, about 1 minute per side.

Slice the scallops crosswise into thin rounds and divide among the toasts. Sprinkle the crostini with a little salt and pepper and top each with a judicious spoonful of the salsa verde. Serve immediately.

To Drink: Grüner Veltliner (Rudi Pichler)

TUNA CROSTINI

Serves 4

For this "tuna salad" crostini, we occasionally poach little pieces (plus any trimmings left over from filleting a large loin) of fresh tuna, but most of the time we rely on good quality Spanish or Italian canned tuna.

8 triangles (about 3 inches long) Focaccia (page 82)
Extra virgin olive oil
1 six-ounce can of tuna packed in olive oil (Ortiz is a
    reliable source)
2 heaping tablespoons mayonnaise
Juice of ½ lemon
2 scallions, finely chopped
2 stalks celery, cut into small dice
1 tablespoon capers, rinsed to remove excess saltiness
Dash of Tabasco
4 small radishes, finely sliced
4 sprigs of parsley, torn into pieces

Preheat oven to 450°F.

Brush the focaccia with olive oil and toast in the oven until the edges are a little crispy, about 10 minutes. Set aside.

Drain the tuna, place in a medium mixing bowl and break up with a fork. Add the mayonnaise, lemon, scallions, celery, capers, and a dash or two of hot pepper sauce and mix thoroughly. Taste and adjust the seasonings.

Arrange 2 toasted focaccia triangles on each of four plates. Spread a layer of tuna onto each piece. Garnish each one with the radishes and parsley and a drizzle of extra virgin olive oil.

To Drink: A cool rosé (La Scola)

CHICKEN LIVER CROSTINI

Makes 8 crostini

This is our variation on one of Tuscany's favorite snacks. In Florence, they coarsely chop the cooked livers and mash them on the crostini. We finely chop half of the pan-seared livers and coarsely chop the rest before combining them. This adds some complexity and provides an interesting contrast of textures. There should be a subtle yet distinguishable flavor of shallot, thyme, and sherry: season to taste and adjust as needed.

8 slices (about ½ inch thick and 2 inches long) Focaccia (page 82), baguette, or other crusty bread

About 3 tablespoons extra virgin olive oil

¼ pound chicken livers, connective tissue and fat removed, patted dry

Kosher salt and freshly ground black pepper

2 shallots, coarsely chopped

4 juniper berries, toasted (see page 256) and ground in a spice or coffee grinder

4 thyme sprigs, leaves removed and chopped

2 tablespoons medium-dry sherry or Marsala, or to taste

1 tablespoon unsalted butter, softened

Coarse sea salt

Arugula leaves, pea tendrils, or tiny sprigs of thyme or rosemary

Preheat the oven to 450°F.

Brush the bread slices with about 1 tablespoon of the olive oil. Arrange on a baking sheet and toast in the oven until crisp, 8 to 10 minutes. Set aside.

Heat 1 tablespoon of the olive oil in a large heavy sauté pan over medium heat. Season the chicken livers assertively with salt and pepper, add to the hot oil, and cook over medium to medium-high heat until browned on both sides, 2 to 3 minutes per side. Be sure to cook until just pink in the center; keep in mind the livers will continue cooking once removed from the heat. Transfer them to a cooling rack.

Add 2 teaspoons olive oil and the shallots to the pan and cook over medium-low heat until the shallots are softened, 1 to 2 minutes. Add the ground juniper berries, thyme, and sherry and cook for 30 seconds more. Remove from the heat.

Add half of the cooked livers to a food processor, along with the shallot-sherry mixture, and pulse to finely chop. Transfer to a bowl.

Coarsely chop the remaining livers with a chef's knife, add to the bowl, and stir in the softened butter. Taste and adjust the seasonings.

Place a small spoonful of the chicken liver mixture on each crostini, spreading it gently, and top with some coarse sea salt, black pepper, and a drizzle of olive oil. Garnish each one with an arugula leaf, sweet pea tendril, or thyme or rosemary sprig.

To Drink: Chianti (Volpaia)

CRUSHED SWEET PEA AND RICOTTA BRUSCHETTA

Serves 4

Grilled bread slathered with fresh mild ricotta and topped with crushed sweet peas is a vibrant healthy snack or hors d'oeuvre, especially pretty when garnished with pink radishes and fresh sprigs of pea tendrils.

4 slices (about 2 inches thick and 3 inches long)
    Focaccia (page 82) or ciabatta
½ cup sweet peas, fresh or frozen, rinsed and blanched
    in boiling water until tender, shocked in ice water,
    drained (frozen peas may be rinsed under hot water)
Sea salt and freshly ground pepper
1 shallot, finely chopped and softened in a pan with
    ½ tablespoon olive oil, about 1 minute
Grated zest and juice of 1 lemon
½ cup fresh ricotta cheese (drained if very wet)
½ cup fresh radishes, washed, dried, and finely sliced
½ cup pea tendrils or fresh mint sprigs
Agrumato lemon oil (see Sources, page 260) or extra
    virgin olive oil

Prepare a fire in a grill or fire up the broiler.

Grill or broil the focaccia slices for 30 seconds per side, until golden brown and crisp.

Place peas in a medium bowl and crush with a potato masher or the back of a large spoon. Season with salt and pepper and add the softened shallot and a little lemon juice. Taste and adjust seasoning.

While the bruschettas are still warm, spread a layer of ricotta across each piece. Spoon some of the crushed peas on top and place them on a serving plate. Garnish with the lemon zest, sliced radishes, and pea tendrils (or mint). Drizzle each bruschetta with the Agrumato lemon oil or extra virgin olive oil before serving.

To Drink: Try an Austrian Riesling from Nigl or Prager

BRUSCHETTA—thick slices of focaccia, a baguette, or ciabatta grilled over an open fire—is traditionally topped with green olive oil, tomato, and basil. But, like their smaller cousin, crostini, bruschetta variations are just about infinite. The recipes given here—for sweet pea and ricotta and crabmeat and avocado—are two that are bound to please.

CRABMEAT AND AVOCADO BRUSCHETTA

Serves 4

Here sweet crabmeat and lush avocado combine for a luxurious snack to be enjoyed during the fleeting season when crabmeat is at its prime. I like the zing of lemon zest and hot pepper, but regulate the spicy kick to suit your tastes.

8 slices baguette (about ½ inch thick)
1 garlic clove, halved
2 ripe Hass avocados
Kosher salt and freshly ground black pepper
½ pound jumbo lump crabmeat, picked over for shells
    and cartilage
Grated zest and juice of 1 lemon
Scant ¼ cup extra virgin olive oil
2 cups arugula
Pinch of cayenne

Prepare a fire in a grill or fire up the broiler.

Grill or broil the baguette slices for 30 seconds per side, until golden brown and crisp. Rub the toasted bread lightly on one side with the cut side of the garlic halves. (The toasts can be made ahead and stored in a tightly closed tin for several days.)

Halve and pit the avocados. Scoop out the flesh and cut it into ¼-inch dice. Place the avocado in a small bowl and season with salt and pepper.

Combine the crabmeat, lemon juice, and 2 tablespoons of the olive oil in another bowl and season with salt and pepper to taste.

Arrange 2 toasted baguette slices on each of four plates. Spoon a layer of the avocado onto each piece, then top with the crabmeat. Garnish each one with arugula, a few drops of the remaining olive oil, a pinch of the lemon zest, and a sprinkle of cayenne.

To Drink: A fruity, plump white wine, such as Grüner Veltliner (Nigl)

snow's bend farm

Getting to Snow's Bend Farm, one of Alabama's most dynamic organic gardens, is an idyllic journey down a dirt road, past pecan orchards and tired cotton fields to a yellow gate that opens to the fields beyond. The expanse of fertile bottomland hugs a huge bend of the Black Warrior River, right outside the "Black Belt" (the area of dark, rich soil prized for its cotton farming in the nineteenth century), west of Tuscaloosa, and is on the site of what was once a Native American village. Situated close to the river and bordered by levees to the south, it is an untouched spot—a place too cumbersome for a farmer to maneuver a tractor. In other words, an ideal place for organic farming.

This is where I found David Snow with his shaggy red beard and old-fashioned farmer's hat and his beautiful girlfriend, Margaret Ann, one day in December. They were tending row upon row of bright green fennel; Swiss chard in multiple hues; bushy-topped golden, red, and candycane beets; turnips, Savoy cabbage, and collard greens; earthy rutabagas; and salad greens of every variety. Their plot constitutes one of the most prolific farming enterprises I've ever seen, and the fruits of their labor are some of the best-tasting vegetables I've ever eaten. And all this productiveness is happening in an early winter garden, when most area farmers have retired for the off-season, forcing the community-at-large to miss out on the wonderful array of cool-weather crops that can be grown locally and enjoyed soon after they are harvested. David and Margaret Ann are setting an impressive example of what farming can become in every community throughout America: imagine our tables supplied by local farmers—foods of the greatest nutritional value and superior taste—and the environmental benefits of sustainable, organically grown local agriculture.

SOUPS

Chilled Tomato Soup with Fruity Olive Oil

Soup

Tuscan White Bean Soup with Wilted Escarole

Spring Minestrone

An Affinity for Shell Beans and Greens

Summer Minestrone

Butter Bean, Lamb, and Orzo Soup with Escarole

Lentil and Chickpea Soup

SALADS

Tomatoes

Fennel with Blood Oranges, Pistachios, Endive, and Gorgonzola

Italian Cobb Salad

Olive Oil

Capri Lunch Salad

Bottega Caesar Salad

Tuscan Egg Salad with Young Lettuces

Tomato Salad with Mozzarella, Basil, and Fruity Olive Oil

Arugula, Charred Onion, and Mushroom Salad

Vinaigrettes and Dressings

PIZZAS AND PIADINE

Basic Pizza Dough

Roasted Sweet Pepper and Tomato Chutney Pizza

Pizza with Wild Mushrooms, Butternut Squash,
    and Wilted Greens

Grilled Chicken, Pesto, Mozzarella, and Aged Provolone Pizza

Smoked Salmon Pizza with Red Onions, Capers,
    and Mascarpone

Caffe Sport Seafood Pizza

Flatbread with Smoked Salmon

Chicken Marinara Piadine

Piadine

Persian Piadine

Focaccia

Muffaletta with Cured Meats and Olive Relish

Salted, Cured, and Simple

OVERLEAF LEFT: *(clockwise from top left) Roasted Sweet Pepper and Tomato Chutney Pizza (page 76); Pizza with Mushrooms, Squash, and Greens (page 76); Smoked Salmon Pizza with Onions, Capers, and Mascarpone (page 77); Grilled Chicken, Pesto, Mozzarella, and Provolone Pizza (page 77);* **OPPOSITE:** *Bottega Café's pizza oven*

CHILLED TOMATO SOUP WITH FRUITY OLIVE OIL

Serves 4

Here is a chilled summer tomato soup—one, I confess, we sometimes make in a simpler version. The easiest way is simply to chop and marinate the tomatoes with sliced shallot and garlic, basil, and sea salt for a few hours, then pass everything through a food mill, chill until ice-cold, brighten with some good vinegar, and serve with a generous drizzle of the best, fruitiest olive oil you can find. The following recipe is more involved, requiring a bit of time at the stove sautéing leeks and onions to sweeten, worthy of a special occasion.

Chill both the soup bowls and spoons to keep the soup refreshingly cold when served on a hot summer day.

Remember: *Never* refrigerate tomatoes—anything below 45° to 50°F, and they break down. Do what our grandparents did, and keep them in a shady spot on a shelf on the north side of your porch or a similar spot.

8 to 12 large ripe mixed heirloom tomatoes, cored and
   coarsely chopped
2 small pickling or kirby cucumbers, peeled, halved
   lengthwise, seeded, and thinly sliced
1 small shallot, thinly sliced
1 small garlic clove, crushed
A small bunch of basil
2 to 4 tablespoons high-quality red wine vinegar, such
   as L'Estornell Spanish garnacha (see Sources, page
   260), or sherry vinegar
2 tablespoons olive oil
Maldon sea salt
1 medium sweet onion, such as Maui or Vidalia, thinly
   sliced
1 leek, white and pale green parts, thinly sliced
2 cups spring water
About ¼ cup finest extra virgin olive oil, chilled in the
   freezer for 2 hours (optional)

OPTIONAL GARNISHES (CHOOSE ONE OR A COMBINATION)
Crabmeat or cooked and peeled tiny shrimp
Small croutons sautéed in olive oil
Basil Oil (page 250)
Cucumber and basil relish (see Note)

Put the chopped tomatoes and cucumbers in a large bowl. Add the shallot, garlic, several sprigs of the basil, 1 tablespoon of the vinegar, and 1 tablespoon of the olive oil.

Season assertively with sea salt, and toss well. Cover and leave at room temperature for 4 to 6 hours.

Heat the remaining tablespoon of olive oil in a medium saucepan, add the onion and leek, and sauté over medium-low heat until softened but not colored, about 10 minutes. Remove from the heat.

Chop 2 of the basil leaves and add to the onion and leek, along with salt to taste.

Remove the garlic and basil sprigs from the marinated tomatoes. Pass the tomatoes and the softened onion and leek through a food mill into a bowl, or puree in a food processor. Add the spring water and stir or process briefly, then strain through a fine strainer into a bowl. Taste and adjust the seasonings with more vinegar, salt, and pepper. Chill until ice-cold. Just before serving, cut the remaining basil leaves into chiffonade. Serve the soup in chilled bowls, drizzled with the chilled (freezing increases viscosity) olive oil. Garnish with the chiffonade of basil and a sprinkle of sea salt, and any optional garnishes you desire.

NOTE: To make a quick cucumber and basil relish, combine 2 kirby cucumbers, peeled, halved lengthwise, seeded, and finely diced, a pinch of salt, 4 basil leaves, chopped, 1 teaspoon red wine vinegar, and 1 tablespoon olive oil.

SOUP My mother's beef and vegetable soup, accompanied by an iron skillet of corn bread and embellished, at least after my travels to Italy, with a liberal drizzle of fruity olive oil, was a favorite lunch, made in winter with "put-up" (frozen) vegetables and in summer with vegetables picked from our garden. It was dark and rich, its broth made from long-simmered beef short ribs or shanks, and it tasted like love. There was such comfort to be found in a bowl of that simple, rustic soup.

And so it is with everyone and every culture, and perhaps with soups more than any other dish: that transparent love that goes into the cooking of a broth nurtured with mountains of aromatics and a little chunk of cured pork, some neck bones, shanks, or ribs, then set to simmer until the house smells divine. Whether ladled into bowls in Nonna's kitchen in Italy or at Grandma's farmhouse table in Alabama, the impact is the same. So make extra—soups are invariably better the day (sometimes two) after they are made.

TUSCAN WHITE BEAN SOUP WITH WILTED ESCAROLE

Serves 8 • Pictured on page 57

In Italy, there are as many versions of this humble restorative soup as there are regions. Greens and cannellini beans are common in Tuscan renditions. At Bottega, the soup is ladled over a mound of wilted escarole, and just before we serve it, we crown the top with a drizzle of fruity olive oil.

Cooking time will vary depending on the age of the dried beans you're using. The time listed is a general guide; be sure to test the tenderness of your beans as they cook, and adjust accordingly.

2 cups dried cannellini, Great Northern, or borlotti
    beans, rinsed and picked over
8 cups spring water
1 tablespoon kosher salt
1 tablespoon extra virgin olive oil
3 garlic cloves, minced
¾ cup diced pancetta (about 4 ounces)
1 tablespoon very finely chopped rosemary
2 medium yellow onions, diced
2 large leeks, white and pale green parts, diced
4 carrots, peeled and diced
4 cups Wilted Greens (page 239; use escarole, spinach,
    chard, or kale)
Fruity green extra virgin olive oil

Combine the beans and water in a large saucepan and bring to a boil over high heat. Turn off the heat and let the beans sit, uncovered, for 1 hour or soak overnight.

Skim off any beans that have floated to the top. Bring the beans to a simmer, add the salt, and let the beans simmer gently, partially covered, over low heat for 45 minutes, or until tender. Make sure that the beans remain covered with 2 inches of liquid at all times.

When the beans are almost tender, heat the olive oil in a large pot over medium heat. Add the garlic and cook for 45 seconds, until it just starts to turn a light golden brown. Toss in the pancetta, give it a stir (this will help prevent the garlic from burning), and cook, stirring occasionally, until the pancetta has rendered its fat and begun to brown. Add the rosemary and stir for 30 seconds, then add the onions and leeks and cook until they just become translucent, 8 to 10 minutes.

Add the carrots, the beans, and the bean cooking liquid to the pot and simmer for 20 minutes.

Place a mound of wilted greens in the bottom of each serving bowl. Ladle the soup over the greens, drizzle with a swirl of fruity olive oil, and serve.

SPRING MINESTRONE

Serves 6 to 8

At Bottega, minestrone is a menu staple that changes with the seasons, and this one heralds spring. For a dramatic and vivid presentation, blanch the green vegetables and shock in a bowl of ice water to set their bright green color and then add at the last minute to warm.

1 tablespoon unsalted butter
2 tablespoons olive oil
2 onions, quartered and thinly sliced
4 bulb onions, thinly sliced (or an additional regular
    onion, thinly sliced)
2 leeks, white and pale green parts, thinly sliced
1 garlic clove, crushed and finely minced
4 carrots, peeled and cut into ½-inch dice
10 small new potatoes, cut into ½-inch dice
½ pound small button mushrooms, quartered
5 cups Chicken Stock (page 241), vegetable stock,
    or spring water
Kosher salt
1 cup sliced asparagus (tips left whole; about 6 to 8
    spears)
1 cup sweet peas
4 small zucchini, cut into ½-inch dice
½ cup shelled fava beans, blanched in boiling water for
    1 minute, cooled in ice water, and peeled
½ cup chopped mint, basil, or parsley or ⅓ cup Pesto
    (page 248)
Extra virgin olive oil (if using the herbs)
Freshly grated Parmigiano-Reggiano
Focaccia (page 82) or ciabatta

Melt the butter with the olive oil in a large pot over medium-low heat. Add the onions, leeks, garlic, and carrots and cook until tender, about 10 minutes.

Add the potatoes, mushrooms, and stock or water and bring to a simmer. Add salt to taste and cook for 10 minutes. Add the asparagus, peas, zucchini, and favas and cook for 5 minutes more, or until the vegetables are very tender.

Ladle the soup into bowls. Top each with a big pinch of chopped herbs and a drizzle of olive oil, or finish each with a dollop of pesto, for a saucier herbaceous garnish. Pass the Parmigiano at the table and serve with wedges of focaccia or slices of ciabatta.

an affinity for shell beans and greens

Tomatoes, shell beans, pole beans, and greens for wilting are ingredients that we Southerners believe to be singularly ours— our own unique heritage of garden goodness. Heated debate often ensues when a gardener declares his homegrown tomatoes the finest, and not long ago, one's wealth correlated with the quantity of shell beans, butter beans, crowders, zippers, lady peas, and October beans that had been "put up," either in the freezer or by drying or canning, for use throughout the gray winter.

Rattlesnake beans, Kentucky Wonder, wax beans, and romano all come under the pole bean category, and a midsummer garden filled with trellises overflowing with climbing bean stalks is a beautiful sight. No self-respecting Alabama farmer would be without these productive vines.

In the American South, there's a particular reverence for a "mess of greens." I'm talking about a tumble of collard, turnip, or mustard greens primarily, but old-timers would add poke salad (poke weed) to that list, as well as dandelion, lamb's-quarters, and other wild greens.

For folks of weak constitution, the distinctive "bouquet" wafting from a pot of simmering greens may be a bit too much. The pungent scent of bitter greens and bacon fat intermingling and simmering are one man's stench and another's perfume. For most, however, the resulting pot liquor is prized, especially suited to "soppin' up" with corn bread and a splash of pepper vinegar.

ABOVE: *Chef Stitt shelling pink-eye peas;* **OPPOSITE:** *Tuscan White Bean Soup with Wilted Escarole (page 55)*

SUMMER MINESTRONE

Serves 6

Since summer brings the greatest variety of vegetables at their flavorful peak, it's the ideal time to make soups to enjoy now or freeze for cooler months. The vegetables in the ingredients list are just suggestions; buy what looks freshest and most appealing at your market.

1 cup dried cannellini beans, soaked overnight in water
   to cover
About 8 cups spring water
One 3-ounce shank-end slice prosciutto di Parma
Kosher salt
¼ cup olive oil
2 large onions, cut into ½-inch dice
1 leek, white and pale green parts, sliced
3 celery stalks, cut into ½-inch dice
2 carrots, peeled and cut into ½-inch dice
2 large garlic cloves, minced
½ small Savoy cabbage, shredded (or substitute kale,
   escarole, mustard greens, or chard)
2 tomatoes, peeled (see page 255), seeded,
   and coarsely chopped
6 basil sprigs, plus 4 basil leaves, chopped
3 bay leaves
Freshly ground black pepper
2 zucchini, cut into ½-inch dice
1 cup small young green beans or haricots verts
Freshly grated Parmigiano-Reggiano
Fruity extra virgin olive oil

OTHER OPTIONS (CHOOSE ONE OR A COMBINATION):
Corn, okra, butter beans, field peas, yellow squash,
   new potatoes

Drain the beans and place them in a heavy pot. Add spring water to cover by 2 inches, then add the prosciutto and a big pinch of salt and bring to a simmer. Reduce the heat and cook at a bare simmer, partially covered, until the beans are tender, about 45 minutes; add a little more water as necessary to keep the beans covered by 2 inches. Remove from the heat and leave the beans in their cooking liquid.

Heat the olive oil in a large pot over medium-low heat. Add the onions, leek, celery, and carrots and cook for 10 to 15 minutes, until the vegetables just begin to turn golden. Add the garlic and cook for another 3 minutes, or until soft. Add the cabbage, tomatoes, basil sprigs, and bay leaves, then add water to cover by 2 inches. Bring to a simmer.

Stir in the cooked beans, with their broth, taste, and add salt and pepper as needed. Cover partially and simmer very gently for 20 minutes. Add the zucchini and green beans and simmer another 10 minutes.

Ladle the soup into bowls, discarding the prosciutto and bay leaves. Garnish each bowl with some of the chopped basil, a little grated Parmigiano, and a drizzle of fruity olive oil, and serve.

BUTTER BEAN, LAMB, AND ORZO SOUP WITH ESCAROLE

Serves 4

In the South, we love our butter beans—limas, as some Northerners call them—both tiny green ones and big fat "speckled" ones. Occasionally you'll find a huge white butter bean that must be a close relative of the *gigante* beans of Italy and Greece. Like the Tuscans, who are called "bean eaters," Southerners recognize the simple beauty of a bowl of beans.

When we have a few leftover lamb shanks, we get excited about the possibility of this delicious soup. Lamb is my first choice for this dish, but leftover braised beef, pork, chicken, or veal work as well. And keep in mind that orzo is a wonderful and easy addition to most hearty soups.

2 tablespoons olive oil

2 medium onions, cut into ¼-inch dice

2 to 3 carrots, peeled and cut into ½-inch dice

2 celery stalks, cut into ½-inch dice

2 garlic cloves, crushed and finely chopped

2 braised lamb shanks, with about 1 cup of their braising liquid

A few mint sprigs

2 to 3 thyme sprigs or a pinch of dried thyme

Pinch of dried marjoram or oregano

3 bay leaves

1 cup peeled (see page 255), seeded, and diced ripe tomatoes, or diced canned tomatoes

2 cups Chicken Stock (page 241) or water

Kosher salt

1 cup cooked (see Note) or frozen small green lima beans

1 heaping cup chopped escarole

Freshly ground black pepper

1 cup cooked orzo (about ½ cup uncooked)

Grated pecorino romano

Fruity extra virgin olive oil

Heat 1 tablespoon of the olive oil in a large pot over medium heat. Add the onions and carrots and cook for 5 minutes. Add the celery and garlic and cook gently for another 5 minutes or until slightly softened.

Meanwhile, remove the lamb from the bones and cut or tear into small pieces; discard the fat and sinew.

Add the lamb and the bones to the pot, along with the mint, thyme, marjoram or oregano, bay leaves, tomatoes, and the braising liquid. Add the stock or water and a pinch of salt and bring to a simmer. Reduce the heat, partially cover, and cook at a very low simmer for 30 to 45 minutes.

Add the lima beans and the escarole and simmer for another 10 minutes. Taste and adjust the seasonings with salt and pepper.

To serve, place the orzo in the bottom of four warm soup bowls and ladle in the soup, discarding the lamb bones and bay leaves. Sprinkle with black pepper and a little grated pecorino; finish with a drizzle of fruity olive oil.

NOTE: To cook fresh butter beans, fill a medium saucepan two-thirds full with water and bring to a boil over high heat. Add 1 teaspoon salt, a sprig of thyme, and 2 bay leaves, if desired, and 1 cup shelled beans. Bring back to a simmer, reduce the heat slightly, and cook for about 25 minutes, or until the beans are tender. Let cool in the cooking liquid, then drain.

LENTIL AND CHICKPEA SOUP

Serves 6 to 8

A tried-and-true comforting favorite, this healthful soup has restorative golden warmth. The choice of using chicken stock or water is yours, but adjust the seasonings to suit your tastes—lots of garlic, perhaps, or a pinch or two of cumin.

A last-second drizzle of vibrant green extra virgin olive oil heightens the flavors. As with many vegetable soups, some cooked barley, farro, or rice makes an interesting addition. Double this recipe and freeze a batch to enjoy on another cold day.

2 tablespoons olive oil

2 garlic cloves, finely chopped

1 medium yellow onion, cut into ½-inch dice

1 red onion, cut into ½-inch dice

Kosher salt and freshly ground black pepper

2 tablespoons chopped flat-leaf parsley

1 teaspoon ground coriander

1 fennel bulb, trimmed, cored, and cut into ½-inch dice

2 carrots, peeled and cut into ½-inch dice

1 celery stalk, cut into ½-inch dice

1 red bell pepper, cored, seeded, and cut into ½-inch
   squares

1½ cups de Puy lentils or brown lentils,
   rinsed and picked over

1 cup canned chickpeas, drained (not rinsed)

2 cups drained canned diced tomatoes

2½ cups Chicken Stock (page 241) or spring water,
   or as needed

Leftover braised meat, such as lamb or veal (optional)

Chopped mint, flat-leaf parsley, or chives or extra virgin
   olive oil for garnish

Heat the olive oil in a large pot over medium heat. Add the garlic and cook, stirring, until golden brown, 2 to 3 minutes. Add the onions and sauté until they are tender but have not begun to caramelize, about 10 minutes. Season with salt and pepper. Add the parsley and coriander and stir for 30 seconds, or until fragrant. Add the diced fennel, carrots, celery, and bell pepper and simmer for 4 to 5 minutes, stirring occasionally.

Meanwhile, combine the lentils in a medium saucepan with water to cover by 2 inches and bring to a rolling boil. Drain the lentils and set aside. (The cooking liquid can be reserved for another recipe or discarded; we don't use it here because it would muddy the soup. The lentils can be cooked in advance.)

Add the lentils, chickpeas, tomatoes, and stock or water to the vegetables. Add the meat, if using, and bring to a simmer. Simmer, partially covered, over low heat for 45 to 50 minutes, until the vegetables are tender. Check the level of the liquid from time to time, replenishing it as necessary. Taste and adjust the seasoning.

Ladle the soup into serving bowls. Garnish with the fresh herbs or a drizzle of extra virgin olive oil.

tomatoes

From the later part of June until the first frost in November, Alabama gardens have the potential to produce world-class tomatoes. However, a sustained harvest of my favorite summer treat can be a bit dicey—a thunderstorm might dump so much rain that the tomatoes split, a hailstorm can wipe out an entire picking, even a blight caused by prolonged high temperatures and humidity will devastate a whole crop. But when conditions are just right—when a cooling breeze drops nighttime temperatures, the thermometer remains steady in the upper 80s, and showers pass—the tomatoes are what a chef's dreams are made of.

I adore cherry tomatoes, the Sweet 100s, Supersweets, and Sungolds, as well as plum tomatoes, all of which are worthy of canning. But it's the big beefsteak tomatoes that win the oohs and ahs—Brandywine, German Pinks, Black Krim, Cherokee Purple, Early Girl, Big Beef, Mortgage Lifter, and Atkinson are just a few of my favorite varieties. The problem, however, is finding these super-quality tomatoes. Most commercial producers are now growing varieties that are just a notch above plain mealy. These are easy to grow, harvest, and ship but have no real flavor or aroma. So count your blessings when you make friends with a farmer or gardener who takes pride in his or her tomato crop, and do everything you can to stay in his or her good graces.

FENNEL WITH BLOOD ORANGES, PISTACHIOS, ENDIVE, AND GORGONZOLA

Serves 4

The tart-sweetness of the citrus mellows the bitter bite of the crisp endive and the earthiness of Gorgonzola. Green pistachios and plump red pomegranate seeds are like little gemstones garnishing this salad of Moorish-influenced Sicilian flavors.

To extract pomegranate seeds, cut the pomegranate in half gently and pry the pulp-coated seeds from the surrounding bitter membrane. Be careful—don't stain your shirt.

½ fennel bulb, halved lengthwise and
    very thinly sliced crosswise
1 Belgian endive, halved crosswise, bottom half trimmed
    and thinly sliced, top separated into leaves
1 head frisée, torn into pieces
½ head radicchio, thinly sliced
Kosher salt and freshly ground black pepper
Scant ¼ cup Balsamic-Sherry Vinaigrette (page 72)
2 blood oranges, peeled, pith cut away,
    and sliced into ¼-inch-thick rounds
1 heaping tablespoon pomegranate seeds
1 heaping tablespoon pistachios, lightly toasted
    (see page 255) and coarsely chopped
¼ pound mountain (naturale) Gorgonzola,
    cut into little pieces

Combine the fennel, sliced endive, frisée, and radicchio in a large bowl. Season with salt and pepper and toss with 2 tablespoons of the vinaigrette.

Artfully arrange the greens on serving plates, distributing them evenly, and placing the endive leaves decoratively around the other greens. Tuck in the slices of blood orange, letting them peek out. Scatter the pomegranate seeds, pistachios, and Gorgonzola evenly over the salads. Drizzle a little more vinaigrette around the edges of the plates and serve.

To Drink: Gewürztraminer (Tramin)

ITALIAN COBB SALAD

Serves 4 • Pictured on page 26

Who doesn't like classic Cobb salad? Here we add endive, watercress, and radicchio instead of romaine and prosciutto in lieu of bacon. The Gorgonzola gives it the final Italian stamp. The ingredients in our Italian Cobb salad are arranged in rows reminiscent of the red, white, and green of the country's flag.

1 Hass avocado
Juice of ¼ lemon
½ head radicchio, thinly sliced
3 tablespoons Sherry Vinaigrette (page 73)
Maldon sea salt and freshly ground black pepper
2 Belgian endive, cut into ⅛-inch-wide slices
2 bunches watercress, larger stems removed,
    rinsed and dried
2 eggs, boiled for 10 minutes, chilled, peeled, and
    chopped
4 thin slices (about 2 ounces) prosciutto di Parma,
    julienned
1 boneless, skinless chicken breast, roasted or grilled,
    chopped
2 tomatoes, peeled (see page 255), seeded, and diced
¾ cup Blue Cheese Dressing (page 73)

Halve and pit the avocado. Scoop out the flesh and cut into ¼-inch dice, then toss with the lemon juice.

Toss the radicchio in a large bowl with 1 tablespoon of the sherry vinaigrette and a pinch each of sea salt and pepper. Arrange in a band on the left side of four large plates. Repeat with the endive and then the watercress, arranging a band of endive in the center of each plate and the watercress on the right side. Season the avocado with salt and pepper and arrange in a little band on top of the endive. Place a band of egg on top of the radicchio and a band of prosciutto and roasted or grilled chicken on the watercress. Scatter the tomatoes around, ladle the blue cheese dressing over, and serve.

To Drink: Rosé, such as Regaleali

olive oil

Most Southern chefs bleed pork fat but I confess that although I love pork in all its many ways, olive oil is my lubricant of choice. The Mediterranean tradition of farming olive trees is of mythic proportions, and I was once lucky enough to travel to the ancient groves of mainland Greece to experience the rite of picking olives and taking them to the mill to be pressed.

Now the demand for high-quality olive oil has skyrocketed, so it pays for the buyer to beware of unscrupulous oil dealers; what the label says and what's in the bottle may be two different things. But there are countless excellent oils from Italy, Crete, Greece, Spain, Turkey, and California—each microclimate of olive groves produces unique variations on a common delicious theme. Since many gourmet food stores allow you to taste before you buy, do this with a couple of friends, and debate the nuances of what you taste to discover your favorites.

ABOVE: *Bottega infused olive oils;* **OPPOSITE:** *Tuscan Egg Salad with Young Lettuces (page 69)*

CAPRI LUNCH SALAD

Serves 2

La Fontellina (see page 131), a dreamy spot nestled between the rocks, cliffs, and blue Mediterranean, serves a classic summer salad of the most intense wild arugula leaves (similar to our favorite *selvetica* variety) in a huge chilled glass bowl. Perched on top of this nest of aromatic greens sits a small mountain of newly picked, still-warm-from-the-sun cherry tomatoes. Everything is anointed with the most vivid green, powerfully olivey olive oil, a little splash of fruity red wine vinegar, and a sprinkling of sea salt. My dear vegetarian wife swoons over it. This is our take.

> 2 tablespoons red wine vinegar
> Maldon sea salt and freshly ground black pepper
> ¼ cup extra virgin olive oil
> 1 cup cherry tomatoes
> 2 cups baby arugula, preferably *selvetica* (wild arugula)
> 1 small bunch basil, leaves only
> 2 ounces fresh mozzarella, thinly sliced

Chill a glass serving bowl.

Combine the vinegar with a pinch each of sea salt and pepper in a small bowl. Gradually whisk in the olive oil to emulsify.

Combine the cherry tomatoes, arugula, and basil in the chilled serving bowl. Season with salt and pepper. Toss the salad with the red wine vinaigrette and garnish with the mozzarella slices.

To Drink: Fiano di Avellino (Feudi di San Gregorio) or white sangria

BOTTEGA CAESAR SALAD

Serves 4

Garnished with delicious focaccia croutons, this salad can be served with or without the grilled chicken.

> 2 heads romaine, washed, dried, and cut or torn
>   into bite-sized pieces
> 2 slices (¾ inch thick and 4 inches long) Focaccia
>   (page 82), cut into ¾-inch cubes and toasted in a
>   300°F oven until golden
> ½ cup Caesar Dressing (page 72)
> Maldon sea salt and freshly ground black pepper
> 4 grilled chicken breasts, cut into thin slices
> ¼ pound Parmigiano-Reggiano or grana padano, grated

Toss the lettuces with the focaccia croutons, dressing, and sea salt and pepper to taste in a large salad bowl. Add the chicken and toss well. Sprinkle with the grated cheese and serve.

To Drink: A simple white wine, such as Soave

TUSCAN EGG SALAD WITH YOUNG LETTUCES

Serves 4 • Pictured on page 67

Chef Cesare Casella introduced me to this unusual and incredibly delicious salad. Cesare's roots reach deep into the Italian countryside outside Lucca. He brings to New York City, via his restaurant Maremma, the hearty and rustic foods of his childhood—dishes infused with his great sense of humor and a generous dose of love and care. At first glance, I thought this warm wilted salad of tender lettuces tossed with soft, pancetta-spiked scrambled farm eggs was very odd, but it took just one bite to realize the brilliance of the dish.

Look for locally or naturally raised eggs rather than the commercial standard—they just taste better. Toast the baguette slices in a 375°F oven for 6 to 8 minutes, or grill them, until crunchy. Use a higher proportion of frisée to the other lettuces in the mix. This salad is a meal in itself.

2 tablespoons extra virgin olive oil

¼ pound pancetta in one piece, unrolled and cut into lardons (¼-by-¾-inch strips)

1 shallot, finely chopped

8 very fresh organic eggs

Maldon sea salt and freshly ground black pepper

Scant 4 cups mixed young lettuces, such as frisée (see headnote), arugula, young Bibb, Romaine, and lolla rossa

2 to 3 tablespoons Sherry Vinaigrette (page 73)

4 slices baguette, rubbed with olive oil and toasted or grilled (see headnote)

Warm the olive oil in a large sauté pan over medium heat. Add the pancetta and cook for 2 to 3 minutes, until it just begins to crisp and render its fat. Add the shallot and cook for 1 minute, or until softened.

Meanwhile, beat the eggs and season with sea salt and pepper. Pour the eggs into the sauté pan and cook over medium-low heat, stirring, until the eggs are just set, 2 to 3 minutes.

Combine the lettuces in a large bowl and season with salt and pepper. Add the vinaigrette and toss.

Add the warm eggs to the salad greens and toss lightly. Divide the "egg salad" among four plates and garnish with the toasts.

To Drink: Orvieto or Vernaccia di San Gimignano

TOMATO SALAD WITH MOZZARELLA, BASIL, AND FRUITY OLIVE OIL

Serves 2

Making this salad is a no-brainer, but there *are* some rules: It should never be prepared before the warm sun of late June appears or after the first frost, and it's a felony to refrigerate tomatoes. Late-summer backyard basil plants are toughened by a long growing season, so stagger your plantings and choose young tender leaves for this and most dishes where the basil is as much a salad green as an herb.

Tune out food snobs who say imported buffalo mozzarella, which is too often slightly rancid or mushy, is the only way to go. Relatively local fresh mozzarella is often a better choice.

I prefer southern Italian—Sicilian or Apulian—olive oil to the Tuscan for dishes like this. Use more oil than you think you should. Add some grilled onions if you want, or some little anchovy fillets, but sea salt and freshly ground black pepper are really the only requirements. If the "regular" tomatoes available are of questionable heritage, consider cherry tomatoes. And you could even substitute fresh mild goat cheese for the mozzarella if you happen to have a local source. Serve with good country bread.

2 or 3 ripe tomatoes, such as Brandywine, German Pinks, Black Crim, Cherokee Purple, or another heirloom variety, cored and sliced ¾ inch thick
4 to 6 ounces fresh mozzarella, cut into ¼- to ½-inch-thick slices
A small handful of tender basil leaves
About 2 teaspoons red wine vinegar or sherry vinegar
Maldon sea salt and freshly ground black pepper
3 tablespoons fruity olive oil, preferably from Sicily or Apulia

Arrange the tomato and mozzarella slices on a large plate, alternating them. Tear the basil leaves over the top. With your thumb over the top of the bottle to control the pour, splash the salad with the vinegar, distributing it evenly. Sprinkle with sea salt and pepper and drizzle with the olive oil.

To Drink: A rosé or a simple, crisp, unoaked white, such as Vermentino (Argiolas) or Soave (Pieropan)

ARUGULA, CHARRED ONION, AND MUSHROOM SALAD

Serves 2

Peppery arugula and shaved Parmigiano with thick, crunchy slices of bittersweet charred onion and white button mushrooms, soft and mild, all brightened by balsamic's syrupy tang—a classic combination.

1 tablespoon aged balsamic vinegar
3 tablespoons extra virgin olive oil
Two ½- to ¾-inch-thick slices Charred Red Onion (page 238)
1 cup thinly sliced cremini or button mushrooms
2 cups arugula
Kosher salt and freshly ground black pepper
Scant ¼ cup shaved Parmigiano-Reggiano

Pour the balsamic vinegar into a small bowl and slowly whisk in the olive oil until emulsified. Set aside.

Arrange the charred onion rings slightly overlapping on two serving plates. Scatter the mushrooms on top of the onions, making sure that some of the onions remain visible. Mound the arugula on top of the mushrooms. Season the salads generously with salt and pepper and scatter the Parmigiano shavings on top. Drizzle with the balsamic dressing and serve.

To Drink: A light, crisp, dry white, such as Pinot Bianco (Tramin)

BALSAMIC VINAIGRETTE

Makes a generous 1 cup

Balsamic vinegar has become a victim of its own success. True artisanal balsamic vinegar is one of Italy's treasures, but there are many more imitation balsamics than the authentic variety, *aceto balsamico di Modena*, which is aged in wood barrels of decreasing size as it matures and concentrates. As with most ingredients, you get what you pay for. An excellent value is *condimento balsamico di Modena*. It's not the ultraluxe version, but it captures balsamic's true spirit—the fruitiness of ripe grapes transformed and matured—and is good for most purposes.

Letting the shallot macerate in the vinegar tames its bite while infusing the vinegar with its flavor.

1 medium shallot, finely minced
⅓ cup balsamic vinegar
½ teaspoon chopped thyme
Kosher salt and freshly ground black pepper
¾ cup extra virgin olive oil

Combine the shallot, vinegar, thyme, and salt and pepper in a small bowl. Set aside to macerate for about 10 minutes.

Whisk in the olive oil and taste and adjust the seasonings. The vinaigrette will keep for several days in a jar in the refrigerator.

BALSAMIC-SHERRY VINAIGRETTE

Makes about ½ cup

I sometimes like to lighten a balsamic vinaigrette with some sherry vinegar—it's less sweet and less intense, and adds complexity of flavor from the Spanish sherry vinegar.

1 shallot, finely minced
2 tablespoons balsamic vinegar
1 tablespoon sherry vinegar
Kosher salt and freshly ground black pepper
½ cup extra virgin olive oil

Combine the shallot, vinegars, and salt and pepper in a small bowl and let macerate for 5 to 10 minutes.

Slowly whisk in the olive oil. Taste and adjust the seasonings. The vinaigrette will keep for several days in a jar in the refrigerator.

CAESAR DRESSING

Makes 1½ cups

We use garlic two ways—a little raw and a little roasted—for a mellower flavor.

1 large garlic clove, crushed and pounded
    to a paste in a mortar
1 teaspoon roasted garlic puree (see page 254)
3 anchovy fillets, rinsed, patted dry, and finely chopped
¼ cup red wine vinegar, such as L'Estornell Spanish
    garnacha (see Sources, page 260)
Juice of ¼ lemon
1 tablespoon Dijon mustard
1 teaspoon Worcestershire sauce
Several dashes of Tabasco sauce
Kosher salt and freshly ground black pepper
1 large egg yolk
1 cup extra virgin olive oil

Combine the garlic, garlic puree, anchovies, vinegar, lemon juice, mustard, Worcestershire, Tabasco, and salt and pepper in a food processor and pulse a few times. Add the yolk and pulse a few more times. Then, with the machine running, add the olive oil in a slow steady stream. The dressing will keep for several days in a jar in the refrigerator.

RED WINE–SHERRY VINAIGRETTE

Makes 1 cup

We use this for our Shrimp Salad Portofino (page 128). Experiment by combining two or three different vinegars. Here an assertive red wine vinegar is paired with sherry—consider trying other options like honey-cider, balsamic, Banyuls, or fig.

½ shallot, finely minced
2 tablespoons L'Estornell Spanish garnacha vinegar (see Sources, page 260) or other good-quality red wine vinegar
2 tablespoons sherry vinegar
Kosher salt and freshly ground black pepper
¾ cup extra virgin olive oil

Combine the shallot, vinegars, and a good pinch each of salt and pepper in a small bowl and let the shallot macerate for 10 minutes.

Whisk in the olive oil in a slow, steady stream. Taste and adjust the seasonings. The vinaigrette will keep for several days in a jar in the refrigerator.

SHERRY VINAIGRETTE

Makes ½ cup

The complex, nutty, and intriguing aroma and flavor of good Spanish sherry vinegar makes this the staple vinaigrette at Bottega.

½ shallot, finely minced
2 tablespoons sherry vinegar
Kosher salt and freshly ground black pepper
6 tablespoons extra virgin olive oil

Combine the shallot, sherry vinegar, and a good pinch each of salt and pepper in a small bowl and let macerate for 10 minutes.

Whisk in the olive oil in a slow, steady stream. Taste and adjust the seasonings. The vinaigrette will keep for several days in a jar in the refrigerator.

BLUE CHEESE DRESSING

Makes about 2¼ cups

We dress our Italian Cobb Salad (page 65) with this rich and creamy dressing. Substitute Stilton or Fourme d'Ambert blue cheese.

½ shallot, finely minced
3 tablespoons white wine vinegar or champagne vinegar
2 tablespoons sherry vinegar or red wine vinegar
½ cup crumbled Gorgonzola
1 cup buttermilk
½ cup heavy cream
½ cup extra virgin olive oil
Kosher salt and freshly ground black pepper

Put the shallot, vinegars, and blue cheese in a food processor and pulse until combined. With the machine running, add the buttermilk, cream, and olive oil. Taste and adjust the seasonings. The dressing will keep for several days in a jar in the refrigerator.

PARMESAN DRESSING

Makes about 1½ cups

This creamy dressing is the pure version of a ranch-style dressing and great when tossed with crisp romaine leaves or used as a dip for crudités.

1 shallot, finely minced
1 cup heavy cream or plain whole-milk yogurt
¼ cup champagne vinegar
Juice of 2 lemons
¼ cup finely grated Parmigiano-Reggiano or grana padano
Kosher salt and freshly ground white pepper
Pinch of sugar

Combine all the ingredients in a bowl, whisking well to blend. Taste and adjust the seasonings. This dressing will remain fresh for about 5 days in a jar in the refrigerator—if you can keep it around that long.

BASIC PIZZA DOUGH

Makes three 7-ounce portions of dough, for three 10-inch pizzas

Bottega's wood-fired oven churns out delicious crusts that get crisp just as the toppings melt, wilt, or warm through. If you want to replicate such a cooking environment at home, put pizza stones or untreated terra-cotta tiles from the home improvement store on the center rack of your oven. Blast your oven as high as it will go—the Bottega oven runs at between 600° and 800°F—and preheat the stones or tiles for at least 30 minutes. Be sure to dust the stones or tiles with coarse cornmeal before sliding in the pizza to help prevent the crust from sticking.

This dough can also be made by hand, but a mixer makes a quick job of it.

1¼ cups warm water (105° to 115°F)
1 tablespoon honey
1 tablespoon active dry yeast
2 cups all-purpose flour
½ cup whole wheat flour
2 teaspoons kosher salt
¼ cup olive oil
Cornmeal for dusting (optional)

Pour the warm water into a small bowl, stir in the honey, and sprinkle the yeast over the top. Set aside to proof until foamy, about 10 minutes.

Combine the flours and salt in the bowl of a stand mixer fitted with the paddle attachment (or use a large bowl and a sturdy hand mixer). Add the yeast mixture and olive oil and mix on low speed until the dough forms a mass on the paddle and pulls away from the sides of the bowl, 4 to 5 minutes.

Remove the dough and divide it into 3 equal portions. Put on a flour-dusted baking sheet, cover with plastic wrap, and set aside in a warm place to rise for 30 minutes, or until almost doubled. (You can make the dough ahead and refrigerate it overnight if necessary; allow it to come to room temperature before continuing.)

The dough is ready to be rolled out and baked. You can hold the rolled dough at room temperature for a short while on a sheet of parchment paper that has been dusted with a little cornmeal.

OPPOSITE: *Grilled Chicken, Pesto, Mozzarella, and Aged Provolone Pizza (page 77)*

ROASTED SWEET PEPPER AND TOMATO CHUTNEY PIZZA

Makes one 10-inch pizza; serves 1 to 2 • Pictured on page 50

Deliciously simple and flavorful. We sometimes add sliced grilled chicken breast and a handful of arugula leaves right as the pizza comes out of the oven, so the leaves just begin to wilt as the dish arrives at the table. If you don't have the chutney on hand, you can substitute sweet, spicy barbecue sauce.

One 7-ounce portion Basic Pizza Dough (page 75)
Coarse cornmeal
1 heaping teaspoon roasted garlic puree (page 254)
1 tablespoon Alecia's Tomato Chutney
   (see Sources, page 260)
1 red or yellow bell pepper, roasted (see page 254),
   peeled, seeded, and sliced into ½-by-2-inch strips
2 ounces Fontina, cut into ½-inch cubes
1½ ounces provolone, shredded

Position a rack in the center of the oven and preheat the oven to 500°F. If using a baking stone, preheat it for 30 minutes.

Roll out the dough on a lightly floured surface to a 10-inch round. Transfer the dough to a 12-inch pizza pan, a large baking sheet, or a pizza peel that has been sprinkled with coarse cornmeal.

Combine the roasted garlic puree with the chutney and spread the mixture evenly over the dough, leaving a 1-inch border all around. Scatter the peppers, Fontina, and provolone on top.

Transfer the pan to the oven or slide the pizza onto the hot stone and bake for 8 to 12 minutes, until the crust is golden brown. Serve immediately.

To Drink: A simple rustic red wine, such as Valpolicella (Allegrini) or Chianti Classico (Fontodi)

PIZZA WITH WILD MUSHROOMS, BUTTERNUT SQUASH, AND WILTED GREENS

Makes one 10-inch pizza; serves 1 to 2 • Pictured on page 50

Autumn ingredients of roasted butternut squash, wild mushrooms, and greens make this a seasonal pizza, but you can adapt your own toppings for any time of the year.

1 tablespoon olive oil
½ yellow onion, thickly sliced
About ½ cup cremini mushrooms, stemmed and
   quartered
2 cups spinach leaves
Kosher salt and freshly ground black pepper
One 7-ounce portion Basic Pizza Dough (page 75)
Coarse cornmeal for sprinkling
1 tablespoon Alecia's Tomato Chutney (see Sources,
   page 260)
½ cup cubed Roasted Butternut Squash and Balsamico
   (page 190)
3 ounces Fontina, cut into ½-inch cubes
Pinch of red pepper flakes

Position a rack in the center of the oven and preheat the oven to 500°F. If using a baking stone, preheat it for 30 minutes.

Heat 2 teaspoons of the olive oil in a large sauté pan over medium heat. Add the onion and cook until golden brown and caramelized, about 10 minutes. Transfer to a plate.

Add the remaining teaspoon of olive oil to the hot pan, then add the mushrooms and sauté for 5 minutes, or until the mushrooms have given up their liquid and are a rich brown. Transfer to the plate with the onions.

Throw the spinach leaves into the hot pan, sprinkle with salt and pepper, and sauté until just wilted, about 30 seconds. Transfer to the plate with the onions and mushrooms.

Roll out the dough on a lightly floured surface to a 10-inch round. Transfer it to a 12-inch pizza pan, a large baking sheet, or a pizza peel that has been sprinkled with coarse cornmeal.

Spread the tomato chutney evenly over the dough, leaving a 1-inch border all around. Top with the spinach, mushrooms, squash, and onions. Dot the top with the cubes of Fontina. Sprinkle with the red pepper.

Transfer the pan to the oven or slide the pizza onto the hot stone and bake for 8 to 12 minutes, until the crust is golden brown and the cheese is bubbly. Serve immediately.

To Drink: Chianti (Badia a Coltibuono)

GRILLED CHICKEN, PESTO, MOZZARELLA, AND AGED PROVOLONE PIZZA

Makes one 10-inch pizza; serves 1 to 2 • Pictured on pages 50 and 74

A popular fixture at Bottega Café, this simple pizza is topped with provolone cheese and sliced grilled chicken breast, perked up with vibrant green pesto. Even kids love it.

One 7-ounce portion Basic Pizza Dough (page 75)
Coarse cornmeal
1 heaping tablespoon Pesto (page 248)
½ to 1 grilled chicken breast, sliced ½ inch thick
2 to 3 ounces fresh mozzarella, torn into pieces
2 ounces aged provolone, shredded

Position a rack in the center of the oven and preheat the oven to 500°F. If using a baking stone, preheat it for 30 minutes.

Roll the dough into a 10-inch round on a lightly floured surface. Transfer it to a 12-inch pizza pan, large baking sheet, or a pizza peel that has been sprinkled with coarse cornmeal.

Spread the pesto evenly over the dough, leaving a 1-inch border all around. Top with the sliced chicken, mozzarella, and provolone.

Transfer the pan to the oven or slide the pizza onto the hot stone and bake for 8 to 12 minutes, until the crust is golden brown and the cheese is bubbling. Serve immediately.

To Drink: Barbera (Marchesi di Gresy)

SMOKED SALMON PIZZA WITH RED ONIONS, CAPERS, AND MASCARPONE

Makes one 10-inch pizza; serves 1 to 2 • Pictured on page 50

This Wolfgang Puck inspiration is perfect cocktail party food. And unexpected though pizza may be for breakfast, a slice of this one is a lighter version of the classic bagel with lox and cream cheese.

One 7-ounce portion Basic Pizza Dough (page 75)
Coarse cornmeal for sprinkling
2 teaspoons extra virgin olive oil
¼ cup thinly sliced red onion
Kosher salt and freshly ground black pepper
2 ounces (¼ cup) mascarpone cheese
1 tablespoon sour cream
1 scant tablespoon chopped dill
Juice of ½ lemon
3 ounces sliced smoked salmon
1 teaspoon capers, drained

Position a rack in the center of the oven and preheat the oven to 500°F. If using a pizza stone, preheat it for 30 minutes.

Roll out the pizza dough to a 10-inch round on a lightly floured surface. Transfer the dough to a 12-inch pizza pan, a large baking sheet, or a pizza peel that has been sprinkled with coarse cornmeal.

Brush the olive oil evenly over the dough, leaving a 1-inch border all around. Scatter half of the red onion on top and sprinkle with salt and pepper.

Put the pan in the oven or slide the pizza onto the hot stone and bake for 8 to 12 minutes, or until the crust is golden brown.

Meanwhile, combine the mascarpone, sour cream, dill, lemon juice, and salt and pepper to taste in a bowl.

Spread the mascarpone mixture evenly over the warm crust, maintaining the border. Top with overlapping slices of the smoked salmon, the capers, and the remaining red onion, and serve immediately.

To Drink: Prosecco

CAFFE SPORT SEAFOOD PIZZA

Makes one 10-inch pizza; serves 2 to 4

I fell in love with the old-time family feel of North Beach, San Francisco's Little Italy, while living there many years ago. North Beach was also home to a humble restaurant called Caffe Sport, along a short street dotted with bars once frequented by the likes of Lawrence Ferlinghetti and other beat poets. It offered a rather uninspired menu of Italian basics, but the local college students and others of meager budget flocked there to enjoy its cheap Sicilian fare. It was always packed, loud, and lively.

In time, someone tipped me off to the kitchen's traditional late-night Friday special: a huge pizza loaded with a massive array of seafood—mussels, clams, prawns, scallops, and even lobster—all cloaked in a garlicky herb-tomato sauce. With my then girlfriend, I went to indulge in this most bizarre yet wonderful creation—elbowing for table space and fueled with plenty of cheap California wine—and be a part of this Friday-night tradition. And though this was a big splurge, the pizza arrived with more shellfish than I had ever seen. It was a rustic-meets-decadent feast, a kind of gustatory celebration of life! Here's my version, but you can tone it down by using just shrimp.

One 1-pound lobster
6 large shrimp (21 to 30 count), peeled and deveined
12 mussels, scrubbed and debearded
6 cockles or small clams, scrubbed and soaked in water
    for 30 minutes
1 large garlic clove, thinly sliced
2 tablespoons olive oil
½ cup plus 1 tablespoon Marinara Sauce (page 246)
One 7-ounce portion Basic Pizza Dough (page 75)
Coarse cornmeal for sprinkling
½ cup cubed mozzarella
A small handful of fresh herb leaves—basil, parsley,
    and oregano—coarsely chopped

Position a rack in the center of the oven and preheat the oven to 500°F. If using a baking stone, preheat it for 30 minutes.

Fit a large stockpot with a steamer basket, add water to come to just below the basket, and bring to a rolling boil over high heat. Add the lobster, cover, and steam for 3 to 4 minutes. Transfer the lobster to a work surface with tongs and, using a towel or oven mitt, break off the claws. Return the claws to the steamer and steam for another 4 minutes. Twist off the tail and discard the body.

Using a large heavy knife or kitchen shears, cut the lobster tail crosswise into 1-inch sections along the natural breaks in the shell and set aside, with the shell intact. Crack the claws and remove all the meat. Use a lobster pick to remove the knuckle meat. In a large bowl, toss the lobster, shrimp, mussels, cockles or clams, and garlic with the olive oil and ½ cup marinara sauce to coat.

Roll the dough into a 10-inch round on a lightly floured surface. Transfer it to a 12-inch pizza pan, a large baking sheet, or a pizza peel that has been sprinkled with coarse cornmeal.

Spread the remaining 1 tablespoon marinara evenly over the dough, leaving a 1-inch border all around. Scatter the mozzarella over the sauce, then top with the seafood mixture.

Transfer the pan to the oven or slide the pizza onto the pizza stone, and bake for 8 to 12 minutes, or until the cockles and mussels have opened, the shrimp are firm, and the crust is golden brown. Top with a sprinkling of the fresh herbs and serve immediately.

To Drink: A rustic light red wine, perhaps Lagrein (Lageder)

FLATBREAD WITH SMOKED SALMON

Serves 2 to 4

An irresistible riff on the bagel with cream cheese and lox, here we roll pizza dough super thin and "dock" it with the tines of a fork (to keep it flat), then bake until crispy. Instead of cream cheese we substitute mascarpone and dill, then add the obligatory red onions and capers. This makes a wonderful party hors d'oeuvre.

> One 7-ounce portion Basic Pizza Dough (page 75),
>   rolled very thin (about 14 inches wide)
> Salt and fresh ground white pepper
> 1 teaspoon extra virgin olive oil
> ½ cup mascarpone
> 1 cup sour cream
> Juice of ½ lemon
> 1 tablespoon fresh dill, finely chopped
> ¼ pound smoked salmon, thinly sliced
> 2 paper-thin slices red onion
> A handful of small tender lettuces
> Heaping teaspoon of rinsed capers

Position a rack in the center of the oven and preheat the oven to 500°F. If using a baking stone, preheat it for 30 minutes.

Once the dough is rolled out, run a "docker" over or prick all over with the tines of a fork. Season with salt and pepper and a drizzle of olive oil and bake in the oven until crispy and light golden—about 3 minutes (depending on your oven).

Place the mascarpone, sour cream, and lemon juice in a mixing bowl, add salt, pepper, and the fresh dill. Taste and adjust the seasonings.

Cut the flatbread into 6 large triangles. Layer each one with a spoonful of the dill mascarpone sauce and then lay the slices of smoked salmon on top. Using three slices apiece, stack into a "tepee" on a serving plate and place the onion slices on top. Scatter the lettuces about and sprinkle the capers over all.

To Drink: Champagne or prosecco

CHICKEN MARINARA PIADINE
Serves 1 to 2

This is a bit like having a healthy chicken and romaine salad and a light pizza at the same time. The pizza dough is rolled ultra thin, very lightly topped with sauce, and cooked until almost crisp, then covered with an herb salad, folded over, and cut on the bias into big "sandwiches." We offer many versions of piadine at Bottega.

  One 7-ounce portion Basic Pizza Dough (page 75)
  2 teaspoons olive oil
  Kosher salt and freshly ground black pepper
  Scant ¼ cup Marinara Sauce (page 246)
  1 grilled chicken breast, thinly sliced
  ⅓ cup ½-inch cubes mozzarella
  ⅓ cup crumbled feta cheese
  1 kirby cucumber, peeled, seeded, and diced
  Heaping 1½ cups chopped romaine
  2 tablespoons Sherry Vinaigrette (page 73)

Position a rack in the center of the oven and put a baking stone or a heavy baking sheet on it. Preheat the oven to 500°F; let the stone or pan preheat for 30 minutes.

Roll out the dough on a lightly floured surface to a 10- to 12-inch round; the dough should be only ¼ inch thick. Brush with the olive oil and sprinkle with salt and pepper. Spread the marinara over the surface of the dough, leaving a 1-inch border all around. Transfer the dough to the hot stone or pan and bake for 6 to 8 minutes, or until cooked through but not crisp.

While the dough bakes, combine the chicken, mozzarella, feta cheese, cucumber, and romaine in a bowl and toss with the sherry vinaigrette to coat. To serve, mound the salad on one side of the hot flatbread, fold it over, and cut in half on the bias. Serve immediately.

To Drink: A light red wine, such as Lagrein (Tramin)

PIADINE are part pizza, part salad, part sandwich. Imagine a very, very thin pizza with a minimum of cheese and almost no sauce. But when it comes out of the oven, it's topped with a salad of assorted ingredients, then folded over, cut in half, and eaten like a sandwich. Piadine are healthier and lighter than traditional American pizzas, and the two recipes here show how they can be inspired even by the flavors of Persia. Build on the piadine idea by creating ingredient combinations to suit your tastes.

PERSIAN PIADINE
Serves 2

My lovely wife, Pardis, and her Persian family introduced me to the custom of serving a platter overflowing with bunches of parsley, mint, chives, and scallions (and sometimes dill and cilantro), along with a bowl of homemade yogurt, chunks of feta, toasted walnuts, and some crisp radishes and cucumbers. Everyone takes a little piece of pita or paper-thin flatbread and makes a little roll-up with all or just a few of these ingredients. I call it our Persian breakfast and serve it at home with a big pot of tea. It seemed only natural to combine these same ingredients in one of our pizza like preparations—the *piadine*. This light version is pure, fresh garden flavor with a hint of the eastern Mediterranean.

  One 7-ounce portion Basic Pizza Dough (page 75)
  1 tablespoon extra virgin olive oil
  Kosher salt and freshly ground black pepper
  2 tablespoons plain fat-free yogurt
  1 tablespoon chopped mint, plus 8 mint leaves, torn
  1 heaping cup watercress leaves
  4 to 5 basil leaves, torn
  2 dill sprigs, torn
  1 teaspoon snipped chives
  2 scallions, chopped
  1 cucumber, peeled and chopped
  2 radishes, thinly sliced
  ⅓ cup crumbled feta cheese
  4 walnut halves, toasted (see page 255) and coarsely chopped
  2 tablespoons Sherry Vinaigrette (page 73)

Position a rack in the center of the oven and put a baking stone or a heavy baking sheet on it. Preheat the oven to 500°F; allow the stone or pan to preheat for 30 minutes.

Roll out the pizza dough on a lightly floured surface to a 10- to 12-inch round; the dough should be only ¼ inch thick. Brush with 2 teaspoons of the olive oil and sprinkle with salt and pepper. Transfer the dough to the hot stone or pan and bake for 6 to 8 minutes, or until it is cooked through but not crisp.

While the dough bakes, whisk together the yogurt, chopped mint, and the remaining teaspoon of oil in a small bowl; set aside. In a large bowl, toss the watercress, torn basil leaves and dill sprigs, chives, scallions, cucumber, radishes, feta cheese, and walnuts with the vinaigrette.

To serve, mound the salad on one side of the warm bread and drizzle with the yogurt sauce. Fold the bread over and slice the piadine in half on the bias. Serve immediately.

To Drink: A dry rosé or Earl Grey tea

FOCACCIA

Makes one 12-by-16-inch bread

A Ligurian staple, this is versatile bread that can be sliced and used for crostini or bruschetta. The top can be embellished simply with kosher salt or coarse sea salt, or further with rosemary sprigs, pine nuts, sultanas, or grated Parmesan cheese—whatever suits your fancy.

  1¼ cups warm water (105° to 115°F)
  1 tablespoon honey
  1 tablespoon active dry yeast
  3 cups bread flour, plus flour for dusting
  1 tablespoon kosher salt
  ¼ cup olive oil
  2 tablespoons extra virgin olive oil
  1 teaspoon coarse sea salt or kosher salt

Put the water in a small bowl, stir in the honey, and sprinkle the yeast over the top. Set the bowl to proof until foamy, about 10 minutes.

Combine the 3 cups flour, salt, ¼ cup oil, and the yeast mixture in the bowl of a stand mixer (or use a large bowl and a sturdy hand mixer) and mix until the ingredients are thoroughly combined and the dough pulls away from the sides of the bowl. Cover tightly with plastic wrap and set aside in a warm area to rest for a few minutes.

Spray a 12-by-16-inch baking pan with cooking spray or lightly grease it. Turn the dough out onto a lightly floured work surface and knead for 2 to 3 minutes, until it is just slightly sticky and firm to the touch. Shape the dough into a ball and place it on the baking sheet. Cover with plastic wrap and let it rise in a warm area for 30 to 45 minutes, until doubled.

Lightly sprinkle flour over the top of the dough, then transfer it to a floured work surface. Using a rolling pin, roll it out into a 12-by-16-inch rectangle. Fold the rolled dough in half, carefully transfer it to the baking pan, and unfold it, fitting it into the pan. Brush the surface with the extra virgin olive oil and sprinkle with the coarse salt. Place the pan in a warm area and let rise until doubled in volume, 30 to 45 minutes.

Preheat the oven to 425°F.

Lightly dimple the dough all over with your fingertips. Bake for 15 to 20 minutes, rotating the pan once halfway through baking, until golden on top and cooked through: the bread should sound hollow when tapped on the bottom. Transfer the bread to a rack to cool before slicing.

MUFFALETTA WITH CURED MEATS AND OLIVE RELISH

Serves 4

This New Orleans classic may not be found in Italy, but I am sure Italians would love it. Focaccia is my choice of bread, but a San Francisco sourdough roll, or even a couple of slices of rye, would work just fine. A small mountain of quality Italian-style cured meats is a must.

You'll want to have at least three different cuts of meat—salami (Genoa, Tuscan, or Neapolitan-style), mortadella (the original bologna), and prosciutto or baked or boiled ham. You can supplement that trio with coppa, spicy cured pork neck or shoulder, and/or pancetta. Adventurous souls may want to add a little guanciale or lardo for a very Italian experience. Mounded on top of the meat is a relishy blend of celery, peppers, olives, scallions, vinegar, olive oil, and herbs, tossed together to provide a little crunch. A few slices of smoky provolone or milky mozzarella, a slice or two of ripe tomato, and a few leaves of arugula wouldn't be out of place, but this sandwich is really about cured meats, with a spicy olive salad embellishment.

FOR THE OLIVE SALAD

¼ cup diced (¼-inch) celery
¼ cup diced (¼-inch) red bell pepper
¼ cup diced (¼-inch) cauliflower (optional)
⅓ cup pitted green olives, coarsely chopped
1 teaspoon dried oregano
Scant 1 teaspoon dried marjoram
4 basil leaves, cut into chiffonade
2 scallions, finely chopped
2 tablespoons red wine vinegar
¼ cup extra virgin olive oil
Pinch of red pepper flakes
Kosher salt and freshly ground black pepper

Four 6-by-4-inch pieces Focaccia (page 82) or ciabatta
8 slices prosciutto
8 slices mortadella
8 slices Tuscan salami
8 slices Genoa salami
8 slices coppa (optional)
4 slices provolone
4 slices mozzarella
8 slices ripe Roma (plum) tomato
A few arugula leaves (optional)

To make the olive salad, combine the celery, bell pepper, cauliflower, if using, olives, oregano, marjoram, basil, scallions, vinegar, olive oil, and red pepper flakes in a medium bowl and toss. Taste the relish and season with salt and pepper.

To make the sandwiches, split the pieces of bread in half and pull out a little of the soft bread from each half to create a cavity for the filling. Layer equal portions of the cured meats on each of the bottom halves, then top with the olive salad, provolone, mozzarella, tomato slices, and arugula leaves, if using. Top with the other halves of the bread, press together, and wrap the sandwiches in plastic. These will only improve over a few hours at room temperature as the flavors meld.

To Drink: Cold beer or a cool Dolcetto

SALTED, CURED, AND SIMPLE Thanks to organizations like Slow Food and people like Paul Bertolli and Armandino Batali, Mario Batali's father, we're seeing a small renaissance of cured meat producers in the United States. There is a renewed interest in the old-fashioned artisanal ways of curing different meats—especially pork, but also venison, beef, goat, and lamb. The cuts range from the belly (pancetta), jowl (guanciale), and shoulder (coppa) to the leg (prosciutto) and fatback (lardo). And the production of salami is the ideal way to combine all the remaining "less beautiful" cuts so that nothing is wasted, with very savory results.

PASTA

DRIED PASTA

Capellini Bottega

Dry versus Fresh

Trenette Genovese

Penne Salad with Sweet Peas, Mint, and Pesto

Pardis's Pasta—or Penne with Spicy Tomato-Fennel Sauce

Garganelli with Spring Onions, Asparagus, and Peas

Spring Vegetable Lasagne

Baked Shells with Ricotta and Fennel Sausage

Café Macaroni and Cheese

Capellini Gratin

Bucatini with Clams, Pancetta, Hot Chile, and Rapini

Pasta with Venison Bolognese

Puttanesca with Shrimp and Linguine

Penne with Chicken Meatballs

Pappardelle with Rabbit, Porcini, and Parmesan

Italian Reds We Love

FRESH PASTA

Pasta Dough

Silk Handkerchief Pasta with Pesto

Train Ride Through Liguria

Tortellini Salad with Chicken, Pine Nuts, Sultanas,
   and Balsamic Vinaigrette

Tortelloni with Crabmeat, Ricotta, and Brown Butter

Ravioli with Pumpkin and Sage Butter

Potato Ravioli with Crawfish, Candied Lemon, and Tabasco

Gnocchi with Prosciutto and Sage

Crespelle

OVERLEAF LEFT: *Ravioli with Pumpkin and Sage Butter (page 114);* **OPPOSITE:**
(clockwise from top left) pappardelle, tortelloni ("bishop's hat"), ravioli, and tagliatelle

CAPELLINI BOTTEGA

Serves 4

This quintessential, humble Bottega dish has only a few ingredients, but when sufficient attention to those ingredients is paid—like carefully and patiently cooking the garlic until just golden and fragrant or adding the chile to the hot oil before the tomatoes—you end up with a spicy, juicy tomato sauce. Instead of the traditional spaghetti, the delicate capellini is a perfect match.

When local vine-ripened tomatoes aren't in season use top-quality canned San Marzano tomatoes. Add them to the pan with the golden soft garlic and chile just after you've put the pasta in to boil. And don't skimp on the basil. The sauce needs to cook just briefly to bring out its aroma and robust flavor. It should be juicy; if it has reduced too much, add some of the pasta water you have reserved. And drizzle with the best Italian olive oil you can find.

⅓ cup extra virgin olive oil

4 to 5 garlic cloves, lightly crushed and peeled

4 dried red chile peppers

½ pound capellini

8 to 10 large basil leaves

10-12 Oven-Roasted Tomatoes (page 238) or canned
   whole San Marzano tomatoes

Kosher salt and freshly ground black pepper

Generous ¼ cup freshly grated grana padano or
   Parmigiano-Reggiano

Bring a large pot of generously salted water to a boil.

Meanwhile, in a large sauté pan, heat 2 tablespoons of the olive oil over medium heat. Add the garlic to the pan, reduce the heat to medium-low, and roll the garlic gently around in the oil to toast it until nicely golden, about 2 to 3 minutes. Add the dried chiles and cook for 30 seconds.

Put the capellini into the boiling water to cook, then add half the basil leaves and the tomatoes to the sauté pan. Raise the heat to medium-high and crush the tomatoes using a wooden spoon for the 2 to 3 minutes that the pasta cooks. Season the sauce with salt and pepper.

When the pasta is al dente, drain it, reserving about 3 tablespoons of the cooking water.

Add the pasta to the sauce and, if the pasta seems dry, add some or all of the reserved pasta water. Toss over medium heat for 30 seconds, then transfer to a warm bowl.

Tear the remaining basil leaves over the pasta, drizzle with the remaining olive oil, and top with the grated cheese. Serve immediately.

To Drink: Chianti (Castello di Volpaia or Isole e Olena)

DRY VERSUS FRESH

I eat much, much more dried pasta than fresh, even though for special menus and occasions nothing beats tender homemade ravioli, tortellini, or delicate silk handkerchiefs. Italians also consume more dried than fresh, despite its availability in neighborhood pasta shops. There's just no way around the convenience of a box in the pantry for a quick meal.

Nowadays a wide variety of artisanal dried pastas is available. Rustichella d'Abruzzo pasta from Manicarette (see Sources, page 260) is one of the best and well worth the cost. The company was founded in the early 1900s in Abruzzo, east of Rome, and the region's durum wheat and spring water produce unparalleled pasta dough. The company uses old bronze dies, some from the 1800s, to extrude the dough, which is then dried for fifty-six hours. This handcrafted product comes in a multitude of shapes, and we keep many of them on hand: penne rigate, pennette, rigatoni, spaghetti, and bucatini, as well as orecchiette, gnocchette, farfalloni, and their delicious egg garganelli.

But on a day when you aren't hurried, take the time to try one of the homemade pasta recipes in this chapter. Admittedly, some work is involved, but the finished product is a very impressive thing to share with guests. Substituting good fresh pasta from your Italian or specialty market is fine. And remember that fresh pastas like ravioli and tortellini freeze very well. Some of the recipes make more pasta than you will need for the particular dish, so you can freeze the extra for later.

Pasta, dried or fresh, is a Bottega specialty. With a salad and a glass of wine, it's pretty much a perfect meal.

TRENETTE GENOVESE

Serves 4 to 6

The Ligurians around Genoa use a pasta similar to linguine, called trenette, in this uniquely regional dish. A bit thicker than linguine, it is usually sold dried but can also be found fresh. The dish is wonderfully subtle: think pesto that is not overwhelmed with garlic, but is more about the perfume of basil from tender young plants. New potatoes are first tossed into the pasta water to cook, and then some thin green beans; they combine with the pasta for a more substantial dish. All of this is tumbled with the fragrant pesto, a bit of pasta water, and a smidgen of butter (optional) for richness. Delicious.

½ pound small new potatoes, scrubbed,
   halved if larger than a golf ball
¼ pound tender young green beans, trimmed
1 pound trenette (see headnote), linguine, or tagliatelle
Pesto (page 248)
1 tablespoon unsalted butter (optional)
Freshly grated grana padano or pecorino romano

Bring a large pot of generously salted water to a rolling boil. Add the potatoes and cook for 10 to 15 minutes, or until tender. Remove with a wire skimmer or slotted spoon and set aside on a plate.

Add the green beans to the boiling water and cook until tender (not crunchy), 3 to 4 minutes. Remove with the slotted spoon and add to the potatoes.

Add the pasta to the boiling water and cook until al dente. Drain the pasta, reserving a little of the pasta water, and return it to the pot. Add the potatoes and green beans and toss together over medium heat. Add ⅔ cup of the pesto and the butter, if using. Toss to thoroughly combine, thinning the sauce with a bit of the reserved pasta water as needed.

Serve in warm pasta bowls, and pass the remaining pesto at the table for those who would like a dollop more, along with the grated cheese.

To Drink: Cinque Terre, Vermentino, or Sauvignon Blanc such as Sancerre

PENNE SALAD WITH SWEET PEAS, MINT, AND PESTO

Serves 6

Pasta salads are of course great for entertaining. This one is relatively easy to prepare and keeps for a couple of days. The flavors are best at room temperature rather than ice-cold from the refrigerator. Frozen peas are a good substitute for fresh, and don't skimp on the fresh mint. You can prepare the pesto and the vinaigrette while the pasta cooks and then cools. Add cubes of grilled chicken for a more substantial dish.

1 pound penne
1½ teaspoons olive oil
½ cup Pesto (page 248)
2 cups cubed (½-inch) fresh mozzarella
   (about 8 ounces)
2 tablespoons Sherry Vinaigrette (page 73)
Juice of ½ lemon
Kosher salt and freshly ground black pepper
1½ cups fresh or frozen tiny sweet peas (if frozen,
   defrost in a sieve under warm water)
1 bunch mint, leaves only

Bring a large pot of generously salted water to a boil. Add the penne and cook until just barely al dente, about 12 minutes.

Drain the pasta and transfer it to a large baking sheet. Toss it with the olive oil to coat, then let cool, giving the pan a shake occasionally.

Transfer the pasta to a large bowl and add the pesto, mozzarella, sherry vinaigrette, lemon juice, and salt and pepper to taste. Toss to combine, then stir in the peas. (The salad can be made to this point up to a day ahead and refrigerated; bring to room temperature before serving.)

Just before serving, chop the mint and add it to the salad. Taste and adjust the seasonings.

To Drink: Sauvignon (Villa Russiz)

PARDIS'S PASTA—OR PENNE WITH SPICY TOMATO-FENNEL SAUCE

Serves 2

It's 11:30 P.M. and my wife and I have finally returned home from the restaurants and cranked up John Hammond, Tom Waits, MC Solaar, or Baba Maal on our sound system. We've fed many but haven't had dinner ourselves. A few glasses of something dry and crisp are in order (an Arneis, Grüner Veltliner, Sancerre, or Tocia) as I begin to sauté some aromatics: onion—sometimes bulb, often red or Vidalia, and much of the time all of the above—plus some leeks; garlic, but not too much; slices of fennel. We sip our wine, listen to the music, and relax while the vegetables soften. Now comes fennel seed, maybe some cumin, and always hot pepper (either jalapeño or dried red chile). I let it all cook a little more, filling our kitchen with a pungent aroma. Good canned tomatoes come next, crushed by hand and allowed to simmer while we change our clothes, consider a red wine, and talk about the day. Once cooked, the pasta gets tossed with the fragrant tomato-fennel sauce, a healthy dose of freshly grated grana padano, and a big slug of fruity olive oil for me, a little less for Pardis. A blessing is offered. We're happy.

Penne is the fallback pasta here, but trenette, orecchiette, and little shells have all stood in.

About 2 tablespoons extra virgin olive oil
1 sweet onion, such as Vidalia or Maui,
    halved and thinly sliced
½ fennel bulb, cut into ½-inch-thick slices
½ leek, white and pale green parts, thinly sliced
    (optional)
1 garlic clove, crushed
1 teaspoon fennel seeds
½ teaspoon cumin seeds
½ jalapeño pepper, thinly sliced
One 28-ounce can whole San Marzano tomatoes
Grated zest of ½ orange
½ pound penne (or another shape; see headnote)
½ cup freshly grated grana padano or Parmigiano-
    Reggiano
Kosher salt and freshly ground black pepper
Several big sprigs of basil, marjoram, parsley, and/or
    oregano, leaves only

Heat 1 tablespoon of the olive oil in a medium saucepan over medium heat. Add the onion, fennel, and leek, if using, and sauté, stirring with a wooden spoon, for 8 to 10 minutes, until softened. Add the garlic, fennel seeds, cumin, and jalapeño and cook until the vegetables are tender and the spices are fragrant, a few minutes more.

Add the tomatoes, crushing them with your hands or the wooden spoon, and their juices, then add the orange zest and cook for 20 minutes, until the tomatoes have broken down and the juices have reduced somewhat.

Meanwhile, bring a large pot of generously salted water to a boil over high heat. Drop in the pasta, give a stir, and cook until the pasta is al dente.

Drain the pasta, reserving a little of the cooking water. Toss the pasta with the tomato sauce and a little of the pasta water until thoroughly coated. Toss with some of the cheese and season with salt and pepper.

Divide the pasta between two bowls and garnish with a drizzle of olive oil, the fresh herbs (tear the bigger leaves as you add them), and the remaining grated cheese.

To Drink: Dolcetto or Barbera (Bruno Giacosa or Aldo Conterno)

ABOVE: *Spring Vegetable Lasagne* (page 95); OPPOSITE: *Garganelli with Spring Onions, Asparagus, and Peas* (page 94)

GARGANELLI WITH SPRING ONIONS, ASPARAGUS, AND PEAS

Serves 4 • Pictured on page 93

When springtime finally brings asparagus spears, bulb onions, and plump sweet peas, we combine them in dishes such as this. Just-picked favas, sugar snaps, carrots, and recently dug new potatoes or ramps would also combine beautifully and celebrate the season. Cut vegetables into bite-sized pieces and give them a quick blanch in boiling water before you add them to the sauce. We finish the dish with mint or other tender herbs for another layer of flavor.

1 teaspoon olive oil

2 tablespoons unsalted butter

1 heaping cup sliced spring onions or leeks
    (white and pale green parts)

12 slender asparagus spears, tough bottoms discarded
    and cut into 2-inch pieces

Sliced baby carrots, sugar snap peas, or other spring
    vegetables (see headnote)

1 cup fresh or frozen sweet peas

¼ cup heavy cream

1 pound garganelli (see Note)

¼ cup chopped mint, plus a little extra for garnish

1 tablespoon finely sliced chives

⅔ cup freshly grated Parmigiano-Reggiano or
    pecorino romano

Finely grated zest of 1 lemon

Kosher salt and freshly ground black pepper

Heat the olive oil and 1 tablespoon of the butter in a large sauté pan over medium heat. Add the onions or leeks and cook for 10 to 15 minutes, until very soft.

Meanwhile, bring a large pot of generously salted water to boil for the pasta. Bring a large saucepan of water to a boil, add the asparagus, and cook for 1 minute. Add the carrots, if using, and cook for 1 minute. Add the sweet peas and cook for about 30 seconds. Add the snap peas, if using, cook for about 30 seconds, then drain. Add the asparagus and other vegetables to the onions, then stir in the cream. Set the pan aside while you cook the pasta.

Add the pasta to the boiling water and cook until al dente. Drain and transfer to the pan with the onions.

Place the pan over high heat and cook, tossing, for 1 to 2 minutes, until the vegetables are hot. Add the mint, chives, ½ cup of the cheese, the lemon zest, and the remaining 1 tablespoon butter and toss well to combine. Season with salt and pepper.

Serve in warm bowls, garnished with more mint and the remaining grated cheese.

To Drink: Pinot Grigio or Pinot Bianco (Livio Felluga)

NOTE: Garganelli is a pennelike cut, but with trapezoid sides and little ridges that collect all the juices from the pan. Many other shapes, such as rigatoni, penne, or even farfalle, work just as well here.

SPRING VEGETABLE LASAGNE

Serves 6 to 8 • Pictured on page 92

This isn't a quick-and-easy dish to prepare. It's what an Italian grandma would dote over for an entire Saturday leading up to a family meal. Plan on a morning or afternoon of leisurely cooking followed by a good rest period for the cooked lasagne and you. The flavors are subtle; green vegetables are lighter stand-ins for a traditional hearty ragù.

½ pound lasagne noodles

2 to 3 tablespoons olive oil

3 to 4 zucchini, trimmed and thinly sliced lengthwise (use a mandoline or vegetable slicer if you have one)

Kosher salt and freshly ground black pepper

1 tablespoon unsalted butter

2 Vidalia or Maui onions or 6 bulb onions, sliced

1 leek, white and pale green parts, thinly sliced

2 garlic cloves, crushed and finely chopped

1½ cups frozen green peas

1½ cups ricotta cheese

1 teaspoon finely grated lemon zest

1 tablespoon finely sliced chives

Pinch of cayenne

2 cups Béchamel Sauce (page 242), warm

1 pounds fresh mozzarella, thinly sliced

⅓ cup grated Fontina

⅓ cup freshly grated Parmigiano-Reggiano

⅓ cup grated pecorino romano

Preheat the oven to 450°F.

Bring a large pot of generously salted water to a rapid boil. Cook the lasagne noodles until just under al dente. Drain, toss with a little olive oil to prevent sticking, and set aside.

Place the zucchini slices on a baking sheet in a single layer. Brush with a little olive oil and season with salt and pepper. Roast for 5 minutes, or until slightly charred and much of the moisture has evaporated from the zucchini. Remove the pan from the oven and set aside. Reduce the oven heat to 350°F.

Heat 1 tablespoon olive oil and the butter in a large sauté pan over medium-high heat. Add the onions, leek, and garlic and sauté until soft, about 5 minutes. Season with salt and pepper and set aside.

Cook the peas in a large saucepan of boiling salted water until very tender, about 30 seconds. Drain, transfer to a food processor, and process to a coarse puree. Set aside.

Combine the ricotta, lemon zest, chives, and cayenne in a small bowl and season with a little salt and pepper. Set aside.

To assemble the lasagne, spoon 1⅓ cups of the béchamel sauce over the bottom of a 9-by-12-inch baking dish. Top with a layer of one-third of the lasagne noodles, then ½ cup of the ricotta mixture, one-third of the onion-leek mixture, one-third of the pea puree, and one-third of the zucchini strips. Season with a sprinkling of salt and pepper. Repeat with two more layers of noodles, ricotta, onion-leek mixture, pea puree, and zucchini, seasoning each layer. Top with a layer of the mozzarella slices, then sprinkle with the grated cheeses. Drizzle the remaining ⅔ cup béchamel sauce over the top.

Bake for 45 minutes, or until the cheese is melted and the top is browned. Let the lasagne rest for 30 minutes before serving.

To Drink: A light red, such as Merlot from Emilia-Romagna

BAKED SHELLS WITH RICOTTA AND FENNEL SAUSAGE

Serves 4

Baked pasta dishes—aromatic and bubbly, with golden brown edges—can be assembled ahead of time and then popped onto the top shelf of a hot oven to heat through. Once the prep is done, it's smooth sailing. All you have to do is make a salad to round out the meal.

1 pound large pasta shells
1 tablespoon olive oil
¾ pound Italian sausage with fennel, removed from casings
2 cups Marinara Sauce (page 246)
1 cup ricotta
Kosher salt and freshly ground black pepper
½ cup freshly grated Parmigiano-Reggiano

Preheat the oven to 475°F.

Bring a large pot of generously salted water to a boil over high heat. Add the shells, stir, and cook until al dente. Drain.

While the pasta cooks, heat the olive oil in a large skillet over medium-high heat. Add the sausage and cook, stirring to break up any clumps of meat, until browned, about 8 minutes. Drain the pan of excess fat. Add the marinara sauce and cook for 2 minutes. Add the ricotta, stir to combine, and season with salt and pepper. Remove the pan from the heat.

Spread a few spoonfuls of the marinara mixture over the bottom of a gratin or baking dish large enough to hold the shells in a single layer. Stuff the shells with more of the mixture and arrange them in the dish. Spoon the remaining sauce over the top and sprinkle with the Parmigiano.

Bake for 15 minutes, then run under the broiler until browned and bubbling hot.

To Drink: Chianti or Rosso di Montalcino

CAFÉ MACARONI AND CHEESE

Serves 8

In our version of this classic baked pasta dish, penne is coated in a rich béchamel sauce flavored with two types of cheddar cheese and grana padano. We mound the pasta in a gratin dish and top it with a handful of grated provolone. The dish comes out of the wood-fired oven bubbly golden brown.

4 cups whole milk
½ yellow onion, chopped
2 bay leaves
1 teaspoon kosher salt
½ teaspoon freshly ground white pepper
8 tablespoons (1 stick) unsalted butter
½ cup all-purpose flour
Dash of Worcestershire sauce
Tabasco sauce to taste
1½ cups shredded sharp yellow cheddar (about 6 ounces)
1½ cups shredded sharp white cheddar (about 6 ounces)
¼ cup grated grana padano
1 pound penne, cooked, drained, and tossed with a little olive oil to prevent sticking
¼ cup shredded provolone

Place an oven rack in the top position and preheat the oven to 500°F.

Combine the milk, onion, bay leaves, salt, and pepper in a large saucepan and bring just to a simmer over low heat. Simmer, stirring occasionally, until reduced by one-quarter, about 15 minutes. Strain the milk and set aside.

Melt the butter in a medium saucepan over medium heat. Whisk in the flour, reduce the heat to low, and cook, whisking constantly, for 3 minutes. Slowly whisk in the milk. Add the Worcestershire and Tabasco, then gradually add the cheddar cheeses, whisking until the cheese is melted. Remove from the heat and stir in the grana padano.

Place the pasta in a large bowl and fold in the cheese sauce until incorporated. Transfer to a buttered gratin dish and top with the shredded provolone.

Bake for 8 to 10 minutes, until bubbly and browned on top. If necessary, give the dish a good blast under the broiler to get the cheese on top a crusty golden brown.

To Drink: Barbera (Luigi Einaudi or Renato Ratti)

CAPELLINI GRATIN

Serves 8 to 12 as a side dish

I attribute this crispy, rich pasta preparation to George Germon from Al Forno in Providence, Rhode Island, who, along with his wonderful wife and partner, Johanne Killeen, so impressed us during the few days they spent in our kitchen years ago. This simple dish is true to their pure, uncomplicated cooking style.

We bake this gratin in a shallow half sheet pan, approximately 12 by 17 inches and 1 inch deep. You could use a smaller, deeper pan, but I like this when it's thin and crisp; otherwise, it becomes a bit too dense and rich. Sheet pans, both full size and half size—which are about the size of a jelly-roll pan—are the workhorses of a professional kitchen, and half sheet pans are a great item to have at home (full sheet pans are too large for most home ovens). Find them at your local kitchenware or restaurant supply store.

Those less concerned with their waistlines may choose to up the richness ante by adding another quarter cup of heavy cream. Serve the gratin with roasted or grilled meats or by itself.

½ **tablespoon unsalted butter**
1 **pound capellini**
½ **cup heavy cream**
1½ **cups freshly grated Parmigiano-Reggiano**
Kosher salt and freshly ground black pepper

Place a rack in the upper third of the oven and preheat the oven to 425°F. Grease a 12-by-17-inch baking sheet (half sheet pan) with the butter.

Bring a large pot of generously salted water to a rolling boil. Add the pasta and cook until al dente. Drain it, reserving about ½ cup of the pasta water.

Combine the cream and ¾ cup of the Parmigiano in a large bowl. Add the pasta and enough of the reserved pasta water to loosen the consistency slightly. Season with salt and pepper, and toss to thoroughly combine. Transfer to the prepared baking sheet, spreading the pasta out evenly. Scatter the remaining ¾ cup Parmigiano over the top.

Bake until golden and crisp around the edges, 15 to 20 minutes (use the convection mode if that is an option). Let the gratin cool for 5 to 10 minutes to set up, then cut into 8 to 12 rectangles.

To Drink: A rustic, fruity red such as Primitivo

BUCATINI WITH CLAMS, PANCETTA, HOT CHILE, AND RAPINI

Serves 4 as a main course, 8 as an appetizer

The classic "linguine and clams," amped up with the big flavors of pancetta and rapini. I prefer hollow bucatini to linguine here because it holds all the flavors of the spicy broth with its notes of sea and earth. Try to find very small clams—they're the most delicate and tender.

Once you master a dish like this, you can adapt it to whatever is on hand—shrimp instead of clams, spinach in place of rapini, even smoky bacon instead of pancetta. Buy a few extra clams in case some fail to open and have to be discarded after cooking. This dish should have the assertive kick of black pepper and red chile, so season generously.

3 tablespoons olive oil

4 garlic cloves

½ cup diced pancetta

2 dried red chile peppers

1½ cups chopped rapini (broccoli rabe)

32 very small littleneck clams, cockles, or Manila clams, rinsed, soaked for 10 minutes, and drained

¾ cup dry white wine

1 pound bucatini

2 teaspoons unsalted butter

Juice of 1 lemon

Kosher salt and freshly ground black pepper

Fruity green extra virgin olive oil for drizzling

1 tablespoon chopped flat-leaf parsley

Bring a large pot of generously salted water to a rolling boil.

Meanwhile, heat a large sauté pan (large enough to hold the clams and pasta) over medium-low heat. Add 2 tablespoons of the olive oil and the garlic cloves, tilt the pan so that the oil pools to one side, and cook the garlic, stirring occasionally, until golden brown on all sides, about 4 minutes.

Set the pan back down over the heat, add the pancetta and chiles, and increase the heat to medium. Cook until the pancetta renders its fat, 3 to 4 minutes. Add the rapini, cover, and cook for 3 minutes.

Add the clams to the pan and cook for 30 seconds to 1 minute. Add the white wine, cover the pan again, give it a vigorous shake, and cook the clams until they open, 5 to 7 minutes.

Meanwhile, drop the pasta into the pot of boiling water and cook until al dente.

Remove the lid from the pan with the clams and give them another shake. (If all the clams are open except for 2 or 3, remove them to a work surface and slip a knife in them as they might just be stubborn—if they are filled with sand, discard them.) If the pasta isn't quite done, turn off the heat under the clams.

Drain the pasta, reserving a generous tablespoon or two of the pasta water, and add the pasta and water to the clams. Shake the pan a few times and toss to coat the pasta. Add the butter and lemon juice and give everything another toss. Taste the sauce and season with salt and pepper, making sure there is a pronounced kick of peppery spice.

Serve in warm pasta bowls, garnished with a drizzle of olive oil and a sprinkling of parsley. No cheese—it would overpower the flavors of the seafood.

To Drink: A crisp white wine, such as Cinque Terre or Frascati

PASTA WITH VENISON BOLOGNESE

Serves 6 to 8

A mixture of meats is essential here—not all beef or pork or veal, but a combination of ground pork, beef, and veal as well as cured meat (prosciutto or pancetta)—and it is all cooked together until a caramelized crust is formed. At Bottega, we add another twist by substituting venison for the traditional veal. (You may need to go to a specialty butcher for the venison and pork belly.) The sauce is spiced with cinnamon, juniper, and a handful of bay leaves for bold flavor. Consider doubling the recipe and reserving a portion for the future; the sauce will keep for 5 to 6 days in the refrigerator and can be frozen for up to 3 months.

1 tablespoon olive oil

¾ pound ground venison

¾ pound ground pork shoulder or belly

¾ pound ground beef chuck

¼ pound pancetta, cut into ¼-inch dice
   (have the butcher cut it into ¼-inch-thick slices)

1 onion, cut into ¼-inch dice

2 celery stalks, cut into ¼-inch dice

3 carrots, peeled and cut into ¼-inch dice

2 garlic cloves, minced

6 juniper berries, toasted (see page 256) and
   ground in a spice grinder

1 cinnamon stick

6 bay leaves

Kosher salt and freshly ground black pepper

1 cup dry red wine

2 cups whole milk

Two 28-ounce cans San Marzano tomatoes,
   drained and finely chopped

1 pound tagliatelle or fettuccine

Freshly grated Parmigiano-Reggiano for serving

Heat the oil in a cast-iron skillet or large heavy pot over medium heat. Add the venison, pork, beef, and pancetta and cook until the fat is rendered and the meat begins to form a crust on the bottom of the pot, about 30 minutes. Drain off the fat and continue cooking until a good crust is formed, 15 minutes more.

Add the onion, celery, carrots, garlic, juniper, cinnamon, and bay leaves, season with salt and pepper, and cook for 15 minutes, or until the vegetables are softened. Add the red wine and cook for 10 minutes, or until reduced by half. Add the milk and tomatoes and simmer gently for 1 to 1½ hours, or until the sauce is very flavorful. Taste and adjust the seasonings.

Meanwhile bring a large pot of generously salted water to a rolling boil. Add the pasta and cook until al dente.

Drain the pasta and toss with the Bolognese sauce. Pass grated Parmigiano at the table.

To Drink: Barbera (Vietti or La Spinetta)

PUTTANESCA WITH SHRIMP AND LINGUINE
Serves 4 to 6

Puttanesca is named, or so the story goes, for *putte,* or streetwalkers, of Palermo and Napoli because it can be thrown together quickly—between tricks. The sauce with racy flavors of anchovy, garlic, red chile pepper, olives, and capers, has been called an aphrodisiac. Luckily, it's one that can be made rapidly in a mere two pans whenever you have the craving. The flavors are intense—salty, spicy, and zesty—and certain to satisfy. Be sure to add some of the reserved pasta water if necessary—the sauce should be loose, but not watery. We like to use large green Italian Cerignola olives, which come from the Adriatic Coast, but you can substitute green Sicilian olives or small Picholines.

Wild American shrimp are like candy from the sea—so sweet, briny, and beautifully pink when cooked. Do try to find these—they are great even frozen and well worth the extra cost.

3 tablespoons olive oil

1 pound medium shrimp (21–30 count),
    preferably wild American, peeled and deveined

1 medium onion, cut into ½-inch dice

3 oil-cured anchovies (or 4 salted, rinsed, soaked in
    water for 10 minutes, and drained), chopped

2 garlic cloves, thinly sliced

1 dried red chile pepper

¼ cup dry white wine

One 14½-ounce can crushed tomatoes

2 tablespoons coarsely chopped Cerignola olives
    (see headnote)

2 tablespoons capers, rinsed

1 pound linguine, bucatini, or spaghetti

Kosher salt and freshly ground black pepper

Pinch of grated orange zest

1 tablespoon chopped flat-leaf parsley

1 tablespoon slivered basil leaves (optional)

Bring a large pot of generously salted water to a boil over high heat.

Meanwhile, heat a large saucepan over medium heat. Add 2 tablespoons of the olive oil and the shrimp and cook the shrimp for approximately 30 to 45 seconds per side, until the flesh just turns pink. Transfer to a plate.

Add the onion, anchovies, and garlic to the pan and sauté for 7 to 10 minutes, until the onion is translucent. Add the chile pepper to the pan, raise the heat to medium-high, and pour in the wine, stirring to deglaze the pan. Bring to a boil and reduce the liquid by two-thirds.

Add the tomatoes, olives, and capers, reduce the heat to low, and simmer the sauce for 10 minutes.

Meanwhile, cook the pasta until al dente. Drain, reserving about ¼ cup of the cooking water.

Add the pasta and the shrimp to the simmering sauce. Toss the pasta with the sauce, shaking the pan so that it is well coated; add some or all of the reserved pasta water as necessary. Stir in the remaining 1 tablespoon olive oil, taste, and adjust the seasoning with salt and pepper if necessary.

Serve the pasta in warm bowls, garnished with the orange zest, parsley, and basil, if using.

To Drink: Greco di Tufo (Feudi di San Gregorio or Terredora di Paolo)

PENNE WITH CHICKEN MEATBALLS

Serves 4

Instead of the typical pork, beef, and veal combinations, we make these meatballs with the lighter and more delicate chicken breasts. For the aromatic vegetables, use a medium-large dice or mirepoix of carrots, onions, and celery—carefully sautéed and removed from the heat before it softens too much. Marjoram and a grating or two of nutmeg add a pleasing aroma. If you don't have a meat grinder, have your butcher grind the chicken for you, or pulse it in a food processor.

FOR THE MEATBALLS

1 pound boneless, skinless chicken breasts, cut into
    small dice and chilled, or 1 pound ground chicken

⅓ pound pork fat, cut into large dice (or use ⅓ pound
    ground pork for leaner meatballs)

2 shallots, finely minced

3 garlic cloves, finely minced

1 marjoram sprig, leaves only

1 thyme sprig, leaves only

Pinch of freshly grated nutmeg

Pinch of cayenne

Kosher salt and freshly ground black pepper

½ cup Bread Crumbs (page 239)

1 large egg

About 1 tablespoon olive oil

FOR THE MIREPOIX

2 tablespoons olive oil

1 large onion, cut into ½-inch dice

2 carrots, peeled and cut into ½-inch dice

2 celery stalks, cut into ½-inch dice

Kosher salt and freshly ground black pepper to taste

1 cup Chicken Stock (page 241), plus more as needed

1 pound penne

2 marjoram sprigs, leaves removed and chopped

2 thyme sprigs, leaves removed and chopped

2 flat-leaf parsley sprigs, leaves removed and chopped

⅓ cup freshly grated pecorino romano or
    Parmigiano-Reggiano

1 tablespoon unsalted butter

To prepare the meatballs, combine the chicken, pork fat (or ground pork), shallots, garlic, marjoram, thyme, nutmeg, cayenne, and salt and pepper in a large bowl. Pass this mixture through the large holes of a meat grinder or pulse in a food processor until it is the consistency of ground beef. Transfer to a bowl.

Add the bread crumbs and egg to the ground chicken mixture and mix with your hands until thoroughly combined (wear plastic gloves if you wish).

To check the mixture for seasoning, heat a little olive oil in a large skillet over medium heat. Roll a tablespoon of the meatball mixture into a small ball, add to the skillet, and cook, turning occasionally, until cooked through, about 8 minutes. Taste the meatball, and adjust the seasonings of the raw meat mixture as necessary. (Set the skillet aside to brown all of the meatballs.) Form the remaining meat mixture into about 20 small meatballs. Set aside.

To make the mirepoix, heat the olive oil in a large sauté pan over medium heat. Add the onion, carrots, and celery and cook until softened, about 10 minutes. Season with salt and pepper, then add the chicken stock and bring to a boil. Reduce to a simmer and cook for 3 minutes. Remove from the heat and set aside.

Meanwhile, bring a large pot of generously salted water to a rolling boil.

While the mirepoix cooks, heat 1 tablespoon olive oil over medium heat in the skillet you used to brown the test meatball. When it is hot but not smoking, add the meatballs and cook, turning to brown on all sides, until cooked through, about 8 minutes.

Add the penne to the boiling water and cook until al dente. Drain, reserving about ½ cup of the pasta water, and return the penne to the pot.

Add the mirepoix to the pasta, along with the chopped herbs. Add the meatballs, cheese, and butter and set over low heat to just warm through. Then add a little of the reserved pasta water and reduce over high heat to concentrate the flavors. The dish should be a little soupy. Spoon into warm pasta bowls and serve.

To Drink: Valpolicella or another light red wine

PAPPARDELLE WITH RABBIT, PORCINI, AND PARMESAN

Serves 4

Unlike most deeply rooted microregional Italian dishes, this braised game and pasta combination can be found from Tuscany to Rome to Turin. I guess it strikes everyone's fancy, and I can certainly understand why. It's made with leftover braised meat—veal shank or shoulder, lamb shank or shoulder, or beef—simmered in red wine. If you're starting from scratch, make the braise ahead; it gets more flavorful after a day or two. The rabbit loins are optional; if they're unavailable, use chicken and toss in some cubes of crisp-cooked pancetta.

Fresh wild mushrooms are fleeting finds of autumn. If they're unavailable, use a variety of cultivated mushrooms, such as oyster and brown beech, along with the cremini and a few slices of reconstituted dried porcini. (A surprisingly good, though extravagant, option is to use flash frozen porcini—a tip my dear fellow chef Tony Mantuano turned me on to.)

2 tablespoons olive oil

3 tablespoons unsalted butter

4 cremini, stemmed and quartered

4 yellowfoot or chanterelle mushrooms

4 hedgehog or oyster mushrooms

4 black trumpet mushrooms (or dried porcini,
    soaked in warm water until softened)

Kosher salt and freshly ground black pepper

1 shallot, finely chopped

1 cup reserved braising liquid or Chicken Stock
    (page 241)

2 rabbit loins or boneless chicken breast halves

1 pound dried or fresh pappardelle

Braised Rabbit Legs or Chicken Thighs (page 160),
    meat removed from bones and shredded

¼ cup freshly grated Parmigiano-Reggiano or
    grana padano, plus more for serving

Bring a large pot of generously salted water to a rolling boil.

Meanwhile, heat a large sauté pan over medium-high heat, and add 1 tablespoon of the olive oil and 1 tablespoon of the butter. When the butter is foamy, add the mushrooms and sauté for 3 to 4 minutes, until partially cooked but still firm. Season with salt and pepper to taste, add the shallot, and cook for 30 seconds. Add the reserved braising liquid or chicken stock and bring to a simmer, then reduce the heat and simmer gently for 5 minutes. Remove from the heat and keep warm.

While the mushrooms cook, heat a medium sauté pan over medium-high heat, and add the remaining 1 tablespoon olive oil. Add the rabbit loins, and cook until the edges begin to brown, about 3 minutes, then turn and cook on the second side for 2 to 3 minutes, or until cooked through. If using chicken breasts, sauté for 5 to 8 minutes per side, until cooked through. Transfer the meat to a rack to rest for a few minutes.

While the meat rests, drop the pappardelle into the boiling water and cook until al dente.

Drain the pasta and return it to the pot. Add the meat from the braised rabbit legs or chicken thighs and the mushrooms. Slice the rabbit loins or chicken breasts on the diagonal into 1-inch-wide slices and add to the pasta. Add the remaining 2 tablespoons butter and the cheese and toss everything together over medium-low heat.

Serve in warm deep pasta bowls, and pass more cheese at the table.

To Drink: Vino Nobile di Montepulciano (Avignonesi)

italian reds we love

The great red wines made near Verona by producers such as Quintarelli, Allegrini, Zenato, and Masi are Amarone (where the grapes are dried on mats until January), Valpolicella Ripasso (where the pulp left over from Amarone is added to Valpolicella as it ferments, to enrich it), as well as the straightforward Valpolicella, with its simpler cherry flavor.

Many of these stunning wines are overlooked due to the mass-marketing of mediocre wines from this region that occurred in the 1960s and 1970s. But passing these by is a big mistake. There is a tremendous joy to be found in the red wines of the Veneto. Farther north, on the slopes of the Alps, the Lagrein grape produces delightful, lighter red wines. Two of my favorite producers are Colterenzio and Gojer.

To me, Italy's greatest red wines are the powerful and complex wines of Piemonte in the northwest. The area around Alba is home to Barolo and Barbaresco, where the Nebbiolo grape is king. Barbaresco is softer and more feminine, while Barolo is a masculine, muscular wine—both rival the complexities of the best Burgundies. With hints of rose, violet, and tar, they're a perfect match with a broad range of hearty dishes. Barbera and Dolcetto are other superb Piemontese red wines that are often more affordable, making them perfect for everyday drinking.

Tuscany is a dreamland of hills, vineyards, forests, and fields of sunflowers. The dark-green olive groves produce refined and elegant olive oil, and the wines are some of the finest in the world. Some of my favorite producers are Badia a Coltibuono, Felsina, Castello di Volpaia, Castello di Fonterutoli, Isole e Olena, San Felice, Altesino, Caparzo, and Avignonesi. They all make full-flavored wines packed with personality and loaded with the Tuscan essence of sun and the soil.

The Marche region, long overlooked by tourists and wine importers, is now becoming more recognized; several small producers, such as Moroder and Le Terrazze, are creating some dramatic and powerful wines.

Deeper into the southern Italian mountains you'll find the penetratingly dark, brooding, and profound wine Aglianco del Vulture. We found this area a bit unnering on a gray and cold winter day (was that a big black bird hovering above?). Try the Aglianco del Vulture while reading some Edgar Allan Poe.

PASTA DOUGH

Makes 12 ounces dough

Making pasta forces you to rely on your senses, especially touch. The goal is a smooth, elastic, slightly tacky dough. Factors like humidity and egg size are variable, so you may get a different result each time. As with anything else, with practice you'll learn to make the necessary adjustments, such as adding more or less flour, to yield perfect results. Here I provide both a hand and mixer method for making the dough.

Fresh pasta keeps from 1 to 2 hours in the refrigerator covered with a damp towel; after that, it oxidizes, darkening in color, and gets tough. If you don't plan to cook it right away, freeze it on a baking sheet in a single layer until firm, then transfer to freezer bags. When ready to cook, drop it into boiling salted water right from the freezer—do not defrost.

1¾ to 2 cups all-purpose flour
1 teaspoon salt
9 extra-large egg yolks

To make the dough by hand, mix the flour and salt and mound on a work surface. Make a well in the center, like the crater of a volcano. Place the egg yolks in the well and, using a fork, mix them together. Start gradually bringing in a little flour from the sides, then continue adding the flour bit by bit until the dough comes together and all the flour has been incorporated. Knead the dough, flouring the work surface as necessary, until it is smooth and elastic, 5 to 7 minutes; it will be a bit sticky. Shape it into a disk, wrap it in plastic, and refrigerate for 30 minutes to 1 hour.

To make the dough in a mixer, combine the eggs and salt in the bowl of a mixer fitted with the dough hook and beat to break up the eggs. Gradually add the flour and mix until the dough just pulls away from the sides of the bowl. It should still be a bit tacky to the touch. Do not overmix the dough, or it will become tough. Press the dough into a disk and wrap it in plastic. Refrigerate for 30 minutes to 1 hour.

Divide the dough into 4 equal portions. Work with one piece at a time, keeping the remaining dough covered with a towel or plastic wrap. Sprinkle a portion of dough with a light dusting of flour, then pass it through a pasta machine at its widest setting. Lay the ribbon of dough on your floured surface and fold it in half, so that the ends meet, and pass it through the same setting a second time. Adjust your pasta machine down a setting and pass the sheet of pasta through. Fold it in half again and pass it through the same setting a second time. Continue in the same fashion until you have passed the sheet of pasta through the thinnest setting twice. When the dough sheet becomes too long to handle, cut it into manageable lengths. Transfer each finished sheet to a lightly dusted work surface and keep covered with a slightly dampened towel to keep the pasta from drying out while you roll out the remaining dough.

The pasta is ready to use.

SILK HANDKERCHIEF PASTA WITH PESTO

Serves 4 to 6 as an appetizer

Only the strong can resist these delicate squares of pasta that the Italians aptly call "silk handkerchiefs," *fazzoletti diseta*, sauced Genovese-style. The pasta water is an important ingredient for moistening the sauce, so reserve a little before draining the pasta. Remember that pesto is best with a minimum of garlic and lots of tender young basil and cheese.

    ½ pound Pasta Dough (page 109), cut into 3 pieces and
        rolled out as directed on page 109
    ½ cup Pesto (page 248)
    3 tablespoons freshly grated Parmigiano-Reggiano
    ¼ cup pine nuts, toasted (see page 255)
    Basil leaves

Bring a large pot of generously salted water to a rolling boil. Meanwhile, cut each pasta sheet into 6-inch squares.

Add the pasta to the boiling water and cook for 1 to 2 minutes. Drain, reserving ½ cup of the pasta water, and transfer to a large serving bowl. Gently toss with the pesto and enough of the reserved pasta water to thin the sauce a bit. Sprinkle with the Parmigiano, toasted pine nuts, and basil. Serve immediately.

To Drink: A simple white wine from Liguria, such as Cinque Terre or Colli di Luni or any simple, crisp, unoaked white wine with low alcohol

TRAIN RIDE THROUGH LIGURIA On early trips to Italy I would take the train from Nice to Tuscany, emerging from the black-as-night depths of seaside mountain cliffs to the bluest sea and a landscape dotted with palms, bougainvillea, and citrus clinging to the southeast-facing elevations; the names of villages on train station signs rushed by in a romantic blur—Rapallo, Portofino, Santa Margarita.

Liguria, a little crescent along the Italian Riviera, and historically cut off from the rest of Italy by a range of mountains, developed its own unique culture and cuisine. It is the region where local wild greens are served with fragrant basil, arugula, and, often, rich walnuts or pignoli. This is food born of meager means, not of a land of cattle and abundant pastures. Here dishes are a blend of what can be fished from the seas—sardines, mussels, clams, an occasional tuna or branzino—or raised on small hillside farms—rabbits are a prized source of protein. Pasta means delicate "silk handkerchiefs" or perfect ravioli or the quintessential spaghetti al pesto with little green beans and tender potatoes added to heighten the pleasure.

TORTELLINI SALAD WITH CHICKEN, PINE NUTS, SULTANAS, AND BALSAMIC

Serves 4

The few times we've dared to replace this dish on the Bottega Café menu, our regular crowd screams in protest. It's deliciously simple once you've assembled all the components, and very satisfying. I have been known to snack on this on those many afternoons when lunch has passed me by.

    ¼ cup Homemade Mayonnaise (page 245) or high-
        quality commercial mayonnaise
    ¼ cup Balsamic Vinaigrette (page 72)
    2 small heads romaine lettuce, sliced into
        1-inch-wide strips
    4 cups (about 1 pound) cooked store-bought
        fresh cheese tortellini
    Four 6-ounce skinless, boneless chicken breasts, grilled
        and cut into large cubes
    1 heaping tablespoon pine nuts, toasted (see page 255)
    ¼ cup sultanas (golden raisins)
    ½ cup cherry tomatoes, halved, or quartered if large
    1 scant tablespoon chopped flat-leaf parsley
    Kosher salt and freshly ground black pepper

Whisk the mayonnaise and vinaigrette together in a small bowl.

Toss the romaine leaves with half of the dressing in a large bowl and divide among four plates. Add the tortellini, chicken, pine nuts, sultanas, half of the tomatoes, and the parsley to the bowl and toss to coat with the remaining dressing. Season with salt and pepper and toss again. Arrange on top of the lettuce leaves, garnish with the remaining cherry tomatoes, and serve.

To Drink: Pinot Grigio (Livio Felluga)

TORTELLONI WITH CRABMEAT, RICOTTA, AND BROWN BUTTER

Serves 4 as an appetizer

The combination of homemade tortelloni filled with herbed ricotta, served in a nutty brown butter sauce, is irresistible. Whenever this appears on the menu in Bottega's main dining room, it's the most ordered dish. In Alabama, fresh jumbo lump crabmeat is available for most of the year (except the dead of winter and early spring). It's truly fantastic, but crawfish and lobster meat (especially the knuckle meat) are great options if crab isn't available.

FOR THE TORTELLONI

2 cups ricotta

1 small russet potato, baked, peeled, and riced or
    mashed (1 cup)

Pinch of freshly grated nutmeg

Kosher salt and freshly ground black pepper

1 tablespoon finely minced herbs, such as chives,
    parsley, mint, or chervil

Pasta Dough (page 109), rolled out as directed on
    page 109 and cut into 24-inch lengths

Cornmeal

FOR THE SAUCE

1 tablespoon unsalted butter

6 ounces jumbo lump crabmeat, picked over for shells
    and cartilage

½ lemon

Kosher salt and freshly ground black pepper

Tabasco sauce (optional)

¼ cup Brown Butter Vinaigrette (page 244)

Flat-leaf parsley leaves

To make the filling, line a sieve with dampened cheesecloth or a damp paper towel and set it over a deep bowl. Put the ricotta in the sieve and let drain for 30 minutes.

Transfer the ricotta to a large mixing bowl. Add the mashed potato (the potato binds and dries out the ricotta), nutmeg, salt and pepper to taste, and herbs and mix thoroughly. Transfer the filling to a pastry bag without a tip or a plastic bag with a ½-inch opening cut in one corner.

To make the tortelloni, lay the pasta sheets on a lightly floured work surface with a long side toward you. Fold each sheet crosswise in half so that the two short ends meet. With a pizza cutter or a sharp knife, cut the folded sheet lengthwise in half. Unfold the sheet and cover with a slightly dampened towel.

Lay one pasta sheet on your work surface and, using a pizza cutter or a sharp knife, cut it into 3-inch squares. Pipe a tablespoonful of the filling onto the center of each square one at a time, fold each square in half to form a triangle, removing any air pockets, and press the edges gently together to seal. Next, bring the two opposite corners of the triangle together to create a "bishop's hat." Then place the tortelloni on a baking sheet dusted with cornmeal. Repeat with the remaining pasta and filling. (You need only 12 tortelloni for this recipe. Arrange the remaining tortelloni on a baking sheet lined with parchment paper until firm, then transfer to heavy-duty freezer bags and freeze for up to 2 months.)

Bring a large pot of generously salted water to a rolling boil. Drop the 12 tortelloni into the boiling water and cook for 2 to 3 minutes.

While the tortelloni cook, make the sauce: Melt the butter in a medium saucepan over medium heat. Add the crabmeat, and toss gently to just heat through. Season with a squeeze of lemon and salt and pepper—you may also wish to add a splash of Tabasco sauce.

When the tortelloni are cooked, lift them out of the water with a slotted spoon or strainer, transfer to the saucepan with the crabmeat, and toss gently. Add 1 tablespoon of the pasta water and gently shake the pan to distribute.

Divide the tortelloni among warm pasta bowls and ladle 1 tablespoon of the brown butter vinaigrette over each portion. Garnish with parsley leaves.

To Drink: Tocai from Friuli (Schiopetto or Venica & Venica)

RAVIOLI WITH PUMPKIN AND SAGE BUTTER

Serves 4 as an appetizer • Pictured on page 84

Pumpkin—*zucca*—is a classic filling for pasta in the Emilia-Romagna region around Bologna. To me butternut squash is more flavorful than our pumpkin, so I usually use it, but if you can find flavorful pumpkins or Hubbard or Delicata squash, don't hesitate to use them. Although some recipes include crumbled almond biscotti in the filling for added texture and sweetness, I prefer this version, which allows you to savor the simplicity of the pasta and the autumn flavor of the filling with just a bit of sage and melted butter.

You can freeze the extra ravioli this recipe makes in batches to pull out as needed. Drop the still-frozen pasta into boiling salted water, and you'll have a delicious meal in less than five minutes.

> Roasted Butternut Squash and Balsamico (page 190),
>   made without the balsamic
> ½ cup ricotta
> Pinch of freshly grated nutmeg
> Kosher salt and freshly ground black pepper
> Pasta Dough (page 109), rolled out as directed on
>   page 109 and cut into 24-inch lengths
> Cornmeal for dusting
> 3 tablespoons unsalted butter
> 4 large sage leaves, torn into pieces
> Freshly grated Parmigiano-Reggiano
> Cracked black pepper

To prepare the filling, combine the squash, ricotta, nutmeg, and salt and pepper in a bowl, mixing well. Refrigerate for 1 hour to firm up the filling.

Remove the filling from the refrigerator and spoon it into a pastry bag without a tip, or a plastic bag with a ½-inch opening cut in one corner.

Fold one pasta sheet in half so that the two short ends meet, to mark the center, then unfold the sheet so that it rests lengthwise in front of you. Working on one side of the crease, starting 2 inches from the end, arrange tablespoonfuls of filling down the sheet at 4-inch intervals. Fold the other side of the pasta back over so that the edges again line up, and press the dough around the mounds of filling to seal. Center a 3-inch scalloped cutter around each mound of filling and cut circles. Press the edges together firmly to seal, without losing the pretty scallop. Place the ravioli on a baking sheet dusted with cornmeal, and repeat with the remaining dough and filling. (You need only 12 ravioli for this recipe. Arrange the remaining ravioli on a baking sheet lined with parchment paper and freeze until firm. Then transfer to heavy-duty freezer bags and freeze for up to 2 months.)

Bring a large pot of generously salted water to a rolling boil. Drop the 12 ravioli into the boiling water and cook for 2 to 3 minutes, until just tender.

While the pasta is cooking, melt the butter in a large sauté pan over medium-high heat. When it is foamy, drop in the sage leaves and cook for 1 minute, or until lightly toasted but not brown.

Lift the ravioli out of the boiling water with a slotted spoon and place in the sauté pan with the sage. Add a small splash of the pasta water and gently toss to coat the ravioli with the butter. Serve in warm pasta bowls, sprinkled with a little grated Parmigiano and cracked pepper.

To Drink: Refosco from Friuli or Lambrusco from Emilia-Romagna

LEFT: *Butternut squash filling for the Ravioli with Pumpkin and Sage Butter (opposite);* **RIGHT:** *Cutouts of ravioli gently pressed to remove air pockets*

POTATO RAVIOLI WITH CRAWFISH, CANDIED LEMON, AND TABASCO

Serves 4 as an appetizer

These tender, mild-flavored ravioli are a perfect foil for the delicate yet distinctive flavor of crawfish tails and the subtle, unexpected sweetness of candied lemon zest. The bulk of our crawfish is farmed in the shallow ponds or paddies where rice is grown earlier in the season, giving the farmer two harvests from the same acreage. Harvested crawfish are boiled and picked—removed from the shell—then packed fresh into one-pound bags. Down in Cajun country, the tailmeats are packed with "fat," or the lush, orangey juices from the head, which are considered a delicacy. Fresh crawfish tailmeat is available from January until June, but Mardi Gras festivities gobble up much of the stock and raise the price until Lent begins. Although you can find frozen imported crawfish, which is cheaper, it isn't worth buying—seek out fresh Louisiana crawfish tailmeat when in season or substitute little shrimp, lobster, or crabmeat.

This dish is easy to throw together if you've made the ravioli in advance; frozen ravioli can be dropped straight into the pot of boiling water and cooked. The candied zest can also be prepared a day or two in advance and stored in an airtight container at room temperature.

FOR THE CANDIED LEMON
Zest of 1 lemon—removed in strips with a zester
1 tablespoon Demerara or natural sugar
    (such as Sugar in the Raw)

FOR THE RAVIOLI
2 cups ricotta
1 small russet potato, baked, peeled, and riced
    or mashed (1 cup)
Pinch of freshly grated nutmeg
Kosher salt and freshly ground black pepper
1 tablespoon finely minced herbs, such as chives,
    parsley, mint, or chervil
Pasta Dough (page 109), rolled out as directed on
    page 109 and cut into 24-inch sheets
Cornmeal for dusting

FOR THE SAUCE
3 tablespoons unsalted butter
1 shallot, thinly sliced
½ garlic clove, crushed
¼ pound fresh crawfish tails with fat (see headnote)
Juice of ½ lemon
1 tablespoon snipped chives or dill
Tabasco sauce
Kosher salt and freshly ground black pepper to taste

Preheat the oven to 200°F. Prepare an ice bath.

To prepare the candied lemon, bring a small saucepan of water to a boil over high heat. Add the strips of lemon zest and blanch for 1 minute. Remove from the boiling water with a slotted spoon and immerse in the ice bath to cool, then remove the zest from the ice bath with the slotted spoon and return to the boiling water again. Blanch for 1 minute more, then drain and immerse in the ice water to cool. Remove the zest from the water and pat dry. (This two-step process removes the bitterness from the zest without overcooking it.)

Place the sugar on a plate and roll the lemon zest in it to coat. Transfer to a small parchment-lined baking sheet and place in the oven for 1 hour, or until thoroughly dry. Remove and set aside to cool.

Meanwhile, line a sieve with dampened cheesecloth or a damp paper towel and set it over a deep bowl. Put the ricotta in the sieve and let it drain for 30 minutes.

To make the filling, transfer the ricotta to a large mixing bowl. Add the mashed potato (the potato binds and dries out the ricotta), nutmeg, salt and pepper, and herbs and mix thoroughly. Transfer the filling to a pastry bag without a tip or a plastic bag with a ½-inch opening cut in one corner.

Fold one pasta sheet in half so that the two short ends meet, to mark the center, then unfold the sheet so that it rests lengthwise in front of you. Working on one side of the crease, starting 2 inches from the end, arrange tablespoonfuls of filling down the sheet at 4-inch intervals. Fold the other side of the pasta back over so that the edges again line up, and press the dough around the mounds of filling to seal. Center a 3-inch scalloped cutter around each mound of filling and cut circles. Press the edges together firmly to seal, without losing the pretty scallop. Place the ravioli on a baking sheet dusted with cornmeal, and repeat with the remaining dough and filling. (You need only 12 ravioli for this recipe. Arrange the remaining ravioli on a baking sheet lined with parchment paper and freeze until firm. Then transfer to heavy-duty freezer bags and freeze for up to 2 months.)

Bring a large pot of generously salted water to a rolling boil. Drop the 12 ravioli into the boiling water and cook for 2 to 3 minutes, until just tender.

Meanwhile, to make the sauce, melt 1 tablespoon of the butter in a small sauté pan over medium heat. Add the shallot and garlic and cook for 1 minute, or until softened. Add the crawfish tails with fat and toss until warmed through. Add a splash of lemon juice, the chives or dill, Tabasco, and salt and pepper. Toss to combine, then taste and adjust the seasonings.

When the ravioli are cooked, use a slotted spoon or strainer to transfer them to the pan with the crawfish. Add the remaining 2 tablespoons butter and a little of the pasta cooking water to loosen the sauce, and toss to combine. Taste and adjust the seasonings.

Serve in warm pasta bowls, garnished with the candied lemon.

To Drink: A light Riesling from Alto Adige

GNOCCHI WITH PROSCIUTTO AND SAGE

Serves 6 as an appetizer

Gnocchi, Italian potato dumplings, should be light and delicate, never heavy or tough. The little pillows carry the flavor of any sauce, whether sage and brown butter, tomato, or olive oil and Parmigiano. Gnocchi make an interesting first course—a change from pasta or risotto—and are also a delicious and unusual side for grilled or braised meats. Be generous with the fresh sage leaves. Chop the leaves if you prefer a more intense flavor or leave them whole for a subtler taste. If you like, substitute little cubes of pancetta, cooked until crisp, for the prosciutto.

There's definitely a learning curve in gnocchi making. Most cooks feel a bit clumsy at first, but you'll get the knack with a little practice. You want the potatoes to be almost overcooked but dry; this will enable you to use less flour, resulting in fluffier, more flavorful gnocchi. Work the flour in gently so the dumplings don't get tough.

Making homemade stuffed pasta or gnocchi requires time and organization but both freeze very well. Arrange the ravioli or gnocchi on a baking sheet lined with parchment paper and freeze until firm. Then transfer to heavy-duty freezer bags and freeze for up to 2 months. To cook, just pull out what you need and toss directly into a pot of boiling salted water—do not defrost.

3 russet potatoes (about 1½ pounds)

2 Yukon Gold potatoes (about 8 ounces)

2½ teaspoons kosher salt

1½ teaspoons freshly ground white pepper

Freshly grated nutmeg

9 tablespoons unsalted butter

About 3 cups all-purpose flour

3 large egg yolks

12 medium sage leaves

6 thin slices prosciutto di Parma, cut into thin strips about 1½ inches long

¼ cup freshly grated Parmigiano-Reggiano

Preheat the oven to 350°F.

Place the potatoes on a baking sheet and bake until tender, 1 to 1½ hours. Let cool slightly.

Bring a large pot of generously salted water to a rolling boil.

When the potatoes are cool enough to handle, peel them and place the warm (not hot) potatoes in a ricer. Add the salt, pepper, a grating of nutmeg, 3 tablespoons of the butter, and a handful of the flour and press through the ricer onto a large wooden cutting board or other work surface. Make sure the potatoes are not too hot, or they will cook the egg yolks. Using a fork, begin working in the egg yolks and remaining flour (you want an approximately equal volume of flour and potatoes). Use a pastry scraper or spatula to gradually incorporate the flour into the potato mixture, being careful not to overwork it. The gentler you are during this phase, the lighter the gnocchi will be.

Melt 2 more tablespoons of the butter in a large sauté pan and keep warm over low heat.

Divide the gnocchi dough into several pieces. Roll each one into a long ¾-inch-thick rope and cut into 1-inch pieces. Press each piece with the back of a fork to create ridges. Once they are all shaped, cook the gnocchi about 15 at a time: Drop them into the boiling water and then once they float to the surface, 30 seconds or so, remove them with a slotted spoon or skimmer and transfer them to the pan of melted butter. When all the gnocchi have been cooked and tossed in the melted butter, transfer them to a platter. (To save gnocchi to serve later, transfer the cooked gnocchi directly to an ice bath to cool rapidly, then place on a baking sheet and cover. Set aside for several hours at room temperature or refrigerate overnight.)

Add the remaining 4 tablespoons butter (or the remaining 6 tablespoons if you cooked the gnocchi ahead) to the sauté pan and cook over medium heat until it melts, takes on a rich brown color, and gives off a nutty aroma. Add the gnocchi to the pan, add the sage, and toss to coat and heat through.

Serve the gnocchi on warm plates, garnished with the prosciutto and a sprinkle of Parmigiano-Reggiano.

To Drink: A light red wine, such as Freisa from Piedmont

CRESPELLE

Serves 6 as an appetizer

Crespelle means "crepe," and the thin pasta dough and filling in this dish are similar in spirit to that traditional Italian preparation. Don't rush home from work and try to pull this recipe off; time and practice are required to get the pasta rolled just right (homemade pasta is mandatory unless you have a source for pasta rolled to request). But this special dish is stunning and certain to dazzle your guests. Imagine a jelly roll, but with cake and jelly replaced by a thin sheet of pasta dough and a delicious filling of ricotta, herbs, and mushrooms. To strengthen the crespelle's structure, we wrap it in a kitchen towel and secure it with twine before gently poaching it. Once it's cooked, the towel comes off, and we're ready to slice and sauce for serving.

- 2 cups ricotta cheese
- 3 tablespoons olive oil
- 4 portobello mushroom caps or 8 cremini mushrooms, cut into ½-inch dice
- 1 medium shallot, finely chopped
- 1 thyme sprig
- 1 small red onion, finely diced
- 2 cups chopped blanched spinach (about 1½ pounds fresh spinach; see page 255)
- Freshly grated nutmeg
- Kosher salt and freshly ground black pepper
- ½ recipe Pasta Dough (page 109), chilled
- 4 tablespoons unsalted butter
- 2 small marjoram sprigs, plus 1 teaspoon marjoram leaves for garnish
- Freshly grated Parmigiano-Reggiano for serving

Line a sieve with dampened cheesecloth or a damp paper towel and set it over a deep bowl. Put the ricotta in the sieve and let drain for 30 minutes.

Meanwhile, heat a large sauté pan over medium-high heat. Add 2 tablespoons of the olive oil, and heat until hot, then add the mushrooms, shallot, and thyme and sauté for 3 minutes, or until the mushrooms are golden but still firm (they will continue to cook once removed from the heat). Transfer to a plate to cool.

Add the remaining tablespoon of olive oil to the pan and heat for a moment over medium-high heat, then add the onion. Cook until it becomes translucent, about 6 minutes. Transfer to a mixing bowl and let cool.

Add the spinach and ricotta to the onion, season with a few scrapes of nutmeg and a pinch each of salt and pepper, and mix well.

Bring a large pot of generously salted water to a boil.

Lightly flour a work surface. Using a floured rolling pin, roll out the pasta dough very thin into a 12-by-18-inch sheet. Transfer it to a baking sheet covered with a clean damp kitchen towel. Spread the spinach filling evenly over the pasta sheet, leaving a 2-inch border all around. Place the mushrooms lengthwise in a line down the center. Fold over the short ends by 2 inches. Using the towel to help you, roll up the dough, starting from a long side, to make a log 3 to 4 inches in diameter. Wrap the towel around the log and tie with kitchen string to secure.

Add the crespelle to the boiling water, reduce to a simmer, and cook for 12 to 15 minutes, until the pasta is thoroughly cooked and the roll feels firm. Carefully remove the crespelle and let cool so that the filling can firm up.

Carefully unwrap the crespelle. Using a chef's knife, slice it into 12 slices.

Divide the butter between two large skillets, add a marjoram sprig to each one, and heat. When the butter is foamy, add the crespelle slices, turning to coat on both sides with butter, and warm through.

Place 2 slices on each serving plate. Garnish with a pinch of fresh marjoram leaves and some grated Parmigiano.

To Drink: Soave (Gini or Suavia)

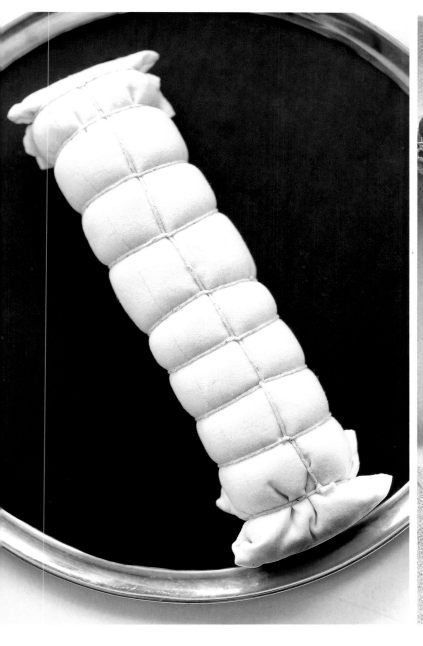

FISH·SHELLFISH

Bottega Salad Niçoise

Shrimp Salad Portofino

Capri Seafood Salad

Capri

Shrimp, Crab, and Shell Bean Salad

Scallops with Porcini Vinaigrette

Mussels Corfu

Lobster Adriatic-Style

Favorite Morsels from the Sea

Shrimp and Tuna with Venetian Agrodolce

Grilled Calamari on Polenta with Hot Chiles

Insalata di Mare

Roast Monkfish with Scallops, Capers, Grilled Lemons,
   and Brown Butter Vinaigrette

White Wines of Italy

Flounder with Little Shrimp, Asparagus, Sweet Peas,
   and Bulb Onions

Skate Wing Pantelleria with Capers, Marjoram,
   and Brown Butter

Tuna with Ligurian Walnut Sauce

Wild Striped Bass with Fennel, Artichokes, and Bay Leaves

Red Snapper in Cartoccio

Roast Grouper with Artichokes, Shell Beans, Fennel,
   and Grilled Lemons

Salmon with Orzo Salad

Fresh Fish from the Redneck Riviera

Roasted Trout with Dill and Lemon

Grilled Trout with Cherry Tomatoes, Herbs,
   and Torpedo Onions

OVERLEAF LEFT: *Roast Monkfish with Scallops, Capers, Grilled Lemons, and*
Brown Butter Vinaigrette (page 137); **OPPOSITE:** *Apalachicola gigged flounder*

BOTTEGA SALAD NIÇOISE

Serves 4

Another of Bottega Café's recipe standards—healthful, colorful, light but substantial. Many of our regulars never even look at anything else on the menu. We've attempted to do a more traditional rendition of this salad using Italian canned tuna, or even our own preserved tuna, but our patrons have come to expect fresh tuna steaks grilled to order. Yes, this is a long list of ingredients, but you can pare it down to suit your tastes or to use what you have on hand.

You might think my geography poor—why include a Niçoise dish in a book on Italian food? Well, because the area between Nice and the Italian border is in its heart and soul a part of what is now called Liguria in Italy. Historically, the area has been a part of Italy for much longer than it has been a part of France, and the food in Nice is far closer to the food of Genoa than to the food of Lyons.

Four 4-ounce tuna steaks
Sea salt and freshly ground black pepper
8 small new potatoes
16 small young green beans
4 large eggs
Olive oil
1 cup canned chickpeas, drained
4 to 6 radishes, thinly sliced
8 black olives, such as Niçoise or Kalamata,
    pitted and halved
½ cup quartered cherry tomatoes
2 small cucumbers, zebra-peeled (alternating stripes of
    unpeeled skin), seeded, and thinly sliced
½ cup Sherry Vinaigrette (page 73)
A heaping cup of mesclun
2 red bell peppers, roasted (see page 254), peeled,
    seeded, and cut into ½-inch-wide strips
4 to 6 basil leaves

Prepare a fire in an outdoor grill or preheat a broiler or stovetop grill.

Season the tuna with sea salt and pepper and set aside.

Put the potatoes in a medium saucepan of generously salted water and bring to a rolling boil. Reduce the heat slightly and cook for 15 minutes, or until tender. Remove the potatoes with a slotted spoon, and set aside until cool enough to handle, then cut into quarters.

Meanwhile, prepare an ice bath. Add the green beans to the boiling water and blanch for 3 to 4 minutes, until tender. With the slotted spoon, transfer to the ice bath to cool, then transfer the beans to a kitchen towel and blot dry. Add the eggs to the pan of water and simmer for 10 minutes. Drain and transfer to the ice bath to cool, then drain, peel, and quarter.

Oil the grill rack using an olive-oil-soaked cloth. Grill the tuna until medium-rare, about 3 minutes per side. Remove to a cooling rack and let rest while you compose the salads.

Divide the potatoes, boiled eggs, green beans, chickpeas, radishes, olives, cherry tomatoes, and cucumbers among four salad plates. Slice each tuna steak into 3 or 4 pieces and arrange on the plates. Drizzle 1 tablespoon of the vinaigrette over each plate. Toss the mesclun with the remaining ¼ cup vinaigrette and salt and pepper to taste. Mound a handful of the dressed greens in the center of each plate and garnish with the roasted peppers. Tear the basil leaves over the salads and serve.

To Drink: A rosé or simple, crisp white wine

SHRIMP SALAD PORTOFINO

Serves 4 as an appetizer

This is my tribute to the home of focaccia and this dreamy seaside village. Crunchy *panzanella,* or bread salad, is heightened with large tender shrimp, briny olives, and just a handful or two of aromatic herbs and tender lettuce leaves. Resist the inclination to toss in a lot of salad greens.

2 small kirbies or other pickling cucumbers
Kosher salt
16 extra-large shrimp (16 to 20 count) in the shell,
    preferably wild American shrimp
About ¼ cup Red Wine–Sherry Vinaigrette (page 73)
Four 2-by-3-inch rectangles Focaccia (page 82),
    grilled or toasted and torn into bite-sized chunks
12 red cherry tomatoes, halved
6 yellow cherry tomatoes, halved
2 tablespoons capers, rinsed
8 caper berries, rinsed and halved
8 Niçoise or Kalamata olives, pitted
1 small bunch flat-leaf parsley, leaves only
1 tablespoon thinly sliced chives
1 small bunch frisée, torn into bite-sized pieces
A small handful of celery leaves
2 scant tablespoons pine nuts, lightly toasted
    (see page 255)

Peel the cucumbers, halve, and thinly slice them. Toss with 1 teaspoon salt, put in a bowl, and refrigerate.

Bring a large saucepan of salted water to a rolling boil over high heat. Add the (unpeeled) shrimp and cook until they curl and are just cooked through, 4 to 5 minutes. Drain and let cool, then peel and devein.

Toss the shrimp with 1 tablespoon of the vinaigrette in a large bowl and let marinate for 5 minutes. Add the focaccia, cherry tomatoes, cucumbers (drained of any liquid), capers, caper berries, and olives to the shrimp, then add 2 tablespoons of the vinaigrette and toss to combine. Set aside for 5 minutes.

Toss the parsley, chives, frisée, and celery leaves in a bowl with a little vinaigrette and mound on four serving plates. Top with the panzanella mixture, then artfully arrange 4 shrimp on each plate, tucking them into the mound haphazardly. Finish with a scattering of the pine nuts over all.

To Drink: Vermentino (Bison)

CAPRI SEAFOOD SALAD

Serves 4

In the hands of those who revere both the sea and being at table, this dish becomes a true expression of Italian pride and confidence in fresh ingredients, cooked simply and dressed, while still warm, with a delicate, unctuous, fruity olive oil. This approach is also applied to the fresh-picked vegetable offerings. Quickly cooked—grilled, sautéed, or blanched—they're bathed in olive oil with just a few herbs, such as marjoram or basil, so that their intrinsic flavors shine. If I make it to heaven, I'm sure this will be served.

1 celery stalk with leaves, plus ½ cup sliced celery

1 bay leaf

16 large shrimp (16 to 20 count) in the shell, preferably wild American shrimp

½ pound cleaned calamari, bodies sliced into ⅛- to ¼-inch rings, tentacles left whole

2 tablespoons olive oil

1 shallot, finely minced

16 small mussels, scrubbed and debearded

1 cup dry white wine

16 small clams or cockles, scrubbed

1 tablespoon red wine vinegar

½ cup extra virgin olive oil, plus more for drizzling

Kosher salt and freshly ground black pepper

6 to 8 small tender basil leaves

4 oregano or marjoram sprigs, leaves only

¼ cup loosely packed flat-leaf parsley leaves

Grated zest of ½ lemon

1 cup halved cherry tomatoes

Extra virgin olive oil

Lemon wedges

1 cup arugula leaves, preferably *selvetica* (wild arugula)

Crusty bread

Bring a large pot of generously salted water, with the celery stalk and bay leaf, to a rolling boil. Toss in the shrimp, reduce the heat to a simmer, and gently poach the shrimp until they are just slightly curled and pink, about 3 minutes. With a strainer or skimmer, transfer the shrimp to a large platter.

Poach the calamari in the pot of simmering water for 45 seconds, or until just firm. Transfer to the platter. When the shrimp are cool enough to handle, peel and devein them (do not rinse them, or you will lose the subtle flavors). Return to the platter and set aside.

Add 1 tablespoon of the olive oil and half the shallots to a large saucepan and cook over medium-low heat just to soften the shallots. Add the mussels and ½ cup of the white wine, cover the pan with a tight-fitting lid, and raise the heat to high. Steam the mussels until they open, 3 to 5 minutes. Transfer the mussels to a bowl and set aside. Pour the juices from the pan into a medium mixing bowl.

Add the remaining oil and shallots to the same pan, and soften the shallots over medium-low heat. Add the clams or cockles and the remaining ½ cup white wine, cover, and raise the heat to high. Steam the clams until they open, 3 to 5 minutes. Transfer the clams to a bowl and set aside. Pour the pan juices into the bowl with the mussel liquid. Remove the mussels from the shells.

Make a "pot liquor" vinaigrette by adding the red wine vinegar to the bowl of cooking juices, then whisking in the extra virgin olive oil. Season with salt and pepper.

Combine the cooked shrimp, calamari, mussels, and clams on a large deep platter and toss with the vinaigrette. Tear the basil leaves over the salad and scatter the oregano or marjoram and parsley leaves over it, then add the lemon zest, cherry tomatoes, and sliced celery and toss well to combine. Taste and adjust the seasonings to suit.

Finish the salad with a splash of extra virgin olive oil, and garnish with lemon wedges and a tangle of arugula in the center. Serve with slices of crusty bread for sopping up the juices.

To Drink: Fiano di Avellino (Terredora)

CAPRI One of the most majestic places I've ever been is the little island of Capri. You come in by boat to the Marina Grande, and from there you take the tram up the cliffs, with Mount Vesuvius and the Bay of Naples in the distance. The beauty of the surroundings engulf you. Below you the earth is abundant with lush gardens. There are lemon trees, eggplants, and tomatoes, and everywhere you turn, you see flowers. The village consists of walking paths that wind their way through the hills, and the heady aroma of lemon blossoms perfume your ascent.

At the top of the tram, you enter a piazza almost like a stage set, surrounded by enchanting little cafès. I start each day at one of the cafès in the main piazza, where I savor a cappuccino and enjoy a pastry while reading the paper and taking in the scene. I try to arrive very early, when most of the tourists are still asleep. The hordes of day-trippers arrive around ten in the morning, and that is when my wife and I make our way to the hundreds of steps leading down the cliff to the cove at La Fontellina.

Typically, we arrive at La Fontellina in the morning and stay until the middle of the day to lunch in the shade on shrimp, calamari, mussels, and lobsters, either in salads or cooked with pasta. This is exquisite food served in the gorgeous setting of 1,000-foot cliffs and sparkling blue sea.

After my many meals at La Fontellina, I became friendly with the family that runs the restaurant and was invited to spend a day in the kitchen. I arrived as the fishermen were bringing in clams, mussels, and assorted fresh fish, and Nonna ("Grandmamma") was busy preparing the eggplant, stews, and sauces.

Each trip to Capri has been inspirational. I come home eager to convey the purity, simplicity, and spirit of that food to my cooks at Bottega. I tell them to choose the ripest tomatoes, the best produce, and then treat them simply and with respect—a toss with lots of good olive oil and vinegar and maybe some shallots and sea salt—and not tinker any more. As the food of Capri illustrates, the best dishes are quite often nothing more than the artful combinations of a few top-quality ingredients beautifully presented so that their essence shines through.

SHRIMP, CRAB, AND SHELL BEAN SALAD
Serves 4 as an appetizer

We use marinated shell beans or tender peas in lieu of cannellini or borlotti beans in our Southern spin on this Italian summer classic. The beans serve as the base for avocado halves filled with delicate lump crabmeat. We garnish the salad with freshly grated lemon zest, chopped cherry tomatoes, and a few boiled shrimp. Try to find a seafood purveyor who carries wild American shrimp.

- 12 extra-large shrimp (16 to 20 count) in the shell, preferably wild American shrimp
- 1½ cups cooked fresh or frozen shell beans (see Note, page 59), such as pink-eyed peas, lady peas, crowder peas, or small favas
- 1 shallot, minced
- ½ cup Sherry Vinaigrette (page 73)
- 1 small bunch basil, leaves only, 8 leaves reserved for garnish, remaining leaves cut into chiffonade
- Kosher salt and freshly ground black pepper
- 2 ripe avocados, halved, pitted, and peeled
- 1 pound jumbo lump crabmeat, picked free of shells and cartilage
- 1 tomato, peeled (see page 255), seeded, and diced, or 8 cherry tomatoes, quartered
- Grated zest of ½ lemon

Bring a large saucepan of salted water to a rolling boil over high heat. Add the (unpeeled) shrimp and cook until they curl and are just cooked through, 4 to 5 minutes. Drain and let cool, then peel and devein.

Toss the beans in a large bowl with the shallot, 2 tablespoons of the vinaigrette, about half of the basil chiffonade, and salt and pepper. Divide among four serving plates.

Gently turn the avocado halves with 2 tablespoons of the vinaigrette and season with salt and pepper. Nestle an avocado half in the beans on each plate.

Dress the crabmeat with 2 tablespoons of the vinaigrette and salt and pepper and mound in the avocados. Top each with a little pinch of the basil chiffonade.

Toss the shrimp with the remaining basil chiffonade and remaining 2 tablespoons vinaigrette and arrange alongside the avocados. Scatter the tomatoes about, garnish with the lemon zest and basil leaves, and serve.

To Drink: Pino Bianco (Tiefenbrunner)

SCALLOPS WITH PORCINI VINAIGRETTE

Serves 4 as an appetizer

There are just a few ingredients in this recipe, so don't even consider making it unless your scallops are pristine and the porcini fresh, firm, and woodsy. Porcini are an extravagance, but if they're not an option, you can use chanterelles, hedgehogs, shiitake, or even cremini. They all have a short shelf life, so use as soon as possible after buying them. Black truffle oil carries a purer aroma than the more powerful white. It's an item worth adding to your pantry—just a little drizzle dresses up almost any mushroom dish, amplifying its inherent earthiness.

8 large sea scallops (about 2 ounces each),
    tough muscle removed
Sea salt and freshly ground black pepper
6 tablespoons olive oil
½ pound porcini or other mushrooms (see headnote),
    trimmed if necessary and sliced ¼ inch thick
1 shallot, finely minced
4 thyme sprigs, leaves only
1 tablespoon sherry vinegar
Splash of dry white wine or water
2 cups arugula, preferably *selvetica* (wild arugula)
Porcini or black truffle oil (see Sources, page 260;
    optional)

Pat the scallops dry and season with sea salt and pepper. Set aside on a plate.

Heat 1 tablespoon of the oil in a large sauté pan over medium heat. Add the mushrooms and sauté until they begin to soften, 6 to 8 minutes. Add the shallot and thyme to the pan and sauté about 45 seconds, to soften the shallot just a bit, then transfer the mushroom mixture to a small mixing bowl. Add the vinegar and whisk in 3 tablespoons of the olive oil. Set aside.

Heat the remaining 2 tablespoons oil in a medium to large cast-iron or French steel skillet over medium-high heat. When the oil is shimmering but not smoking, add the scallops and cook for 2 minutes per side, or until golden. Transfer the scallops to warm serving plates.

Deglaze the pan with a splash of white wine or water, scraping up the flavorful browned bits and juices on the pan bottom, then reduce until the liquid is syrupy. Whisk this into the porcini vinaigrette.

Drizzle the scallops with the warm vinaigrette. Garnish with the arugula leaves, and finish with a drizzle of porcini or truffle oil.

To Drink: Chardonnay (Au Bon Climat)

MUSSELS CORFU

Serves 2

I usually keep cheese away from seafood so its funky, earthy aromas don't compete with the clean saline flavors of fresh shellfish. But I diverge from that rule when it comes to these mussels in a zesty garlic-tomato broth, enhanced by tangy feta cheese and creamy butter. Don't skip the grilled sourdough—it's very useful for sopping up all of the flavorful juices.

¼ cup olive oil
2 shallots or ½ small red onion, finely minced
2 garlic cloves, smashed and finely chopped
4 fresh or canned Roma (plum) tomatoes, peeled
    (see page 253), seeded, and chopped
2 pounds mussels, scrubbed and debearded
4 large thyme or marjoram sprigs
1 small bunch basil, leaves only
1 cup dry white wine
1 cup crumbled French or Greek feta (about 4 ounces)
4 tablespoons salted butter
½ lemon
Kosher salt and freshly ground black pepper
4 slices sourdough bread, grilled or toasted and drizzled
    with olive oil

Heat 2 tablespoons of the olive oil in a large casserole or pot over medium-high heat. Add the shallots or onion and garlic and cook until fragrant but not colored (lower the heat if necessary), about 3 minutes. Add the tomatoes, mussels, herbs (reserve 4 basil leaves for garnish), and wine, cover with a tight-fitting lid, and raise the heat to high. Let the mussels steam for about 4 minutes, shaking the pot occasionally. Remove the lid and check to see that the mussels have opened—cover and cook a bit longer if necessary.

Once the mussels have opened, lift them out with a slotted spoon and transfer to two serving bowls. Reduce the broth over high heat until concentrated and slightly thickened, about 3 minutes. Add the feta, butter, a squeeze of lemon juice, and salt and pepper and shake and whisk to incorporate. Taste and adjust for seasonings.

Ladle the broth over the mussels and tear the reserved basil leaves over the mussels to garnish. Serve with the grilled bread.

To Drink: Pinot Gris (Eyrie Vineyards)

LOBSTER ADRIATIC-STYLE

Serves 4

These buttery basil-and-lemon-scented lobsters make me dream of sailing off the Dalmatian Coast. Even if I can't be there, this preparation makes dinner a celebration.

Four 1½-pound live lobsters
½ pound (2 sticks) butter
1 large leek, white and pale green parts,
    cleaned and cut into ½-inch pieces
1 large garlic clove, finely minced
5 cups Bread Crumbs (page 239)
1 large bunch basil, leaves removed and finely chopped
1 bunch flat-leaf parsley, leaves removed and
    finely chopped
Grated zest and juice of 2 lemons
Kosher salt and freshly ground black pepper
Cayenne to taste (optional)
Melted butter (optional)

To quickly kill the lobsters, place the tip of a large heavy chef's knife at the midsection of the underbelly (thorax) and slice down and through the head without going all the way through the other side of the shell (see Note). Turn the lobster around and slice lengthwise through the tail section in the same manner to butterfly the lobster, rocking the knife back and forth to slice through the tail, again being careful not to cut all the way through. Remove the tomalley and any coral, then remove the grain sacs from the heads of the lobsters. Pull off the claws and knuckles and cut through the shell of each claw with heavy kitchen shears so that the meat will be easy to remove after roasting. Set aside.

Preheat the oven to 425°F.

Melt the butter in a large sauté pan over medium-low heat. Add the leek and garlic and cook until the leek is softened, 10 to 12 minutes. Transfer to a large bowl and add the bread crumbs, basil, parsley, lemon zest and juice, salt and pepper, and cayenne, if desired. Mix well.

Divide the stuffing into fourths (you will have a little less than 1 cup for each lobster) and spoon the filling into each lobster from the head to the tail.

Arrange the stuffed lobsters on a baking sheet, along with the cracked claws, and roast for 15 to 20 minutes: the bread crumbs should be browned and the lobster meat opaque and glistening with butter.

Drizzle with more melted butter, and dig in.

NOTE: If you'd rather not split the cooked lobsters, bring a large pot of salted water to a boil. Drop the lobsters in and cook for 3 minutes, then remove and plunge into a bowl of ice water. Proceed as directed, but reduce the baking time by 5 minutes.

To Drink: Chardonnay (DuMol)

FAVORITE MORSELS FROM THE SEA Our Southern seafood hamper offers a luscious bounty, and at the top of my list are crawfish tails, so vibrantly pink and fleshy with their creeklike flavors and superb texture. (They're "crayfish" to most of the world, but down South we say "crawfish" or "crawdad.") I admit, though, nothing can beat the exquisite texture and flavor of lump crabmeat freshly steamed or boiled, the meat picked free of the shell. Both of these divine meats—heated with some butter, maybe a bit of garlic, some scallions, lemon juice, a sprinkling of chives, and a final splash of Tabasco—embellish many of our sautéed, broiled, or grilled fish.

SHRIMP AND TUNA WITH VENETIAN AGRODOLCE

Serves 4

Venetian merchants made fortunes dealing in spices during the late fifteenth and early sixteenth centuries—cloves, pepper, saffron, cinnamon, nutmeg, coriander, mustard seed, fennel, basil, parsley, sage, rosemary, bay, and borage, among them. From the Arab stronghold in nearby Sicily came other uncommon flavors, most notably sugarcane. Mixing piquant spices with tart vinegar and a dose of sugar became an immediate hit in Italy, and there remains today a keen fondness for *agrodolce,* "sweet-and-sour," sauces.

At Bottega, we make sweet-tart agrodolce onions to serve with various seafood dishes, such as delicate fish fillets, dredged in bread crumbs and panfried, or as here, big meaty shrimp and chunks of firm fresh tuna. You may have to call the fishmonger ahead of time to get the 2-inch slabs of tuna.

FOR THE AGRODOLCE

1 tablespoon olive oil
3 large onions, quartered and thinly sliced
8 bay leaves
½ teaspoon fennel seeds
2 whole cloves
1 star anise
2 tablespoons vinegar, such as cider-honey or white wine
1 heaping tablespoon brown sugar
2 tablespoons sultanas (golden raisins),
    soaked in warm water for 10 minutes
1 tablespoon pine nuts, toasted (see page 255; optional)
Kosher salt and freshly ground black pepper

12 extra-large shrimp (16 to 20 count), peeled
    and deveined
Four 2-inch-thick 4-ounce squares tuna steak
Maldon sea salt and freshly ground black pepper
1 tablespoon olive oil
Celery leaves or borage leaves for garnish
Fruity extra virgin olive oil

To make the agrodolce, heat the olive oil in a large saucepan over medium heat. Add the onions and cook for 5 minutes. Add the bay leaves, fennel seeds, cloves, star anise, vinegar, sugar, and sultanas and cook, covered, over medium-low heat for 10 minutes, or until the onions are very soft. Keep warm over very low heat while you cook the shrimp and tuna.

Season the shrimp and tuna with sea salt and pepper. Heat the olive oil in a large heavy skillet over high heat. Add the shrimp and tuna and sear for about 2 minutes. Turn and cook for another 2 to 3 minutes, until the shrimp are just cooked through and the tuna is medium-rare in the center (or to your taste).

Just before serving, stir the pine nuts into the agrodolce onions and season with salt and pepper.

Arrange 3 shrimp and 1 piece of tuna on each plate, along with some of the agrodolce onions. Garnish with the celery or borage leaves and a drizzle of fruity olive oil.

To Drink: Pinot Bianco (Schiopetto)

GRILLED CALAMARI ON POLENTA WITH HOT CHILES

Serves 4

Fried calamari may be a great way to introduce squid to tentative palates, but once you taste this lighter, simpler preparation, you'll come to love squid's unique flavor. There's an old saying that calamari must be cooked either for just a few moments, until no longer raw, or for hours, as in many Sicilian and Provençal recipes. For this recipe, have your grill hot and your guests seated, ready to dig in—it comes together that quickly.

> 4 fresh or frozen squid (about 4 to 5 inches plus tentacles)
> 1 tablespoon olive oil, plus extra for brushing
> 1 red jalapeño, thinly sliced (some seeds removed)
> 1 dried red chile pepper
> 1 garlic clove, crushed and finely chopped
> Sea salt and freshly ground black pepper
> Four 4-inch squares Firm Polenta (page 206)
> 2 cups arugula
> 1 red bell pepper, roasted (see page 254), peeled, seeded, and cut into small dice
> ¼ cup Sherry Vinaigrette (page 73)
> 1 lemon, halved

If the squid hasn't been cleaned, pull out the insides; remove and discard the beak, the sharp inedible bony structure where the tentacles meet the body. Rinse and pat dry. Cut each squid lengthwise in half. Score the inner sides of the bodies in a ¼-inch crosshatch pattern.

Toss the squid with the olive oil, jalapeño, dried chile, and garlic in a bowl. Let marinate for 30 minutes at room temperature.

Prepare a fire in an outdoor grill or preheat a cast-iron grill pan over medium-high heat.

Season the squid assertively with sea salt and pepper. Brush the polenta on both sides with a little olive oil and grill for 1 to 2 minutes per side, to add grill marks and just warm it through. Add the squid to the grill at the same time and cook for about 1 minute per side.

Place a square of polenta on each plate and place the squid on top. Scatter the arugula over and top with the diced roasted pepper. Drizzle with the sherry vinaigrette, and give everything a squeeze of lemon before serving.

To Drink: Pino Bianco (Lageder)

INSALATA DI MARE

When I was a kid vacationing on the American Gulf Coast, I used to order platters of fried seafood at the beach. These were delicacies I couldn't get easily back home in Cullman, and certainly not all at once on the same large platter—scallops, shrimp, oysters, crab, sometimes even lobster—it was incredible. The freshness, quality, and care in preparation was usually suspect, but we greeted the platters with an "It won't kill ya" frame of mind (figuring at least it was cooked), and fascination with the world of shellfish persisted for this boy from north Alabama.

With that, you can imagine my reaction when I encountered insalata di mare in Italy as a teenager, with its array of shimmering, glistening shellfish: octopus in shades of magenta to deep violet; snowy white calamari; mussels so shiny black they looked blue; quarter-sized mahogany clams; fat scallops with orange roe hugging their sides; and sometimes odd creatures straight from *20,000 Leagues Under the Sea*. The sheer beauty and purity of the varied flavors and textures still astound me, as does the unbelievably simple, commonsense Italian approach.

There's no need for fuss: Just pour freshly squeezed lemon juice over a couple of cloves of garlic and allow the cloves to macerate for an hour to infuse the citrus juice with the garlic flavor, then discard the garlic. Poach the seafood in salted water (discard any mollusks that fail to open). Combine the garlic-infused lemon juice with a little olive oil, chopped parsley, sea salt, and cracked pepper, and toss with the seafood. Marinate the salad for anywhere from 10 minutes to 2 hours so that the flavors come together. On a warm, sunny summer day, nothing could be better.

ROAST MONKFISH WITH SCALLOPS, CAPERS, GRILLED LEMONS, AND BROWN BUTTER VINAIGRETTE

Serves 4 to 6 • Pictured on page 122

Again, a preparation that's about using the freshest fish you can find, whether monkfish or flounder, snapper, dolphin-fish, or pompano: almost any variety of fish can be prepared in this fashion. One taste of our brown butter vinaigrette, and it will become a go-to sauce whenever you have fresh fish on hand. And the grilled lemon slices—warm, tender, and slightly caramelized—are a sunny garnish that can be eaten in their entirety.

One 24-ounce monkfish tail fillet
12 dry-packed scallops, preferably day-boat
Sea salt and freshly ground white pepper
2 lemons, washed, sliced ¼-inch thick, and seeds removed
2 tablespoons plus about 1 teaspoon olive oil
1 tablespoon capers, rinsed
Chopped flat-leaf parsley or other herbs for garnish
About ¼ cup Brown Butter Vinaigrette (page 244)

Preheat the oven to 425°F. Season the monkfish and scallops on both sides with sea salt and white pepper and set aside.

Heat a large heavy skillet over medium-high heat; depending on the number of lemon slices you have, you may need to cook them in batches—or use two large pans, if you have them. (Alternatively, preheat the broiler.) Rub the lemon slices with a tiny amount—about 1 teaspoon—of the olive oil, add to the hot pan, and char on both sides until just blackened. (Or arrange the slices on a baking sheet lined with parchment paper and caramelize under the broiler.) Remove to a rack.

Heat a large heavy skillet over medium-high heat. Add 1 tablespoon of the olive oil and when it shimmers, add the monkfish. Reduce the heat to medium and cook the fish until the edges turn opaque, about 6 minutes.

Turn the fish and cook it on the second side until almost done, about 5 minutes more. (The fish will continue cooking once it is removed from the heat, so it is important to remove it before it is cooked through.) Transfer the fish to a cooling rack and cover loosely to keep warm while you prepare the scallops.

Heat a large heavy skillet over medium-high heat. Add the remaining 1 tablespoon olive oil and heat until hot, then place the scallops in the pan with space around each so that they will sear, not steam. When they are opaque one-third of the way up, about 2 minutes, turn them and cook for about 2 minutes more, until golden.

Place the fish on a large platter and arrange the scallops around it. Scatter the lemon slices over and around the seafood and garnish with the capers, parsley or other herbs, and a spoonful of the brown butter vinaigrette. Pass the remaining vinaigrette in a sauceboat at the table.

To Drink: Chardonnay (Kistler)

white wines of italy

For all of us who love bright, fresh, light, yet minerally, white wines, with hints of citrus and fruit, Italy produces a vast array of choices. Modern wine making advances mean fewer flat and oxidized white wines. With temperature-controlled fermentation, even the warm climates of Southern Italy can produce good crisp wines, unlike years past when you were better off opting for a more reliable red wine.

The northeastern Italian regions of Friuli, Alto Adige, and the Veneto, with the cool mountain air of the Alps, are the country's richest trove of white wines. Be sure to try the varieties produced in these hills—Tocais, Pinot Biancos, Sauvignons, and Pinot Grigios. Soaves's best producers create interesting and extremely versatile wines at good value.

Prosecco comes from this region in the foothills that give rise to the Alps, and is a wonderful alternative to the much more costly French Champagne.

From the northwest, near the Swiss and French borders, there's a sensational white of great value—Erbalace. Arneis, a perfect-first-course white and the major white wine of Piedmonte, was only recently revitalized and now there are numerous producers, such as Cerreto, Corregia, and Gicacossa.

The coastal regions from Liguria to Campania insist on local wines to accompany their pristine seafood, so, from the hills outside La Spezia, look for Bison Vermintino and the delicate wines from Cinque Terre.

Farther south, outside Naples, the ancient grape growing tradition has been rekindled by wineries such as Feudi di San Gregorio, Terredorra di Paolo, and Mastrobernadino. With all seafoods, try the Falanghina, Greco di Tufo, and Fiano di Avallino.

FLOUNDER WITH LITTLE SHRIMP, ASPARAGUS, SWEET PEAS, AND BULB ONIONS

Serves 4

Reflecting both Venetian and South Carolina cuisines, this dish captures what I crave in both these coastal culinary traditions—spanking-fresh fish, local shellfish (in this case, little bay or creek shrimp), and vegetables that sing of the season (a spring ragout of bulb onions, peas, and tiny asparagus). Use whatever freshly caught fish you can find: triggerfish, snapper, or pompano could all be substituted for the flounder. Cook the small shrimp first so you can use some of the flavorful broth when preparing the vegetable ragout.

FOR THE SHRIMP

4 cups water

Three ½-inch-thick onion slices

3 lemon slices

1 celery stalk, sliced

4 parsley sprigs

Kosher salt

5 black peppercorns

½ pound small shrimp (21–30 count)

2½ tablespoons unsalted butter

4 bulb onions, quartered lengthwise

Kosher salt and freshly ground black pepper

12 small new potatoes, halved or quartered, blanched in boiling salted water for 15 minutes, or until tender, and drained

½ cup fresh or frozen sweet peas, blanched in boiling salted water until tender and drained

2 tablespoons olive oil

4 flounder or other fish fillets (see headnote)

Maldon sea salt

Several sprigs of mint, tarragon, or dill, leaves only

12 small asparagus spears, trimmed, blanched for 2 minutes, shocked in ice water, and sliced into 1½-inch pieces

½ lemon

To cook the shrimp, combine the water, onion slices, lemon slices, celery, parsley sprigs, salt to taste (season aggressively), and peppercorns and bring to a boil. Add the shrimp and cook until the shrimp curl and turn pink. Remove the shrimp with a strainer, then strain the broth for use in this and other recipes. When they are cool, peel the shrimp and set aside.

Melt ½ tablespoon of the butter in a medium saucepan over medium heat. Add the bulb onions and cook for 5 minutes, or until softened. Add a splash of water and cook until the onions are glazed and tender, about 4 minutes more. Season the onions with salt and pepper, then add the potatoes, sweet peas, and 1 cup of the reserved shrimp broth and bring the liquid to a gentle simmer; keep warm over very low heat.

Heat a large heavy well-seasoned cast-iron skillet or nonstick skillet over high heat, and add the olive oil. Season the fish with sea salt and pepper, add to the pan, and cook until the edges turn opaque, 2 to 3 minutes. Turn the fish, reduce the heat to medium, and cook until just cooked through, 4 to 5 minutes, depending upon the thickness of the fillets. Transfer the fish to a rack, and keep warm.

Meanwhile, chop the herbs. Bring the shrimp broth back to a gentle simmer and add the shrimp and blanched asparagus. Swirl in the remaining 2 tablespoons butter, then add the herbs. Season with salt and pepper and brighten with a squeeze of lemon juice.

Spoon the vegetables and shrimp into the center of four deep serving bowls or dishes, top with the fish fillets, and serve.

To Drink: Sauvignon Blanc

SKATE WING PANTELLERIA WITH CAPERS, MARJORAM, AND BROWN BUTTER

Serves 4

Not so long ago, skate would have been a long-shot entice-ment for most Southerners. Now, in large part because of French bistro offerings, many have learned to love this ten-der, flavorful, and inexpensive fish.

We serve skate with the irresistible combination of rich brown butter vinaigrette, salty and tangy capers (a specialty from the little Sicilian island of Pantelleria), and lots of marjoram and parsley. Traditional recipes often call for oregano, but most of the varieties I encounter today seem a bit diluted in flavor, so I prefer to use oregano's more direct cousin, marjoram. This is a good standard recipe to have as a part of your repertoire: brown butter vinaigrette makes any fish taste simply delicious. Serve with steamed new potatoes.

> Four 7-ounce skate wing fillets (or flounder, John Dory, or sole)
> Sea salt and freshly ground white pepper
> Flour for dusting
> 2 tablespoons olive oil
> 2 tablespoons unsalted butter
> 3 tablespoons capers, preferably salt-packed, rinsed
> 1 heaping tablespoon caper berries
> ¼ cup Brown Butter Vinaigrette (page 244)
> 4 sprigs marjoram, leaves only
> 4 sprigs flat-leaf parsley, leaves removed and chopped

Season the skate with sea salt and pepper and dust with flour, shaking off the excess.

Heat two large skillets over medium-high heat and add half of the oil and butter to each one. When the butter is foamy, add the skate and cook for approximately 4 minutes per side, until golden brown. Place the fillets on serving plates.

Pour the fat out of one of the pans, and add to it the capers, caper berries, and brown butter vinaigrette and bring to a boil.

Spoon the vinaigrette, capers, and caper berries over the fish, garnish with the marjoram leaves and chopped parsley, and serve.

To Drink: Trebbiano d'Abruzzo (Nicodemi)

TUNA WITH LIGURIAN WALNUT SAUCE

Serves 4

I find great pleasure in this rather quirky sauce of walnuts. Its earthy nuttiness is enhanced further with walnut oil, making it a wonderfully full-flavored embellishment for a hearty fish like tuna and a rich and slightly exotic sauce for pasta. The sauce is best if the vinegar mixture is combined with the nuts at the last second. Try it with Silk Handkerchief Pasta with Pesto (page 110) or linguine.

> Four 6- to 7-ounce tuna steaks
> Maldon sea salt and freshly ground black pepper
> 1 shallot, thinly sliced
> 2 tablespoons red wine vinegar
> ⅓ cup delicate extra virgin olive oil, plus oil for the grill or skillet
> 2 tablespoons walnut oil
> ¾ cup walnut halves, toasted (see page 255)
> ¼ cup pine nuts, toasted (see page 255)
> 2 tablespoons capers, rinsed
> ¼ cup coarsely chopped flat-leaf parsley
> ¼ cup pitted Picholine or Niçoise olives, coarsely chopped
> Yolks from 2 hard-boiled eggs, chopped (optional)

Season the tuna with sea salt and pepper and set aside.

Prepare a hot fire in a grill. (If you wish to cook the tuna on the stovetop, see below.) While the grill is heating, combine the shallot and vinegar with sea salt and pepper in a medium bowl. Set aside to macerate for 10 minutes.

Rub the grill grate with an olive-oil-soaked cloth (or heat 1 tablespoon olive oil in a large skillet over medium-high heat). Put the fish on the grill (or in the hot pan) and cook until the edges begin to turn opaque, about 2 minutes. Turn and cook for about 2 minutes more for medium-rare. Transfer the fish to a rack and tent with foil to keep warm.

Whisk the olive and walnut oils into the shallot-vinegar mixture. Add the walnuts, pine nuts, capers, parsley, and olives and toss thoroughly to combine.

Place the fish on warm plates and serve with a heaping spoonful of the walnut sauce. Top with the chopped egg yolk, if desired.

To Drink: Cinque Terre or other simple, light, young white wine

WILD STRIPED BASS WITH FENNEL, ARTICHOKES, AND BAY LEAVES

Serves 4

Wild striped bass is the king of the Mediterranean. This beautiful fish is unsurpassed for its delicate texture and exquisite flavor. Here we opt for traditional accompaniments: fennel (both fresh and dried seeds), young artichokes, lots of crushed garlic, and bay leaves, moistened with fruity green olive oil.

Thin fish fillets often curl at the edges as they cook on the skin side. To prevent this, dry the fillets thoroughly and make several slits in the skin before placing the fish in the hot pan. Scraping the skin of the fillets with the back of a knife before searing them helps remove excess moisture and will make the skin extra crisp.

FOR THE VEGETABLES

2 fennel bulbs, trimmed and cut lengthwise into sixths

8 fingerling potatoes, halved lengthwise

4 baby artichokes, trimmed (see page 254) and
    quartered

8 garlic cloves, crushed lightly with skin on

⅓ cup olive oil

Maldon sea salt and freshly ground black pepper

1 teaspoon fennel seeds

12 bay leaves

½ cup dry white wine

FOR THE FISH

Four 6- to 8-ounce skin-on striped bass fillets
    (or red snapper or halibut)

Kosher salt and freshly ground white pepper

2 tablespoons olive oil

Flour for dredging

1 tablespoon unsalted butter

Juice of ½ lemon

½ teaspoon thyme leaves

Preheat the oven to 400°F.

To prepare the vegetables, toss the fennel, potatoes, artichokes, and garlic with the olive oil in a large roasting pan. Season assertively with sea salt and pepper, and add the fennel seeds and bay leaves. Spread the vegetables out and roast for 20 to 25 minutes, until slightly charred and just tender when pierced with a knife.

Set the pan over high heat, add the wine, and bring to a boil, scraping up all the browned bits. Boil until reduced to a syrupy glaze. Adjust the seasoning if necessary, and set aside, loosely covered to keep warm.

To cook the fish, pat the fillets dry and cut several diagonal slashes in the skin of each one. For extra-crisp skin, scrape the skin with the back of a knife and pat dry again (see headnote). Season the fillets with salt and white pepper.

Heat a skillet large enough to hold the fillets without crowding over high heat. Add 1 tablespoon of the oil to the hot pan. Quickly dredge each fillet in flour, shaking off the excess, and place skin side up in the pan. Cook for about 3 minutes—the fish will release from the pan easily when it is ready to flip. Turn the fish, add the remaining tablespoon of olive oil, the butter, lemon juice, and thyme, and cook the fish for about 3 minutes more, until just opaque throughout. Baste the fish with the pan sauce as it finishes cooking.

Transfer the fish to warm plates and serve the vegetables alongside.

To Drink: Arneis

RED SNAPPER IN CARTOCCIO

This is a simple way to wow your dinner guests. Any delicate fish is welcome here—sole, striped bass, halibut, or branzino—nestled in a parchment cocoon with sweet onions, tomatoes, fresh herbs, lemon, and a generous pat of butter. In the oven, the packages puff up like golden balloons. As the guests carefully open the dramatic *cartoccio* at the table, the intoxicating aroma casts its spell. Do not attempt this unless the fish is absolutely fresh—the delicate sea aroma is essential—and be generous with the butter.

2 ripe tomatoes, peeled (see page 255), seeded, and diced

Sea salt

Scant 1 tablespoon olive oil

1½ sweet onions, such as Maui or Vidalia, halved and thinly sliced

Kosher salt and freshly ground black pepper

6 tablespoons butter, cut into 4 slices, plus butter for the parchment

1 lemon, scrubbed, thinly sliced, and seeds removed (you need 8 slices)

Four 6- to 7-ounce skin-on red snapper fillets

6 basil leaves, cut into chiffonade

6 chives, thinly sliced

6 flat-leaf parsley sprigs, leaves removed and finely chopped

6 sprigs lemon thyme, leaves only

Grated zest of 1 lemon

1 egg, beaten with a splash of water (optional)

Place the tomatoes in a bowl with a little sea salt and let macerate for 30 minutes to 1 hour.

Preheat the oven to 475°F.

Heat the olive oil in a large sauté pan over medium heat. Add the onions and sauté until softened, about 10 minutes. Season with salt and pepper and set aside.

Drain the tomatoes in a mesh strainer, gently pressing out the excess liquid. Place the tomatoes in a small bowl.

Cut four 16-by-20-inch sheets of parchment paper or heavy-duty foil. Fold each one crosswise in half and trace a half-heart shape from near the top to near the bottom of the folded edges. Cut out the traced shape and unfold the parchment to reveal a heart. Rub a little butter over where the fish will lie on each heart, and place 2 slices of lemon on the buttered portion. Top with the fillets, skin side down, and season assertively with sea salt and pepper. Place the sautéed onions on the fish, slightly to one side. Top with the diced tomato and the herbs. Place a slice of the butter on top of each fish and sprinkle with a little lemon zest. Fold the parchment or foil over so that the edges align and, beginning at one end, seal with small overlapping folds, each about an inch long, making sure to seal the ends securely. (The packets can be refrigerated for a few hours; return to room temperature before proceeding.)

Place the packets on a baking sheet. If desired, brush the parchment with the beaten egg to give the packets a deeper golden color when baked. Place the pan in the oven and cook for 10 minutes (a little longer if your fillets are thicker than ½ inch).

Transfer to serving plates and rush to the table, allowing each guest to carefully open his or her packet with a scissors or knife. Inhale the aroma and dig in.

To Drink: An elegant, aged Chablis (Raveneau)

ROAST GROUPER WITH ARTICHOKES, SHELL BEANS, FENNEL, AND GRILLED LEMONS

Serves 4

Roasted fish perfumed with fennel is a dish I adore. Here, shell beans in a flavorful broth make a hearty and homey base for the grouper—and the grilled lemons are an aromatic and beautiful garnish. You could, if you like, substitute Roasted Fingerling Potatoes with Herbs (page 196), boiled new potatoes, or cannellini beans for the shell beans. The artichokes combine beautifully with the carefully cooked beans.

> Four 6- to 8-ounce skinless grouper, striped bass, snapper, or halibut fillets
> About ¼ cup extra virgin olive oil, plus extra for the fish
> 1 tablespoon fennel seeds
> 8 baby artichokes, trimmed (see page 254) and quartered
> 2 small fennel bulbs, trimmed and cut into 1-inch wedges
> 1 small red onion, cut into 1-inch wedges
> 4 unpeeled garlic cloves, lightly crushed
> 8 bay leaves
> Sea salt and freshly ground white or black pepper
> 2 cups Cooked Shell Beans (page 195)
> 1 lemon, washed, sliced ¼ inch thick, seeds removed

Position a rack in the upper third of the oven and preheat the oven to 475°F.

Place the fish fillets on a platter, rub with a little olive oil, and sprinkle with about ¼ teaspoon of the fennel seeds. Set aside.

Put the artichokes, fennel wedges, onion, and garlic on a baking sheet or in a gratin dish and toss with the bay leaves, fennel seeds, sea salt and pepper to taste, and about 2 tablespoons of the olive oil. Roast until the edges of the vegetables are charred and the vegetables are tender when pierced, about 20 minutes; rotate and shake the pan halfway through for even cooking. Remove from the oven and cover to keep warm.

Meanwhile, heat the shell beans in a saucepan over medium heat.

While the beans are warming up, heat a large heavy ovenproof skillet over medium-high heat, then add 1 tablespoon of the olive oil to the pan. Season the fish with sea salt and pepper, and when the oil is almost shimmering in the pan, add the fish and cook until the edges just turn opaque, 5 to 7 minutes, depending upon the thickness of the fillets. Turn the fillets over, place the pan in the oven, and roast until the fish is just cooked through, about 5 minutes more. Transfer to a cooling rack to rest for a few minutes.

While the fish is in the oven, heat a grill pan over high heat. Add the lemon slices to the pan and cook, turning once, until they develop a light char on both sides, about 3 minutes per side.

Spoon the borlotti beans onto serving plates and arrange the artichokes, fennel, onion, garlic, and bay leaves over and around them. Top with the fish and a drizzle of olive oil. Garnish with the hot grilled lemon slices.

To Drink: Vernaccia di San Gimignano or other medium- to full-bodied white wine

SALMON WITH ORZO SALAD

Serves 4

This is an ideal recipe: relatively few ingredients, bold flavors, quick and easy to prepare, and very healthy. You can substitute other fresh fish—grouper, tuna, or striped bass—but the richness of seared salmon with its buttery texture makes it my favorite choice here. When corn is out of season, consider sweet peas in spring or roasted butternut squash in the cooler months. The orzo is served at room temperature, so it can be made ahead—a great choice for a buffet platter.

1½ cups orzo

About 1 tablespoon olive oil

Four 6-ounce skinless salmon fillets, any pinbones removed

Sea salt and freshly ground black pepper

1 cup corn kernels (from about 3 ears of corn)

1 cup quartered cherry tomatoes

1 shallot or ¼ red onion, minced

¼ cup pitted Kalamata or Niçoise olives, coarsely chopped

¼ cup basil leaves, torn into little pieces or cut into chiffonade, plus 4 small sprigs for garnish

Kosher salt

2 tablespoons L'Estornell Spanish garnacha vinegar (see Sources, page 260) or other good-quality red wine vinegar

3 tablespoons extra virgin olive oil

Grated lemon zest for garnish (optional)

Preheat the oven to 375°F.

Bring a large pot of generously salted water to a boil. Add the orzo and cook until al dente, 5 to 7 minutes. Drain and transfer to a large bowl. Toss with a splash of olive oil.

Heat a large ovenproof skillet over high heat, then add just enough olive oil to barely coat the bottom of the pan. Season the salmon with sea salt and pepper, place in the hot skillet, and cook until the fish is lightly golden on the first side and the edges are beginning to turn opaque, about 4 minutes. Turn the salmon and transfer the pan to the oven to finish cooking, about 4 minutes for medium-rare, or about 6 minutes for medium. Transfer the fillets to a rack and keep warm.

Stir the corn, tomatoes, shallot or onion, olives, torn basil, and salt and pepper to taste into the orzo. Add the vinegar, drizzle in the extra virgin olive oil, and toss to coat. Taste for seasonings and adjust to your liking.

Place a large spoonful of the orzo on each serving plate and top with a salmon fillet. Garnish each plate with a little lemon zest, if desired, and a sprig of basil.

To Drink: A rosé (Domaine Tempier)

FRESH FISH FROM THE REDNECK RIVIERA Alabamians and many who vacation on the Gulf Coast's sugar-white sands stretching from Apalachicola to the shores of Mobile Bay lovingly refer to the area as "the Redneck Riviera." The hordes of tourists are always dumbfounded that fresh local fish is so hard to come by at beachside restaurants there, yet available to them here in Birmingham. We can thank the original Greek, Italian, and Lebanese restaurateurs of Birmingham for setting the bar high when it comes to seafood. We remain the beneficiaries of the relationships they built with suppliers.

The Gulf is only a few hours from us and it teems with an incredible array of seafood—plump shrimp of all sizes, salty Apalachicola oysters, speckled trout, gigged flounder, succulent grouper, prized Gulf American red snapper, and, perhaps my most favorite, the pompano. I must not leave out the delicate, meaty blue crabs that yield the "jumbo lump" and claw "finger" meat we use in countless ways.

My friends Greg Abrams and Lee Fish, competing seafood dealers, deliver the Gulf's finest seafood (if not some of America's) to our kitchen doors. They are behind the quality and freshness we are known for in our seafood dishes. Although in today's global economy we can get wild salmon from the Northwest and striped bass from the East Coast flown directly to us within eight hours of being caught, we continue to believe, as the Italians do, in the importance of showcasing the local, regional seafood we are lucky to have.

ROASTED TROUT WITH DILL AND LEMON
Serves 4

Rainbow trout is one of my favorite farm-raised fish, and I happen to think the fish are quite beautiful. Try it sautéed, smoked, poached, or, as here, stuffed with aromatics and roasted in a hot oven. Beyond its good looks, trout is a healthy choice with a clean light flavor and a firm yet delicate texture. The oven really needs to be super-hot to crisp the skin, so preheat it to the maximum temperature, with a rack near the top, and be quick about opening and closing the oven door to minimize heat loss (at Bottega, we place the stuffed trout in our extremely hot pizza oven and roast it directly near the fire). Then just remember to be generous with your seasonings, and use lots of fresh dill.

    4 whole boneless rainbow trout
    Sea salt and freshly ground black pepper
    1 bunch dill
    8 thin lemon slices
    1 scant tablespoon unsalted butter
    1 tablespoon olive oil
    2 cups watercress leaves
    4 radishes, thinly sliced
    ¼ cup walnuts, toasted (see page 255)
        and coarsely chopped
    2 tablespoons Sherry Vinaigrette (page 73)
    ¼ cup crème fraîche

Position a rack in the upper third of the oven and preheat the oven to 500°F.

Season the cavity of each trout assertively with sea salt and pepper. Stuff each one with 2 to 4 dill sprigs and 2 lemon slices. Set aside.

Melt the butter with the olive oil in a large ovenproof skillet over medium-high heat. When the butter is foamy, add the trout, place the pan in the oven, and cook for 4 to 5 minutes. Rotate the pan for even cooking and continue cooking until the skin on top is crusty and crispy golden brown, another 4 to 5 minutes. The flesh should just be opaque throughout; be careful not to overcook the fish.

While the fish roasts, toss the watercress, radishes, and walnuts with the sherry vinaigrette. Mound the salad on one side of each of four dinner plates. Place the trout on the plates and spoon a dollop of crème fraîche next to each one. Serve immediately.

To Drink: Soave (Pieropan or Gini)

GRILLED TROUT WITH CHERRY TOMATOES, HERBS, AND TORPEDO ONIONS

Serves 4

Farmed seafood is the fastest-growing segment of the fishing industry. No doubt the controversies over the problems aquaculture creates need to be better addressed, but from a taste and sustainability standpoint, rainbow trout farming seems to be quite successful. Rainbow trout is a beautiful fish, delicate yet firm, and well suited to most types of cooking. For this dish at Bottega, the fish gets bathed in smoke over a hot wood fire or in our big hickory-burning oven. At home, you can grill or broil it.

The relish works with all kinds of fish and is ideal during the warm summer months when tomatoes and corn are at their prime. Large red torpedo onions are prized in various parts of Italy, and Venetians are especially fond of them.

¼ cup plus 1 tablespoon extra virgin olive oil

4 whole boneless rainbow trout

Sea salt and freshly ground white pepper

1 large torpedo onion or other red onion,
    sliced ¾ inch thick

3 ears corn, shucked and silk removed

½ cup red cherry tomatoes, quartered

½ cup yellow cherry tomatoes, quartered

1 tablespoon sherry vinegar

1 small bunch basil, leaves only

2 to 3 flat-leaf parsley sprigs, leaves only,
    plus extra for garnish if desired

2 to 3 mint sprigs, leaves only, plus extra for garnish
    if desired

2 tablespoons finely sliced chives

Grated zest of ½ lemon

Kosher salt

Prepare a fire in an outdoor grill or preheat the broiler.

Drizzle the 1 tablespoon olive oil on the trout and season with sea salt and white pepper. Set aside.

Grill or broil the onion and corn, turning occasionally, until well charred, about 10 minutes.

Chop the onion into ¼-inch dice and transfer to a large bowl. Cut the kernels from the corncobs and add to the bowl, along with the cherry tomatoes. Stir in the vinegar. Coarsely chop the basil, parsley, and mint and add to the bowl, along with the chives and lemon zest. Season the relish with salt and white pepper, then drizzle in the remaining olive oil.

Place the trout skin side up on the grill and cook for 3 to 4 minutes, until the flesh side is well colored with grill marks. Carefully flip the fish over and cook for 3 to 4 minutes more, or until just cooked—with the tip of a knife, take a peek at the thickest part to be sure the fish is just opaque throughout.

Transfer the fish to serving plates, top with some of the relish, and garnish with additional parsley and mint, if desired. Pass the remaining relish at the table.

To Drink: A delicate, light white wine, such as Bianco di Custoza

OVERLEAF LEFT: *Short Ribs and Oxtail with Gremolata and Green Olives* (page 184); **OPPOSITE:** *Chef Stitt with a skillet of braised lamb shoulder*

CHICKEN PAILLARDS WITH WATERCRESS AND TOMATO CHUTNEY VINAIGRETTE

Serves 4

Extremely thin-pounded chicken breasts are quickly grilled and form the base for a salad of grilled red onions, thinly sliced raw mushrooms, spicy watercress, and slightly sweet, tangy tomato chutney vinaigrette—perfect luncheon fare.

4 skinless, boneless chicken breast halves, preferably from naturally raised chicken, rinsed and patted dry
Kosher salt and freshly ground black pepper
¼ cup red wine vinegar (or equal parts sherry vinegar and red wine vinegar)
1 shallot, finely minced
2 thyme sprigs, leaves only
1 heaping tablespoon Alecia's Tomato Chutney (see Sources, page 260)
1 cup extra virgin olive oil
2 to 3 cups watercress, larger stems removed, washed, and dried
1 Charred Red Onion (page 238), cut into large dice
1 cup (3 ounces) button mushrooms, thinly sliced
¼ cup shaved Parmigiano-Reggiano or grana padano

Prepare a hot fire in a charcoal or gas grill.

Place the chicken breast halves between sheets of waxed paper or plastic wrap and pound to an even thickness, about ⅛ inch thick. Season the chicken with salt and pepper.

Rub the grill grate with an oiled rag. Place the chicken on the grill and cook until the edges turn opaque, about 2 minutes. Turn and cook on the other side until just cooked through, about 2 minutes more. Remove to a cooling rack.

Combine the vinegar(s), shallot, thyme, chutney, and salt and pepper in a small bowl. Slowly whisk in the olive oil. Taste and adjust the seasonings.

Combine the watercress, red onion, and mushrooms in a large bowl and season with salt and pepper. Toss with 3 tablespoons of the vinaigrette.

Place the watercress salad in the center of four serving plates, distributing the onions and mushrooms equally. Slice the chicken breasts on the diagonal and arrange around the salad. Garnish with the shaved Parmigiano and serve.

NOTE: The extra vinaigrette will keep in the refrigerator, tightly sealed, for 4 to 5 days.

To Drink: Tocai from the Veneto or Grüner Veltliner from Austria

CHICKEN UNDER A BRICK

Serves 4

Cooking chicken under a brick is a classic technique in Italy because weighting the chicken results in tender, juicy meat. We use our very hot pizza oven to get a good char, so turn your oven up as hot as it goes—and turn on your exhaust fan. The marinade, loaded with garlic and rosemary, fills the kitchen with a delicious aroma as the chicken cooks (note that the chicken must marinate overnight). Use oven mitts to remove the hot bricks, and put them safely at the back of the stove.

We serve this with a rich, crusty Capellini Gratin (page 98) and a few lettuce or arugula leaves.

½ cup olive oil
1 tablespoon rosemary leaves, roughly chopped
6 garlic cloves, thinly sliced
1 teaspoon kosher salt
1 teaspoon freshly ground black pepper
Four 10- to 12-ounce bone-in, skin-on chicken breasts, preferably from naturally raised chicken, rinsed and patted dry

Combine the olive oil, rosemary, garlic, salt, and pepper in a small bowl.

Arrange the chicken breasts skin side down in a ceramic or glass baking dish. Pour the marinade over the breasts, turning to coat. Cover with plastic wrap and refrigerate overnight.

Preheat the oven to 500°F. Wrap 4 clean bricks in heavy-duty aluminum foil.

Place the chicken breasts skin side down on a baking sheet and top each one with a foil-covered brick. Press each brick down to flatten the breasts.

Place the pan in the oven and cook for 10 to 12 minutes. Remove the pan from the oven and carefully remove the bricks with an oven mitt. Turn the breasts over, return the pan to the oven, and cook for 5 to 6 minutes more, until cooked through. Let rest for 3 to 5 minutes before serving.

To Drink: A fruity, medium-bodied red wine, such as Dolcetto (Einandi di Gresy)

CHICKEN SALTIMBOCCA

Serves 4

Saltimbocca is a traditional preparation of a thinly pounded veal cutlet topped with a slice of prosciutto, some mozzarella, and a sage leaf. We've borrowed that idea, substituting plump bone-in chicken breasts and layering the toppings underneath the skin. Cooking the stuffed breasts skin side down gives them a wonderful, golden-brown, crisp skin, which seals in the filling. Heads turn when this dish makes the journey from kitchen to table.

Four 10- to 12-ounce bone-in, skin-on chicken breasts, preferably from naturally raised chicken, rinsed and patted dry

Kosher salt and freshly ground black pepper

4 large sage leaves

Eight ¼-inch-thick slices (about 10 ounces) fresh mozzarella

4 very thin slices prosciutto di Parma

2 tablespoons olive oil

1 shallot, finely chopped

1 garlic clove, minced

¼ cup dry vermouth

1 tablespoon fresh lemon juice

4 tablespoons unsalted butter

½ cup fresh or frozen sweet peas, cooked in boiling salted water until tender and chilled in ice water (optional)

Creamy Polenta (page 206) or mashed potatoes

Preheat the oven to 425°F.

Slip a finger under the skin of each chicken breast, being careful not to tear the skin, and gently fold it back without detaching it completely. Season the exposed meat lightly with salt and pepper. Place a sage leaf on top of each breast and layer 2 slices of mozzarella and a slice of prosciutto on top of each leaf. Carefully stretch the skin back over the stuffing.

Heat a large ovenproof skillet over medium heat, then add the olive oil and swirl it around the hot pan. Place the chicken breasts skin side down in the pan and cook for 6 to 8 minutes.

Transfer the pan to the oven and cook for 10 to 12 minutes more, until the breasts are cooked through. Transfer the chicken to a rack to rest.

Pour off the excess fat from the pan, add the shallot and garlic, and cook over medium heat until translucent. Remove the pan from the heat and whisk in the vermouth, scraping up the crusty bits of chicken from the bottom of the pan. Return the pan to medium-low heat and simmer to reduce the liquid by half.

Add the lemon juice and remove the pan from the heat. Whisk the butter bit by bit into the sauce, then stir in the peas, if using. Season to taste with salt and pepper.

Serve the chicken on a bed of polenta or mashed potatoes and spoon the sauce over all.

To Drink: Barbera (Conterno Fantino)

BOTTEGA CHICKEN SCALOPPINE

Serves 4

This is the most-ordered dish at Bottega Café—it's just the right combination of crisp, golden crust and juicy, moist chicken. We serve it on Creamy Polenta (page 206) with a little salad of tender lettuces, and the acidic tartness of capers and the lemon sauce brings it all together. The chicken can be breaded well in advance: place on a small parchment-lined baking sheet and refrigerate until ready to cook. Be sure to dust off excess flour before dipping the chicken into the egg to make a lighter breading. And pay attention to the bread crumbs—not too fine, not too coarse, but a good mix of irregular sizes.

4 boneless, skinless chicken breasts, preferably from naturally raised chicken, rinsed and patted dry

Kosher salt and freshly ground black pepper

½ cup all-purpose flour

2 eggs, beaten

1 cup Bread Crumbs (page 239)

2 tablespoons olive, canola, or grapeseed oil

1 cup dry white wine

½ cup sherry vinegar or champagne vinegar

1 shallot, finely chopped

1 dried red chile pepper

1 bay leaf

1 tablespoon heavy cream

½ pound (1½ sticks) unsalted butter

Juice of ½ lemon

2 tablespoons diced tomatoes

1 tablespoon capers, rinsed

Preheat the oven to 350°F.

Season the chicken on both sides with salt and pepper. Set out three shallow plates in assembly-line fashion. Put the flour in one, the beaten eggs in the next, and the bread crumbs in the third. Dredge each seasoned chicken breast in the flour, shaking off the excess, then dip in the eggs, and finally press them into the bread crumbs to coat thoroughly on both sides. Set the breaded chicken on a plate.

Heat a large ovenproof sauté pan over medium-high heat, and add the oil. Brown the chicken breasts on both sides until golden, about 3 minutes per side; regulate the heat as necessary to achieve a uniformly browned crust.

Transfer the pan to the oven and cook the chicken until cooked through, 10 to 15 minutes. Transfer the chicken to a rack to rest briefly.

Meanwhile, combine the wine, vinegar, shallot, chile, and bay leaf in a saucepan, bring to a boil over medium-high heat, and cook until the pan is almost dry. Add the cream and simmer until it reduces to about a teaspoon. Whisk in the butter little by little over medium-low heat until the sauce is creamy and emulsified. Strain the sauce through a fine-mesh strainer into a bowl. Add salt and pepper to taste and the juice of the lemon half.

Slice the chicken on the bias and arrange on serving plates. Spoon the sauce over the top and garnish with the diced tomatoes and capers.

To Drink: Chardonnay (Calera or Tiefenbrunner)

GUINEA HEN WITH PANCETTA AND DOLCETTO
Serves 4 to 6

Guinea hens were one of my grandmother's favorite farmyard animals, partly because they announced the arrival of anyone who came along the winding gravel road leading to her back porch. She also loved them for the delicious eating they provided. Speckled black with grayish feathers, her birds were truly free range. Like chicken, but with darker, more flavorful flesh, guinea hens are prized in Italy and France. A server's assistant at Bottega told us that they're known as "son-in-law birds" in Africa because the son-in-law is one of the few people esteemed enough to be feted with them.

If you find cutting up the hens daunting, have your butcher do it. We serve this with risotto made with butternut squash.

> Two 3- to 4-pound guinea hens, cut into 6 pieces each:
>   2 bone-in breasts (wing tips removed), 2 thighs and
>   2 legs (see page 256), patted dry
> Kosher salt and freshly ground black pepper
> Sixteen ¹⁄₁₆-inch-thick slices pancetta (about 1 pound)
> 5 tablespoons olive oil
> 5 carrots, cut into 2-inch pieces
> 4 medium onions, diced
> 3 celery stalks, cut into 2-inch pieces
> 3 garlic cloves
> 1 thyme sprig
> 1 parsley sprig
> 2 bay leaves
> 4 to 6 dried porcini, soaked in hot water until softened
>   (optional)
> 2 cups dry red wine, such as Dolcetto
> 4 cups Chicken Stock (page 241)
> Basic Risotto (page 201), made with butternut squash
>   (½ squash, cut into ½-inch cubes, tossed with olive
>   oil and salt and pepper and baked on a sheet pan in
>   a 450°F oven for 15 minutes), prepared through the
>   last addition in stock and still hot

Season the guinea hen breasts lightly with salt and pepper. Unroll each slice of pancetta, so that you have long pieces like strips of bacon. Lay 4 pancetta lengths side by side, overlapping them slightly; the meatier side of each slice should overlap the fattier side of the next. Place a seasoned breast in the center and wrap the pancetta around it, leaving the wing bone and tip of the breast exposed. Trim away any excess pancetta and reserve for another use. Repeat with the remaining pancetta and breasts. Set aside.

Heat a large Dutch oven over medium-high heat, and add 3 tablespoons of the olive oil. Season the guinea hen legs and thighs, add to the hot oil, and sauté until they are a deep golden brown on all sides. Transfer them to a rack and pour off all but about 1 tablespoon of the fat from the pot. Add the carrots, onions, celery, and garlic to the pot and sauté for 10 minutes, or until tender.

Add the thyme, parsley, bay leaves, porcini, and wine to the vegetables and bring to a simmer. Once the wine has evaporated, add the stock and bring back to a simmer.

Return the legs and thighs to the pot and bring the stock to a simmer again. Cover the pot tightly with foil and then the lid, transfer to the oven, and cook for 1 to 1½ hours until the meat is very tender and almost falling off the bone. Remove from the oven, but leave the oven on.

Transfer the legs and thighs to a platter and strain the liquid into a saucepan; discard the vegetables. Place the pan over medium heat and bring to a simmer, skimming frequently; if you have one side of the pan off the heat, the fat will accumulate there, making it easy to skim the fat; then keep warm over very low heat. While the legs and thighs are still warm, remove the meat from the bones and put in a bowl; add a spoonful or two of the braising liquid to keep it moist, and cover to keep warm while you sear the breasts.

Heat an ovenproof sauté pan over medium heat, then add the remaining 2 tablespoons olive oil. When the oil is hot, place the breasts in the pan, skin side down, and cook for 6 minutes per side, turning each breast as necessary to brown the pancetta evenly. Transfer the pan to the oven and cook for about 5 minutes, until cooked to medium. (Guinea hen breast goes from undercooked to overcooked very quickly, so watch carefully; remember the internal heat will continue cooking the breasts after they are removed from the pan.)

To serve, toss the braised leg meat into the risotto and stir in ½ cup of the reserved braising liquid, along with the butter and Parmesan (in the risotto recipe), and cook, stirring until hot. Taste and adjust the seasonings. Slice the guinea hen breasts on the bias and serve with the risotto and more of the braising liquid in a sauceboat to pass at the table.

To Drink: Barbaresco (Bruno Giacosa or Paitin)

DUCK WITH PEACHES AND MOSCATO

Serves 4

Passionate cooks love to work with duck because it demands attention to detail—the breasts require one form of cooking and the legs another. The breasts should be carefully trimmed, seared, and then roasted to medium-rare; the legs are best slowly braised. The crisped skin is a decadent delight, and cooking in the rendered duck fat makes anything delicious, especially onions, turnips, and potatoes. The deep red breast meat has a hint of a wild flavor that isn't too overpowering for the timid, and its richness makes a good red wine taste even better.

Air-dry the duck breast in the fridge on a rack set over a plate for a few hours or up to a day or two ahead to firm up the fat. This will yield crisper skin when cooked.

With duck, I find quince, apples, and figs a bit more interesting than the ubiquitous orange, but peaches in season lend a luscious sweetness to duck. Moscato, a slightly effervescent sweet wine, adds the faint perfume of magnolia or orange blossom and is a pretty complement to the peach. We like to serve this with polenta, grilled or creamy (see page 206).

10 black peppercorns

2 allspice berries

3 juniper berries

4 boneless Pekin (Long Island) duck breasts,
    fat trimmed and skin scored in a crosshatch pattern

Kosher salt

2 firm but ripe peaches, blanched in boiling water for
    10 seconds, peeled, halved, and pitted

¼ cup Moscato (Italian dessert wine)

¼ cup hazelnuts, lightly toasted (see page 255) and
    chopped (optional)

4 small mint sprigs

Combine the peppercorns, allspice, and juniper berries in a small dry skillet and toast over medium heat, shaking the pan from time to time, until fragrant. Transfer to a spice or coffee grinder and coarsely grind.

Rub the duck with salt and the spice mixture. Place on a plate in the refrigerator to air-dry for at least a couple of hours, or overnight, to infuse the flavor.

Preheat the oven to 475°F.

Heat a large heavy ovenproof sauté pan over medium heat. Add the duck breasts, skin side down, and sear until golden, about 12 minutes.

Pour off the excess fat (reserve it for cooking, if desired—see headnote), turn the duck over, and add the peaches to the pan. Transfer the pan to the oven and cook for about 10 minutes, until medium-rare (135°F on an instant-read thermometer). Remove the pan from the oven and place the duck on a rack to rest, loosely covered to keep warm.

Carefully pour off the fat from the pan, add the Moscato, and cook over medium-high heat until the peaches are almost melting, about 5 minutes. Remove from the heat.

Thinly slice the duck breasts on the bias and arrange on warm plates. Place the peaches next to the duck. Pour the pan juices over the duck, and garnish with the hazelnuts, if using, and the mint sprigs.

To Drink: Barolo (Bartolo Mascarello)

BRAISED RABBIT LEGS OR CHICKEN THIGHS

Serves 4

Pan-searing followed by braising—long, slow cooking in liquid in a covered pot—yields flavorful, juicy meat. Humble cuts like rabbit legs and chicken thighs are perfect candidates for the technique. Some of the recipes in this book call for leftover braised meat, because I like to have such succulent morsels on hand to fold into a risotto or to add to a salad or soup. I often pair braised legs with their counterparts—loin or breast—grilled and thinly sliced. The juxtaposition of flavors and textures is always interesting. Use this recipe as a jumping-off point, braising any of the cuts (shanks, shoulder, cheeks, etc.) that need slow, moist cooking to make them tender.

2 tablespoons olive oil

4 bone-in rabbit legs or chicken thighs

Kosher salt and freshly ground white pepper

2 tablespoons unsalted butter

2 medium onions, cut into medium dice

3 medium carrots, sliced ½ inch thick

1 cup Madeira or medium-dry sherry

1 cup dry white wine

2 cups Chicken Stock (page 241)

A few thyme sprigs

3 bay leaves

Preheat the oven to 325°F.

In a large heavy sauté pan, heat the olive oil over medium-high heat. Season the rabbit or chicken thighs with salt and pepper and sear on all sides until browned, about 10 minutes. Transfer the meat to a rack and set aside. Wipe the pan clean with a paper towel.

Melt 1 tablespoon of the butter in the pan over medium-high heat. Add the onions and carrots and cook until golden and softened, about 10 minutes. Add the Madeira or sherry and white wine and bring to a boil and reduce by three-quarters. Add the stock, thyme, and bay leaves and bring to a simmer.

Place the browned meat in a casserole and pour the stock and vegetables over it. Cover with a round of parchment paper, placed directly on the meat, and then the lid. Transfer to the oven, and cook until the meat is tender, 1 to 1½ hours. Remove the meat from the braising liquid and transfer to a rack.

Strain the braising liquid into a saucepan and bring to a simmer, with the pan half on and half off the burner, to make skimming easier. Reduce the liquid by half, skimming off all of the fat as it rises to the cooler side of the pan.

Swirl the remaining tablespoon of butter into the braising sauce to finish, and check the seasoning. Add the braised meat to the sauce and serve.

To Drink: Pinot Noir (DuMOL, Arcadian Winery, or Au Bon Climat)

RABBIT CACCIATORE

Serves 4 to 6

Cacciatore means prepared "hunter-style," and this simple, rustic rabbit or chicken preparation, found throughout Italy, is especially popular in Tuscany. The dish is built around the prizes a hunter might bring back from a romp through the woods in the fall or winter months: a meaty rabbit and a basket of wild mushrooms—porcini, if he's lucky. These trophies, along with some good red wine, home-canned summer tomatoes, garlic, and onions are simmered together into what has become an Italian classic.

We love to cook and eat rabbit, but this also works beautifully with chicken thighs, or even guinea hen. I prefer the legs and thighs of chicken in a braise; the breasts are better suited to quick cooking over direct heat. Instead of serving the meat on the bone, you could remove and shred it, then toss it into a dish of pasta or risotto, moistened with some of the braising broth.

1 rabbit, cut into 8 pieces: 2 hind legs, 2 shoulders,
    2 flanks, and loin cut crosswise in half
Kosher salt and freshly ground black pepper
3 tablespoons olive oil
1 large onion, cut into 1-inch dice
3 carrots, peeled and cut into 1-inch dice
2 celery stalks, sliced
2 garlic cloves, finely chopped
4 juniper berries, toasted (see page 256; optional)
1 ounce (a very small handful) dried porcini
One 28-ounce can whole tomatoes, drained and
    coarsely chopped
Bouquet garni: several thyme and marjoram sprigs plus
    1 bay leaf tied in a leek green
2 cups dry red wine
4 cups Chicken Stock (page 241)
1 pound fresh porcini or cremini mushrooms,
    quartered or cut into large pieces
½ shallot, finely chopped
2 thyme sprigs, leaves only

Season the rabbit with salt and lots of pepper.

Heat a large Dutch oven over high heat. Add 2 tablespoons of the olive oil, and when it is almost shimmering, add the rabbit, reduce the heat to medium, and cook until an even golden brown crust forms on the first side, about 8 minutes. Turn and cook for 8 minutes more, or until golden brown. Transfer the meat to a rack to rest.

Add the onion, carrots, and celery to the pot and cook until tender and lightly colored, about 10 minutes. Add the garlic and cook for 1 minute. Add the juniper berries, if using, the dried porcini, tomatoes, bouquet garni, and red wine, bring to a boil over high heat, and boil until the wine is reduced by half, about 10 minutes.

Preheat the oven to 325°F.

Add the stock to the vegetables and bring to a simmer. Return the rabbit to the pot, cover, and transfer to the oven to cook until the meat is tender; the large hind legs will probably need 45 minutes; after about 25 minutes, check the loin pieces to test for doneness, pierce the meat with a paring knife to see if the juices run clear, or use an instant-read thermometer: the meat should reach an internal temperature of 150°F. As the pieces are done, transfer to a platter.

Set the pot over high heat and reduce the braising liquid by half, skimming off any fat that accumulates on the top.

Meanwhile, heat a large sauté pan over high heat. Add the remaining tablespoon of olive oil and the fresh mushrooms and sauté for 3 minutes, or until tender. Toss in the shallot and thyme leaves and sauté for 30 seconds more. Remove from the heat.

To serve, place the rabbit back in the reduced braising broth to warm through, then add the mushrooms. Remove the bouquet garni and serve family-style. Pair with rice or roasted or boiled potatoes.

To Drink: A Tuscan red (Badia a Coltibuono)

RABBIT TORINO

Serves 6

In the cozy, unassuming dining room of an out-of-the-way restaurant in Turin, I enjoyed a fabulous dish of slices of boned rabbit stuffed with dried plums, rosemary, onions, and pancetta and served with the liver and kidneys. This recipe is based on my recollection of that fine meal.

Deboning a rabbit is an ambitious project, so ask your butcher to do it for you if you prefer.

One 2- to 2½-pound rabbit, liver reserved
Kosher salt and freshly ground black pepper
5 tablespoons olive oil
1 large shallot, chopped
1 teaspoon thyme leaves
¼ cup dry Marsala
4 sweet onions, such as Vidalia or Maui Maui
14 pitted prunes
2 cups port
1½ cups coarse Bread Crumbs (see page 239)
5 rosemary sprigs, 1 finely chopped, 6 left whole
¼ cup chopped flat-leaf parsley
1½ cups blanched coarsely chopped Swiss chard
   (see page 255) (about 1 pound uncooked greens)
8 tablespoons (1 stick) unsalted butter, melted
1 pound very thinly sliced pancetta, unrolled
Extra virgin olive oil for drizzling

Rinse the rabbit and pat dry with paper towels. Lay the rabbit on its back on a cutting board. With a sharp boning knife, remove the front legs by slicing through the shoulder joint; reserve for another use. Remove the shoulders and save them for a braise. Carefully slide your knife along the top of the rib bones nearest the stomach and work your way along the ribs, gently folding back the meat as you go. Once the ribs are free, slide your knife down the backbone; when you have exposed the backbone, use the tip of your knife to "ride" underneath the spine, freeing the meat as you go. Work your way down to the thigh and hip joint, free the leg and remove the thigh/femur and shin bone. The thigh will be "butterflied."

To bone the hindquarters, make an incision along the hip joint of the hindquarters and use the tip of your knife to work around the leg bone to the knee. Remove the leg bone at the shin and roll away the loose cartilage.

Use a meat mallet to pound the meat evenly to about a ½-inch thickness. The tenderloin and hindquarter need the most pounding: it helps to make "butterfly" incisions in the hindquarter. Season the inside of the rabbit with salt and pepper; set aside.

Heat a large sauté pan over medium heat. Add 1 tablespoon of the olive oil, then add the reserved liver, shallot, and thyme leaves, and sauté until the liver is medium-rare, 7 to 8 minutes. Season with salt and pepper, then deglaze with the Marsala, stirring up the browned bits. Cook for 2 to 3 minutes more, until the liver is medium. Set aside to cool, then coarsely chop the liver (discard the pan drippings).

Heat a large cast-iron skillet over medium heat. Add 1 tablespoon olive oil and the onions. Cook, stirring occasionally, until the onions are lightly golden, about 15 minutes. Set aside to cool.

Meanwhile, combine the prunes and port in a saucepan, bring to a simmer, and cook until the prunes are plump and the port is reduced to ½ cup syrupy glaze, 15 to 20 minutes. Let cool.

Combine the bread crumbs, onions, chopped rosemary, parsley, liver, and chard in a large mixing bowl. Add the melted butter and the remaining 3 tablespoons olive oil and mix well. Season to taste with salt and pepper.

Set an oven rack in the top third of the oven and preheat the oven to 425°F.

To stuff the rabbit, arrange the prunes evenly down the indentation left by the backbone, between the tenderloins, in a tight row from head to tail. Place the stuffing on top of the prunes, packing it lightly. Fold the flank and hindquarters up and over the stuffing, overlapping the skin. Overlap the two sides of the loin by about an inch; they will be a little tacky and stick together.

Neatly arrange the unrolled pancetta slices side by side on your work surface, overlapping them a bit. Place the stuffed rabbit across the center of the pancetta slices. Lift the ends of the strips up and over the rabbit so that they overlap. Tie a couple of pieces of twine around the ends to secure the stuffing. Place the rabbit seam side down on a baking sheet.

Roast for 20 to 25 minutes, until the rabbit reaches an internal temperature of 130°F when tested with an instant-read thermometer. The pancetta should be uniformly crisp and golden brown. Transfer to a rack to rest briefly.

Slice the rabbit into ¾-inch-thick slices and arrange on the plates. Garnish with the rosemary sprigs and a drizzle of olive oil.

To Drink: Barbaresco (Produttori di Barbaresco or Castello di Nieve)

ROAST PORK WITH VENETIAN SPINACH AND TOMATO CHUTNEY AÏOLI

Serves 4

Charring a meaty chop in Bottega's blasting-hot pizza oven gives it a delicious browned crust. The pork is served atop a mound of garlicky spinach spiked with golden raisins and pine nuts and finished with a spoonful of aïoli, turned orange thanks to an embellishment of tomato chutney. This is an impressive melding of flavors, so you might consider preparing a whole pork rack in this manner to serve for a buffet or dinner party.

You can make aïoli up to 1 to 2 days ahead and keep it refrigerated until ready to use. And you can prepare the polenta an hour or so ahead, leaving out the cheese until just before serving.

1 large onion, quartered

Kosher salt and freshly ground black pepper

1 tablespoon olive oil

Four 12-ounce center-cut pork chops, about ½ inch thick

Creamy Polenta (page 206)

Venetian Spinach (page 191)

Tomato Chutney Aïoli (page 245)

Preheat the oven to 475°F.

Season the onion with salt and pepper. Place on a small baking sheet and roast until tender, approximately 30 minutes. Remove from the oven and set aside in a warm spot.

Heat the olive oil in a large ovenproof skillet over high heat. Add the pork chops and sear until golden on the first side, about 5 minutes. Turn the pork, transfer the pan to the oven, and cook until medium (145°F on an instant-read thermometer), about 10 minutes. Transfer the meat to a rack and cover loosely to keep warm.

Meanwhile, reheat the polenta if necessary (stir in the cheese if you haven't already done so). Reheat the spinach.

To serve, ladle a generous spoonful of creamy polenta onto each warm serving plate. Top with a roasted onion quarter and place a helping of spinach to one side. Prop a pork chop against each onion quarter and garnish with a dollop of the chutney aïoli.

To Drink: Chianti (Felsina or Castello di Volpaia)

HENRY FUDGE arrives in the restaurant parking lot with a large enameled cooler tethered in the back of his pickup truck. Inside are pale pink pork shoulders streaked with pure white fat and loins of impressive diameter nestled on the array of cuts ordered by his customers, mostly chefs and specialty grocers. Mr. Fudge is an energetic character whose rapid-fire manner of speaking belies his north Alabama drawl. He has such enthusiasm for his hog-hobby-turned-business venture that it's hard to believe he's been up since dawn zigzagging the northern part of the state, crossing into Tennessee and Mississippi in order to pick up mature hogs from Amish coproducers to whom he leases his breeding stock. Years ago, these Amish families lost their income to large commercial pork factories who eliminated the need for outside sources. Mr. Fudge is changing all that.

His passion for hogs began when, as a young man, he bought nine acres outside of Huntsville, Alabama, with dreams of becoming a rancher. Knowing his small acreage could never maintain a herd of cattle, he turned to raising hogs instead. He didn't want to raise just any old hog—only the finest, but it took years to determine that the best hogs were a combination of his purebred Durocs of African origin and the Berkshire hog, the mother breed of all European breeds.

Mass-produced commodity pork comes from hybridized hogs that have been bred to the point that they have lost their natural hog frame and stature. "Somebody along the way decided that wide meant fat and narrow meant lean," Henry says. So you have these hogs that are long and thick like a Tootsie Roll yet have a mere one percent leaf fat—the supple pure fat that marbles the meat and carries that distinctive pork flavor. Once cooked, this pork is about as tasty as cardboard. By breeding his Durocs with his old-line Berkshires, Mr. Fudge gets pork comprised of about five percent leaf fat. That means quality meat that is light pink instead of that darker grocery store hue—this pale color is one indicator of the incomparable flavor within.

Another reason his pork tastes so good is the way the hogs are raised. In addition to the natural corn fed to them, they are also allowed to forage. After a corn crop has been harvested, the hogs are moved to the field to consume the remaining corn left there. This symbiotic relationship allows the hogs to roam, clean the fields, eat weeds and roots, and, in the process, till and fertilize the soil. Eventually, Mr. Fudge hopes to convince his Amish producers to grow old-fashioned, open-pollinated corn. The Amish already avoid using hybridized corn as feed, having noted that their hogs prefer the naturally grown variety. If a hog can sniff out a truffle, it must know good corn when it sees it. One taste of Henry Fudge's pork, and you'll know you've tasted the best there is too.

PORK SCALOPPINE WITH GREENS AND POLENTA

Serves 4

Here we pound the pork to create medallions that cook quickly. Seek out Berkshire pork (see "Henry Fudge," page 165) for its flavor and juiciness.

2 to 3 tablespoons olive oil, or as needed
1 large sweet onion, such as Vidalia or Maui Maui, sliced
2 garlic cloves, 1 crushed, 1 minced
1 thyme sprig
4 cups roughly chopped turnip greens, Swiss chard,
  or mustard greens
Kosher salt and freshly ground black pepper
1 cup all-purpose flour
Eight 3-ounce slices pork loin, pounded to ⅛ inch thick
1 shallot, finely minced
¼ cup dry Marsala
1 cup Chicken Stock (page 239)
2 tablespoons cold unsalted butter
3 cups Creamy Polenta (page 204)
¼ cup pine nuts, toasted (see page 253)
¼ cup freshly grated Parmigiano-Reggiano or
  pecorino romano

Heat a large sauté pan over medium heat. Add 1 tablespoon of the olive oil, the onion, crushed garlic clove, and thyme sprig and cook until the onion is lightly colored, about 12 minutes. Add the chopped greens, cover the pan, and cook for 10 minutes, or until the greens are soft. Then season to taste with salt and pepper, transfer to a bowl, and set aside to cool. (Set the pan aside.)

Season the flour with salt and pepper; spread on a plate. Return the pan to medium-high heat and add 1 tablespoon of the olive oil. Dust each scaloppine with flour, shaking off any excess. Working in batches to avoid crowding, add the pork to the pan and cook until browned on both sides and medium-rare, 1 to 2 minutes per side. Transfer the slices to a rack as they are done and cover loosely to keep warm; add more oil to the pan as necessary.

Add the minced garlic and shallot to the pan and cook for 1 minute more. Add the Marsala and simmer to reduce by half. Add the stock and reduce again by half. Whisk in the cold butter bit by bit, and season to taste. Remove the pan from the heat.

Spoon a portion of the soft polenta into the center of each plate, place 2 scaloppine on top, and ladle the sauce over the pork. Serve with a generous spoonful of the greens, garnished with the pine nuts and cheese.

To Drink: Côtes du Rhône or Châteauneuf du Pape (Vieux Télégraphe)

VEAL SCALOPPINE WITH ASPARAGUS, SPRING ONIONS, AND SWEET PEAS

Serves 4

Although this dish is not difficult, it must be prepared at the last minute and is best if you have two hot sauté pans going, so it's a recipe for cooks capable of handling choreographed pressure! The key is to have all the vegetables and herbs sliced or chopped and ready. Make sure to shake off excess flour after dredging so that the scaloppine is light and golden, not gummy. Serve with crushed new potatoes or over Creamy Polenta (page 206).

Eight 3-ounce veal medallions, pounded thin
  and patted dry
Kosher salt and freshly ground black pepper
Flour
2 to 3 tablespoons olive oil, or as needed
3 tablespoons unsalted butter
2 bulb or spring onions, halved lengthwise and
  thinly sliced
½ cup dry vermouth or dry white wine
8 medium asparagus, tough ends cut away, stalks cut on
  the diagonal into 1-inch slices, blanched in boiling
  water until tender, chilled in ice water, and drained
½ cup frozen sweet peas, rinsed under hot water to thaw
Juice of ½ lemon
1 tablespoon chopped flat-leaf parsley
Chopped chives, marjoram, mint, or thyme leaves for
  garnish (optional)

Season the veal with salt and pepper and dredge in the flour, shaking off the excess. Heat two large heavy sauté pans over high heat. Add 1 tablespoon of the oil and ½ tablespoon of the butter to each pan and heat until foamy. Working in batches, carefully place the veal in the hot pans, without crowding, and brown on both sides, about 1 minute per side; reduce the heat slightly if necessary. Transfer the veal to a cooling rack and cover loosely to keep warm. Add more oil to the pans as necessary, allowing it to get hot before adding more veal to the pan.

Wipe out one of the pans and add to it 1 tablespoon of the butter and the onions and cook until the onions are tender, 8 to 10 minutes. Add the vermouth or wine and boil gently to reduce by three-quarters. Add the asparagus and peas and cook until warmed through, about 1 minute. Add the lemon and parsley, then stir in the remaining tablespoon of butter to incorporate.

Place the veal on warm serving plates and top with the sauce. Sprinkle with the herbs, if desired.

To Drink: Valpolicella (Zenato)

VEAL MILANESE

Serves 4

Making bread crumbs properly is worth the effort; the result is a combination of crunchy, fine, and coarse. The mild, tender veal, cloaked in its crisp coating, is the perfect canvas for the lemon-herb butter sauce with its hint of vermouth. A definite crowd pleaser.

Flour for dredging

2 eggs

1 tablespoon water

1 heaping cup Bread Crumbs (page 239)

Four 4- to 6-ounce slices boneless veal top round or
    tenderloin, pounded thin

Kosher salt and freshly ground black pepper

2 tablespoons olive oil

3 tablespoons unsalted butter

1 shallot, minced

¾ cup dry white wine or dry vermouth

Juice of ½ lemon

1 tablespoon chopped herbs such as flat-leaf parsley,
    chives, and/or basil

Spread the flour on a plate. Beat the eggs with the water in a shallow bowl. Put the bread crumbs on another shallow plate. Season the veal with salt and pepper. Dredge it in the flour, shaking off the excess, dip in the eggs to coat, and then transfer to the bread crumbs, turning to coat evenly. Place the meat on a sheet of wax paper or on a cooling rack. (The veal can be prepared to this point up to 1 hour ahead and refrigerated; bring to room temperature before cooking.)

Heat the oil in a large heavy sauté pan over medium-high heat until shimmering but not smoking. Working in batches, add the veal, without crowding, and cook until a golden crust forms on the first side, about 2 minutes. Regulate the heat as necessary to evenly brown. Turn and cook for 2 minutes more, or until golden. Transfer to a cooling rack and keep warm while you prepare the sauce.

Add about a teaspoon of the butter and the shallot to the pan and soften over medium heat, about 30 seconds. Season with salt and pepper, add the wine or vermouth, and increase the heat to high. When the wine has almost evaporated, whisk in the remaining butter bit by bit while shaking the pan. Add the lemon juice and chopped herbs, then taste and adjust the seasonings. Serve the veal with the sauce spooned over it.

To Drink: Anything from a white to a medium-weight red wine—consider a Chinon or Barbera (Conterno Fantino)

VEAL CHEEKS WITH BUTTERNUT–SWEET POTATO PUREE

Serves 4, with leftovers

These plump nuggets may be the most tender and delicious of all cuts. They're very similar to the choicest part of an osso buco, or braised veal shank. Have your butcher trim away the layer of sinew that runs along one side of the meat, or use a sharp boning knife to lift up a little flap of the silverskin or sinew, then slide your knife underneath it to remove.

Cheeks are very economical and, since this classic braise only gets better on standing, you may wish to double the recipe and refrigerate half for another dish. You could use the braised meat in a pasta or risotto, moistened with some of the braising broth. Here we pair the meat with a butternut squash and sweet potato puree for a delicious cool-season main course, but you can certainly substitute other seasonal vegetables to suit your tastes—sweet peas, asparagus, and bulb onions in springtime perhaps, or tomato, basil, and shell beans in summer.

FOR THE VEAL CHEEKS

2 tablespoons olive oil

4 pounds untrimmed veal cheeks (see headnote) or
    2 pounds trimmed cheeks

Kosher salt and freshly ground black pepper

2 onions, finely chopped

2 carrots, finely chopped

2 celery stalks, finely chopped

2 garlic cloves, crushed and finely chopped

3 or 4 sprigs thyme and a few bay leaves, tied together
    with kitchen twine to form a bouquet garni

One 2-inch piece cinnamon stick

2 cups dry white wine

6 cups Chicken Stock (page 241)

1 tablespoon unsalted butter

FOR THE BUTTERNUT–SWEET POTATO PUREE

3 sweet potatoes, scrubbed

½ butternut squash, halved and seeded

Kosher salt and freshly ground black pepper

Olive oil

2 tablespoons unsalted butter

12 cipollini onions, glazed (see page 255)

2 carrots, cut into 1-inch batons and glazed
    (see page 255)

Preheat the oven to 300°F.

To prepare the veal cheeks, heat 1 tablespoon of the olive oil in a large Dutch oven over high heat. Pat the veal cheeks dry and season with salt and pepper. Working in batches, add to the pot and brown over medium heat until golden, about 5 minutes per side. Transfer the meat to a rack to rest.

Wipe out the Dutch oven, add the remaining 1 tablespoon olive oil, and heat over medium heat. Add the mirepoix— onions, carrots, and celery—and cook until softened, about 10 minutes. Add the garlic and cook for 1 minute. Add the herbs, cinnamon, and white wine, bring to a boil over high heat, and boil until the wine reduces by half.

Add the chicken stock and, when it comes to a simmer, return the veal to the pot. Bring the liquid back to a simmer, cover, and transfer to the oven. After 5 minutes, check to make sure that the braise is not cooking too slowly or too fast; there should be just the slightest bubble occasionally breaking the surface of the liquid. Adjust the heat of the oven as necessary, and cook for 2 to 2¼ hours, until the meat is easily pierced with a fork.

Meanwhile, after the veal has cooked for about 1 hour, pierce the sweet potatoes with a fork and place them on a baking sheet. Season the cut surfaces of the butternut squash with salt and pepper and a drizzle of olive oil. Place cut side down next to the potatoes. Bake for 45 minutes to 1 hour, until the potatoes and squash are tender. Remove and let cool slightly.

While they are still quite warm, scoop out the flesh from the sweet potatoes and butternut squash and puree through a food mill into a bowl. Stir in the butter and salt and pepper to taste. (Alternatively, puree in a food processor with the butter, then season.) Cover loosely to keep warm.

When the veal is very tender, transfer it to a platter. Strain the braising liquid into a saucepan and bring to a simmer over medium-high heat, skimming any fat that comes to the surface. Simmer until reduced by about half and slightly thickened, 10 minutes.

Just before serving, warm the veal in the reduced braising broth. Swirl in the butter, then taste and adjust the seasonings.

Rewarm the glazed vegetables and the puree, if necessary.

To serve, place a generous spoonful of puree in the bottom of each warm serving bowl and top with the veal and sauce. (Reserve any extra puree for another meal.) Garnish with the glazed cipollini and carrots.

To Drink: Dolcetto (Renato Ratti)

VEAL BREAST GENOESE

In the states, securing veal breast usually requires placing a special order with your butcher. But in Genoa, one of the great culinary cities of Italy, there's a long tradition of cooking veal breast—sometimes boned, sometimes not; sometimes stuffed with a mosaic of filling, cooked, cooled, and served chilled; sometimes served in a meaty ragù with pasta. Rely on your butcher for boning the breast. The meat isn't especially lean; even when it's been trimmed of most fat and sinew, some will remain, lending a rustic quality to the dish.

FOR THE STUFFING

2 tablespoons extra virgin olive oil

3 onions, diced

4 cups Swiss chard or spinach, blanched (see page 255) and chopped

1 garlic clove, minced

2 tablespoons finely chopped flat-leaf parsley

½ cup pine nuts, toasted (see page 255)

8 tablespoons (1 stick) unsalted butter, melted

1 cup Bread Crumbs (page 239)

3 ounces mortadella in one piece, cut into 1-inch pieces (¾ cup)

¼ teaspoon freshly grated nutmeg

3 large eggs, lightly beaten

¾ cup freshly grated Parmigiano-Reggiano

Kosher salt and freshly ground black pepper

FOR THE VEAL

One 4- to 5-pound boneless veal breast

Kosher salt and freshly ground black pepper

2 tablespoons olive oil

3 onions, coarsely chopped

3 celery rib stalks, coarsely chopped

2 carrots, coarsely chopped

1 garlic clove, finely chopped

1 bay leaf

5 cups Chicken Stock (page 241)

Heat 1 tablespoon of the olive oil in a large sauté pan over medium-low heat. Add the onions and slowly brown them, stirring often with a wooden spoon, about 15 minutes. Remove from the heat and let cool.

In a large mixing bowl, combine the onions, chard, garlic, the remaining tablespoon of olive oil, parsley, pine nuts, butter, bread crumbs, mortadella, nutmeg, eggs, Parmigiano, and salt and pepper and mix well.

Open the veal and pat it dry. Season the inside liberally with salt and pepper. Spread the stuffing over the meat, leaving a 1-inch border all around. Starting from a long side, roll up the veal jelly-roll fashion into a compact log. Using kitchen twine, tie the roast at 3-inch intervals.

Preheat the oven to 315°F.

Heat a large Dutch oven over medium-high heat. Add 1 tablespoon of the olive oil, and brown the meat on all sides. Transfer to a rack and wipe out the pot.

Place the pot back over medium-high heat and add the remaining tablespoon of oil. Add the mirepoix—onions, celery, carrots, garlic, and bay leaf—and cook until just softened, about 8 minutes.

Return the veal to the pot, add the stock, and bring to a simmer. Cover the pot, place in the oven, and braise for 3 to 3½ hours, until the veal is very tender.

Transfer the veal to a rack or cutting board (making sure to save any juices that pool around the meat), and let rest for 20 minutes.

Strain the braising liquid into a saucepan, pressing down on the solids to extract all the flavorful juices. Simmer the liquid over low heat for 20 minutes to reduce it, skimming off the fat that rises to the top. Add any accumulated juices from the veal.

Untie the veal breast and slice into ½-inch-thick slices. Arrange on plates and spoon the sauce over the meat.

To Drink: Pinot Noir (Chambolle Musigny by Bertheau, or Au Bon Climat)

VEAL LIVER VENETIAN-STYLE
Serves 4 to 6

As a child, I hated liver. Frozen, thawed, then overcooked, the beef liver I knew was horrible. So you can imagine my surprise when I experienced how delicate and faintly sweet fresh, beigy pink veal liver can be.

It's no secret that Harry's Bar in Venice is one of my favorite restaurants, and their veal liver is the standard to which we aspire. Thin slices of perfectly trimmed fresh liver, gently sautéed, united with oh-so-sweet caramelized onions, and served atop polenta, either grilled or creamy, soaking up the buttery pan juices, could make a grown man cry. Calvin, a young cook (as big as an NFL tackle) at Bottega from north Birmingham, grew up loving his mother's hard-cooked beef liver. But when he tried this delicate liver, his big brown eyes misted over. "This is the greatest thing I've ever eaten!" he exclaimed.

FOR THE CARAMELIZED ONIONS

1 tablespoon olive oil

2 red onions, cut into julienne

1 yellow onion, cut into julienne

Kosher salt and freshly ground black pepper

1 thyme sprig

1 bay leaf

2 tablespoons sherry

2 pounds veal (calves') liver, membranes removed and
    veins trimmed away

1½ cups all-purpose flour

Kosher salt and freshly ground black pepper

2 tablespoons olive oil

2 small garlic cloves, chopped

2 tablespoons plus 1 teaspoon unsalted butter

¾ cup Chicken Stock (page 241)

1 teaspoon fresh lemon juice

Scant 1 tablespoon flat-leaf chopped parsley

Creamy Polenta (page 206)

Freshly grated Parmigiano-Reggiano for serving (optional)

To prepare the caramelized onions, heat the olive oil in a large cast-iron skillet over medium-low heat. Add the onions and slowly cook them, stirring often with a wooden spoon, until soft, about 15 minutes. Add a pinch each of salt and pepper, the thyme sprig, and bay leaf and continue cooking until the onions caramelize to a coffee-brown color, about 15 minutes more. Remove the pan from the heat and stir in the sherry, then transfer the onions to a plate and set aside. (The onions can be prepared 2 to 3 hours in advance.)

Slice the trimmed liver into thin medallions, about ⅛ inch thick. Season the flour with salt and pepper. Just before cooking, lightly dust the liver with the seasoned flour, shaking off the excess.

Heat a large skillet over medium-high heat, then add the olive oil. Add the veal liver, in batches, reduce the heat to medium (if the heat is too high, the liver will char and become bitter), and cook for approximately 20 seconds per side, until the exterior is golden brown but the liver is still light pink in the center. Transfer the pieces to a rack to rest and allow the juices to settle.

Add the chopped garlic and 1 teaspoon of the butter to the pan and cook over medium heat until the garlic is golden. Add the remaining 2 tablespoons butter and the stock and whisk to combine, then add the caramelized onions and liver. Finish with the lemon juice and parsley.

To serve, place the grilled or soft polenta onto serving plates and top with the veal medallions and sauce. Sprinkle with Parmigiano-Reggiano, if desired.

To Drink: Valpolicella Ripasso (Zenato)

OTHER CUTS Years ago on a visit to Florence I was hit by a funky aroma wafting up from a rickety old street cart. I had stumbled upon a vendor whom I'd heard about, selling trippa à la fiorentina. The tripe had been prepared over many days—washed and bleached and cleaned and then cooked forever. It was then added to a wonderfully flavorful tomato sauce with lots of Parmesan and cooked some more. It was delicious.

Such exotic dishes fascinate. For people who couldn't afford choice cuts of meat, secondary cuts like spleen or tripe became regional specialties. All the fabulous Italian sausages came out of this same frugal tradition of using the whole animal.

I'd love to see us return to an appreciation of the diverse cuts of meat, thereby giving greater respect to the animal that was sacrificed for our table. From cheeks to oxtails, an inquisitive and patient cook can fashion endless dishes. If you get the chance, visit Fergus Henderson's wonderful restaurant St. John in London, or check out his cookbook, *The Whole Beast, Nose to Tail Eating*—he is a master of using every morsel.

PISTACHIO-CRUSTED LAMB LOIN

Serves 4

The contrast of green pistachios and pink lamb loin is an impressive sight at a dinner party, and the abundance of cool mint adds a wonderful herbal aroma. To make things easy, get a jump-start by searing the lamb and coating it with the pistachios several hours in advance, then pop it into the oven just before serving to finish cooking. I urge you to seek out high-quality lamb such as that from Jamison Farms (see Sources, page 260). The Butter Bean and Mint Pilaf (page 204) is a perfect pairing to round out the meal.

Four 6-ounce boneless lamb loins, silverskin removed (see page 256)
Kosher salt and freshly ground black pepper
1 tablespoon olive oil
2 tablespoons Dijon mustard
½ cup shelled pistachios, coarsely chopped
Mint Oil (page 250) for drizzling
Mint leaves for garnish

Preheat the oven to 500°F.

Season the lamb loins with salt and pepper. Heat a large heavy sauté pan over high heat, then add the oil and heat until hot. Sear the lamb until well colored on all sides but still rare, 2 to 3 minutes per side. Transfer to a cooling rack and let the meat rest for at least 10 minutes.

When the lamb is cool, brush the Dijon mustard over the lamb to coat, then roll the loins in the pistachios. (You can prepare the lamb to this point several hours in advance and refrigerate it; bring to room temperature before proceeding.)

Place the lamb in a roasting pan and roast until it is medium-rare (125°F on an instant-read thermometer), about 6 to 8 minutes. Let the lamb rest on a rack for 5 minutes.

Slice the lamb on the bias and serve drizzled with a little mint oil and garnished with fresh mint.

To Drink: Cabernet from Napa (Ladera, Corison, or Cakebread) or a Super Tuscan

LAMB SHOULDER WITH PORCINI, PINE NUTS, AND CANNELLINI PUREE

Serves 4 to 6, with leftovers

When off-duty chefs talk about their favorite foods or preferred cuts of meat it's often cheeks, sweetbreads, liver, shanks, feet, and so on. And when it comes to lamb, there's unanimous praise for the shoulder—the flavor and richness that can be cajoled from this "poor man's" cut amounts to culinary perfection, in some ways more satisfying and robust than the elegant rack, loin, or tenderloin.

Boning a lamb shoulder can be a great lesson in anatomy and knife skill. If you're up for it, know that the trick is simply to follow the natural contours of the bone with a very sharp knife. I'd strongly recommend visiting a butcher and watching him perform the task first. The shoulder is actually better—and easier to slice—if prepared a day in advance. Gently reheat the sliced lamb in the reduced braising liquid before serving.

FOR THE STUFFING

2 tablespoons extra virgin olive oil
1 onion, quartered and thinly sliced
2 garlic cloves, crushed and finely chopped
¼ cup dried porcini, soaked in warm water until softened and chopped
1½ cups Bread Crumbs (page 239)
2 tablespoons pine nuts, toasted (see page 255)
1 small bunch flat-leaf parsley, leaves removed and chopped
1 teaspoon each chopped thyme, savory, and rosemary
Grated zest of 1 lemon
Kosher salt and freshly ground black pepper

FOR THE BRAISE

One 3- to 4-pound boneless lamb shoulder
Kosher salt and freshly ground black pepper
2 tablespoons plus 2 teaspoons olive oil
1 onion, sliced
2 carrots, sliced
1½ cups dry white wine
6 cups Chicken Stock (page 241) or beef or lamb stock
Several sprigs thyme, savory, and rosemary and 1 bay leaf, tied together with kitchen twine to form a bouquet garni
½ pound porcini or cremini mushrooms, sliced
1 teaspoon thyme leaves (optional)

Cannellini Bean Puree with Roasted Garlic (page 196)

Heat 1 tablespoon of the olive oil in a large sauté pan over medium heat. Add the onion and sauté until soft and translucent, 8 to 10 minutes. Add the garlic and cook until softened, about 1 minute. Add the porcini and toss for a few seconds. Transfer to a large mixing bowl and fold in the bread crumbs, pine nuts, chopped herbs, lemon zest, salt and pepper, and the remaining 1 tablespoon olive oil.

Open the lamb shoulder on a cutting board and remove any excess fat. Season with salt and pepper. Spread the stuffing over the meat, leaving a 1-inch border all around. Starting from a long side, roll up and tuck the meat to enclose the stuffing. Using kitchen twine, tie the roll into a neat, secure package—kind of like a football. Season with salt and pepper.

Preheat the oven to 310°F.

Heat 1 tablespoon of the olive oil in a large Dutch oven over medium-high heat. Add the lamb shoulder and brown it on all sides. Transfer the meat to a rack to rest.

Wipe the fat from the pot with a paper towel and return the pot to the stove. Add 1 tablespoon olive oil and heat over medium-low heat. Add the onion and carrots and cook until tender, about 15 minutes.

Add the wine, bring to a boil over high heat, and boil for 1 minute. Add the stock and bring to a simmer. Add the bouquet garni, and return the lamb to the pot. Bring the liquid back to a simmer, then cover with the lid and transfer the pot to the oven. Cook until the lamb is tender, about 2½ hours.

Meanwhile, heat the remaining 2 teaspoons olive oil in a large skillet over medium heat. Add the mushrooms and sauté until tender, about 5 minutes. Season with salt and pepper, and the thyme leaves, if using. Set aside.

When the lamb is tender, remove it to a rack to rest.

Place the pot of braising liquid over high heat and bring to a boil, skimming all the fat from the surface. Reduce the liquid by half.

Warm the cannellini bean puree. Reheat the mushrooms; toss the whole cannellini beans from the puree recipe into the skillet with the mushrooms to warm through.

Slice the lamb into ½-inch-thick slices. Spoon the puree onto warm serving plates and arrange the lamb on top of the puree. Spoon the broth over all, and garnish with the sautéed mushrooms and cannellini beans.

To Drink: Barbaresco or California Cabernet

LAMB SPIEDINI WITH SICILIAN COUSCOUS AND YOGURT SAUCE

Serves 4

Picture a summer cookout with friends: The grill is fired up and rosemary "arrows" skewer lamb kebabs, imparting a wonderful woodsy flavor. A mound of Sicilian couscous, infused with fragrant cinnamon, rosemary, and basil, is loaded with sweet, colorful peppers and chickpeas. Yogurt sauce makes a refreshing accent.

FOR THE LAMB

3 garlic cloves, crushed

3 rosemary sprigs

3 basil sprigs

2 tablespoons olive oil

2 pounds boneless leg of lamb, cut into 2-inch cubes

Kosher salt and freshly ground black pepper

Four 10-inch-long thick rosemary sprigs,
    soaked in water for 10 minutes

FOR THE SICILIAN COUSCOUS

1 cup water

1 tablespoon unsalted butter

2 cups Israeli couscous

Kosher salt and freshly ground black pepper

3 tablespoons olive oil

2 red bell peppers, cored, seeded, and cut into
    2-inch pieces

2 yellow bell peppers, cored, seeded, and cut into
    2-inch pieces

1 red onion, cut into 1-inch dice

1 garlic clove, smashed

1 rosemary sprig

1 basil sprig

½ teaspoon ground cinnamon

1 cup canned chickpeas, drained

Scant pinch of cayenne

1 bunch basil, leaves removed and torn into pieces

FOR THE YOGURT SAUCE

1 cup plain low-fat yogurt

1 tablespoon mint cut into chiffonade

Squeeze of lemon juice

Kosher salt

Pinch of freshly ground white pepper or a dash
    of Tabasco sauce

Minced scallions or garlic (optional)

Combine the garlic, rosemary, basil, and olive oil in a shallow bowl. Add the lamb, massaging the marinade into the meat. Refrigerate for at least 4 hours, or overnight.

To make the rosemary skewers, remove most of the leaves from each sprig, leaving 1 to 2 inches of leaves at the very top. Cut off the very bottom of each sprig on an angle to create a sharp point. Thread 4 to 5 cubes of lamb onto each skewer, and set aside on a platter to come to room temperature.

To prepare the couscous, combine the water and butter in a small saucepan and bring to a boil. Meanwhile, toast the couscous in a large dry skillet over medium heat until nutty brown, about 3 to 4 minutes. Transfer to a bowl.

Pour the boiling water over the couscous, cover the bowl tightly, and let sit for 15 minutes. Fluff the couscous with a fork to separate the grains. Season with salt and pepper and set aside.

Prepare a fire in an outdoor grill.

Meanwhile, heat 1 tablespoon of the olive oil in a large sauté pan over medium heat. Add the red and yellow bell peppers, onion, garlic, rosemary and basil sprigs, and cinnamon and sauté until the vegetables are soft and slightly caramelized, about 10 minutes. Transfer to the bowl with the couscous and add the remaining 2 tablespoons olive oil, the chickpeas, cayenne, and torn basil. Toss well, then taste and adjust the seasonings.

Season the lamb spiedini with salt and pepper. Grill, turning occasionally, for 6 to 7 minutes total for medium-rare. Transfer to a rack to rest.

Meanwhile, to prepare the yogurt sauce, combine the yogurt, mint, lemon juice, salt to taste, and white pepper or Tabasco in a small bowl. Transfer to a serving bowl, and sprinkle with the scallions or garlic, if desired.

Spoon the couscous onto one side of a large platter. Place the skewered lamb on the other side, flanked by the bowl of yogurt sauce.

To Drink: A Sicilian red, such as Regaleali, or Zinfandel (Ridge)

LAMB RAGÙ WITH ARTICHOKES, OVEN-ROASTED TOMATOES, AND BASIL

Serves 6 to 8

Fresh lamb shoulder is extremely forgiving if you cook it very slowly and for a long time, as we do with this simple braise. I love the addition of artichokes and concentrated tomato with mint and basil, but choose the accompanying vegetable and seasonings to suit the season.

2½ pounds boneless lamb shoulder, trimmed of excess
    fat and cut into 2-inch chunks
Kosher salt and freshly ground black pepper
2 tablespoons olive oil
2 onions, quartered and sliced ¼ inch thick
2 carrots, peeled and sliced 1 inch thick
1 leek, cleaned and sliced 1 inch thick
1 head garlic, cut horizontally in half
3 dried porcini soaked in warm water until softened
5 thyme sprigs
3 bay leaves
½ teaspoon fennel seeds
2 cups dry red wine
3 cups Chicken Stock (page 241)
Braised Artichokes (page 238)
Oven-Roasted Tomatoes (page 238)
2 mint sprigs, leaves removed and chopped
2 basil sprigs, leaves removed and chopped
Fruity extra virgin olive oil for drizzling

Preheat the oven to 310°F.

Season the lamb generously with salt and pepper. Heat a large Dutch oven over medium-high heat, then add 1 tablespoon of the olive oil. Add the meat, in batches so that you do not crowd the pot, and sear on all sides until well browned, about 8 minutes per batch. Remove to a rack.

Add the remaining 1 tablespoon olive oil to the Dutch oven and heat until hot. Add the onions, carrots, leek, garlic, porcini, thyme, bay leaves, and fennel seeds and sauté for 5 to 6 minutes, until the onions begin to turn translucent. Pour in the wine, bring to a boil, and reduce by half.

Add the stock and bring to a simmer. Add the lamb and place a round of parchment directly on top of it, then cover the pot with the lid. Transfer the pot to the oven and cook for 1½ to 2 hours, until the lamb is tender.

When the meat is cooked, transfer it to a plate. Strain the braising liquid through a fine-mesh strainer into a pot, pressing on the vegetables with a spoon to extract all the flavorful juices. Bring to a boil and reduce the liquid by half, skimming the fat. (Set the pan so that it is half on and half off the burner, and the fat will collect on the cooler side of the pan making it easier to skim.) Taste and adjust the seasonings.

Add the lamb, artichokes, and tomatoes to the sauce and reheat gently. Serve garnished with the chopped mint and basil and a splash of fruity olive oil.

To Drink: Rosso di Montalcino (Altesino or Caparzo)

LAMB SHANKS WITH SWEET PEAS AND MINT

Serves 4

Lamb has always been a favorite of mine, and this particular recipe, lamb shanks partnered with the bright green flavors of spring, brings a big smile to my face—and those seated with me at table. Long, slow braising breaks down the tough muscle fibers and makes the meat uncommonly moist and tender. Throw a few extra shanks in the pot so you'll have leftovers for soups and pasta dishes.

2 tablespoons olive oil

4 lamb shanks, trimmed and patted dry

Kosher salt and freshly ground black pepper

1 onion, quartered and thinly sliced

2 carrots, peeled and thinly sliced

2 cups dry white wine

6 cups Chicken Stock (page 241) or beef or lamb stock

Several sprigs of thyme and mint plus a couple of bay leaves, wrapped in a leek green and tied to form a bouquet garni

8 cipollini (optional)

1 tablespoon extra virgin olive oil, plus a splash if using the cipollini

1 tablespoon unsalted butter

1 leek, cleaned and finely sliced

2 small spring bulb onions or 1 Vidalia onion, halved and sliced

1 small garlic clove, crushed

2 cups fresh or frozen sweet peas

¼ cup mint leaves, finely chopped, plus a few leaves for garnish

1 small bunch flat-leaf parsley, leaves removed and finely chopped

Rice Pilaf (page 204) or Basic Risotto (page 201)

Preheat the oven to 325°F.

Heat a heavy sauté pan large enough to accommodate the shanks in a single layer over medium-high heat, and add 1 tablespoon of the olive oil. Season the shanks with salt and pepper and sear until golden brown on all sides, about 10 minutes. Transfer to a Dutch oven or heavy casserole.

Wipe out the sauté pan, and heat the remaining 1 tablespoon olive oil over medium heat. Add the onion and carrots and cook until softened, about 10 minutes. Add the wine, bring to a boil over high heat, and reduce by half. Add the stock and herbs and bring to a simmer.

Pour the stock and vegetables over the shanks. Place a round of parchment paper on top of the lamb. Cover the pot with the lid, place it in the oven, and reduce the heat to 300°F. Cook at the barest simmer until the lamb is tender, 2 to 2½ hours.

Meanwhile, if using the cipollini, to make peeling them easy, put them in a bowl, pour boiling water over to cover, and let stand for 10 minutes. Drain and peel. Film the bottom of a sauté pan just large enough to hold the cipollini in a single layer with a little olive oil. Add the onions, season with salt and pepper, and cook over medium heat, stirring occasionally, until lightly golden, about 8 to 12 minutes. Set aside.

Heat the remaining 1 tablespoon olive oil and the butter in a medium sauté pan over medium heat. Add the leek, bulb onions, and garlic and cook for 10 to 12 minutes, until softened and lightly colored. Add the peas and a splash of water and cook until tender. Stir in the mint, parsley, and salt and pepper to taste. Set aside.

When they are tender, transfer the shanks to a rack. Strain the braising broth into a small saucepan and boil over high heat to reduce by half, skimming off the fat.

To serve, reheat the shanks, vegetables, and optional cipollini. Place the rice pilaf or risotto on warmed serving plates, top with the shanks, and garnish with the pea mixture, optional cipollini, and fresh mint.

To Drink: A medium-bodied red wine with a taste of the ancient Mediterranean, such as Aglianico (Terredora di Paolo)

eating and drinking in piemonte

There is simply no better place for complex, subtle, and distinguished wine and food than the Piedmont region of northern Italy. The incredible *tajarín*—homemade pasta colored yellow with the bright yolks of farm eggs, cut into shapes, and tossed with the local truffles and butter—is heaven on earth. From October through Christmas, the region is scented with the elusive fragrance of white Alba truffles, and tajarín may be the perfect foil for showcasing this distinctive fungus. But a rich cheese fonduta anointed with a copious shaving competes for top honors too, as does my favored "peasant" dish—a couple of lightly fried farm eggs finished with a shower of truffle shavings.

As for wine, the local Arneis, a recently revived varietal from the Roero region, supplies the first-course partner before you move into all the glorious reds—Dolcetto, Barbera, Nebbiolo, Barbaresco, and Barolo. The producers here are similar to those in the Burgundy region of France in that they often tend their own land and know every row of vines intimately. The result is wines of the utmost personality, flavor, and character.

BEEF FLATIRON WITH PANZANELLA
Serves 4

The flatiron cut of beef was practically unknown here ten years ago. I can't understand why—this well-marbled, intensely flavorful, relatively tender steak is remarkably well priced. (Once the word gets out, though, it may no longer be a bargain.) Ask your butcher to save this cut for you and to remove the sinew that bisects the top. If you can't find it, skirt, flank, or hanger steak is a worthy substitute.

Panzanella, the Tuscan bread salad, is a great accompaniment for the steak, as well as for most any meat or seafood. Summer is the season for tomatoes, making this an ideal side dish when you are cooking outdoors on the grill. Toast the bread on a hot grill or in the oven until crisp, then rub each piece with the cut side of a garlic clove before cutting into cubes.

FOR THE PANZANELLA

1 small red onion, quartered lengthwise and
    thinly sliced crosswise
3 tablespoons red wine vinegar
1 red bell pepper, roasted (see page 254), peeled,
    seeded, and cut into 1½-by-½-inch strips
1 yellow bell pepper, roasted (see page 254), peeled,
    seeded, and cut into 1½-by-½-inch strips
6 tomatoes, halved, seeded (see page 255), and
    cut into 1-inch chunks
2 cups cubed (1-inch) toasted sourdough bread
½ cup extra virgin olive oil
½ cup brine-cured black or green olives
    (such as Niçoise or Picholine), halved and pitted
2 small firm cucumbers, such as kirby, peeled, halved
    lengthwise, seeded, and cut into ¼-inch slices
Kosher salt and freshly ground black pepper
⅔ cup torn basil leaves
¼ cup flat-leaf parsley leaves

FOR THE BEEF

Two 1-pound beef flatiron steaks,
    main center sinew removed
Kosher salt and freshly ground black pepper
Olive oil
Fruity extra virgin olive oil

For the salad, combine the onion and vinegar in a large bowl and let macerate for 10 to 20 minutes.

Prepare a fire in a charcoal or gas grill, or preheat a cast-iron pan when ready to cook the beef.

Add the roasted peppers, tomatoes, toasted bread cubes, olive oil, olives, cucumbers, and salt and pepper to taste to the onion and vinegar and toss to combine. Let marinate for 10 minutes.

Season the beef with salt and lots of pepper and rub it with a little olive oil. Cook over a high heat until charred on the first side, about 4 minutes. Turn the meat and cook for another 4 minutes, or until medium-rare. Transfer to a cooling rack to rest for 5 minutes.

Add the basil and parsley to the panzanella, then taste and adjust the seasonings.

Thinly slice the meat on the bias and serve with the panzanella. Pass the fruity olive oil at the table for those who may want a drizzle.

To Drink: Vino Nobile di Montepulciano (Poliziano)

TUSCAN PORTERHOUSE WITH LEMON, OLIVE OIL, AND ARUGULA

Serves 4

A big splurge—porterhouse steaks add drama to any cook-out. The seasonings used here—olive oil, lemon, and arugula—provide the perfect counterpoint for the spectacular thick steak. These big 2- to 3-inch-thick porterhouses are meant to be shared—each one serves 2 to 3 people. If you have time, air-dry them overnight in the refrigerator and let them come to room temperature before grilling.

Serve with roasted red potatoes or Roasted Fingerling Potatoes with Herbs (page 196).

Two 32-ounce porterhouse steaks, 2 to 3 inches thick
2 whole garlic heads
About 2 tablespoons olive oil
Kosher salt and freshly ground black pepper
2 rosemary sprigs, leaves only
4 cups loosely packed arugula
½ lemon
Maldon sea salt

Pat the steaks dry and set aside on a plate. Or air-dry overnight in the refrigerator.

Prepare a fire in a charcoal or gas grill. Place the garlic heads on a double sheet of aluminum foil, drizzle with 1 tablespoon of the olive oil and sprinkle with salt and pepper and rosemary needles. Wrap the garlic in the foil to form a pouch and place it on the grill, off the direct heat, and cook for 30 minutes, or until soft. (Alternatively, bake the garlic in a 325°F oven for 45 minutes to 1 hour.) Let cool slightly, then unwrap and cut horizontally in half.

Meanwhile, season each steak generously with salt and pepper on each side. Place the steaks on the grill and cook for 10 to 12 minutes per side for medium-rare. Remove to a rack and let rest, loosely covered with aluminum foil, for 5 to 10 minutes.

Toss the arugula with lemon juice to taste, 2 to 3 teaspoons olive oil, and salt and pepper. Place a mound of greens on each of four plates. Place the roasted garlic next to the greens and dress with a little more olive oil.

Slice the meat off the bone: Remove the strip portion first, sliding the tip of a chef's knife along the bone. You can rest the porterhouse on its T-bone with the tip of the steak in the air for greater stability. Then cut away the filet. Slice the strip against the grain into 8 slices. Slice the filet into 4 slices. Arrange on the serving plates and garnish with a sprinkle of sea salt, a few leaves of rosemary, and a drizzle of olive oil.

To Drink: Brunello di Montalcino (Caparzo)

SHORT RIBS AND OXTAIL WITH GREMOLATA AND GREEN OLIVES

Serves 4 to 6 • Pictured on page 150

Carefully braised short ribs and oxtails are extremely tender, moist, and so beefy tasting. Long, slow cooking makes the meat soft and keeps the flavorful broth clear; too fast, and the braising liquid will become cloudy. The parsley and orange zest gremolata and green olives provide contrast and balance to the creamy richness of the beef and polenta.

Four 2½-inch-long kosher-cut short ribs
  (about 4 pounds), trimmed of excess fat
1¼ pounds oxtail, in 4 pieces
¼ cup olive oil
Kosher salt and freshly ground black pepper
1 yellow onion, cut into ½-inch dice
2 celery stalks, cut into ½-inch dice
5 carrots, cut into ½-inch dice
2 garlic cloves, crushed
¼ cup medium-dry sherry
2 cups dry red wine
About 4 cups Chicken Stock (page 241) or beef stock,
  heated
3 thyme sprigs
3 parsley stems
1 bay leaf, broken into pieces
1 ounce dried porcini mushrooms, broken into pieces
  and rinsed
Creamy Polenta (page 206)
½ cup green Greek or Sicilian olives, pitted and
  coarsely chopped
Parsley and Orange Zest Gremolata (page 249)

Preheat the oven to 425°F. Bring the meat to room temperature. Have at the ready a roasting pan large enough to hold the short ribs and oxtails snugly in a single layer.

Heat 2 tablespoons of the olive oil in a very large cast-iron skillet or Dutch oven over medium-high heat. Salt and pepper the meat. Add the short ribs to the hot oil, in batches, and brown well all over, about 4 to 5 minutes per side. Transfer to a rack to rest. Add the oxtails to the pan and brown well all over. Transfer to the rack.

Add the remaining 2 tablespoons olive oil to the pan and heat over medium heat. Add the onion, celery, and carrots, and sauté for 5 minutes. Add the garlic and cook for 5 minutes more, until the vegetables are tender and the onion is translucent. Add the sherry, scraping up the browned bits, bring to a boil, and boil until thick and syrupy. Pour in the red wine, bring to a boil, and reduce until it becomes syrupy. Remove from the heat.

Arrange the short ribs and oxtails in the roasting pan. Add the vegetables and their cooking liquid, along with enough warm stock to come three-quarters of the way up the sides of the meat. Add the thyme, parsley stems, bay leaf, and porcini. Cover with a piece of parchment placed directly on the meat, then cover the pan tightly with aluminum foil.

Place the roasting pan in the oven and reduce the heat to 310°F. Cook for 2 to 2½ hours, until the meat is very tender—check for doneness by transferring an oxtail and short rib to a cutting board: the meat should be falling off the bones. If it isn't, return the meat to the pan, cover with the parchment and foil, and continue cooking until it is tender.

When the meat is done, transfer it to a cutting board and let it rest, uncovered.

Strain the braising liquid through a fine-mesh strainer into a saucepan, pressing on the vegetables with the back of a spoon or spatula to release all the concentrated flavors. Place the saucepan half on and half off a burner and bring to a very gentle simmer over medium to medium-low heat, skimming off the fat that accumulates on the cool side of the pan. Continue simmering and skimming for 20 minutes, until the liquid is slightly reduced and no fat remains.

Transfer the short ribs and oxtails to a pot, add a little of the braising broth, and warm gently over low heat.

Serve the meat on the warm creamy polenta, with more of the braising liquid spooned over. Garnish with the green olives and gremolata.

To Drink: Barolo (Elio Grasso or Luigi Einaudi)

GRILLED VENISON WITH FARRO, POMEGRANATE, AND PARSLEY SALAD

Serves 4

Farro, one of the oldest cultivated grains, is similar to barley but more nutty tasting, flavorful, and nutritious. When cooked, the grain soaks up and takes on the flavors of the cooking liquid, becoming tender and plump.

Venison is lean and best served medium-rare to rare; it becomes dry if cooked longer. When grilling or pan searing venison, you want to create a nice crust, almost charred but not burnt—especially desirable if you are slicing the venison very thin.

Big, ripe pomegranates full of juicy seeds have a distinctive flavor and sweet-tart crunch that makes this dish especially attractive. We use lots of parsley for the salad, as you would watercress, arugula, or lettuce.

2 pounds boneless venison leg, loin, or tenderloin,
    cut into 4 equal portions

FOR THE MARINADE
6 parsley sprigs
1 rosemary sprig
8 to 9 juniper berries, toasted (see page 256)
    and lightly crushed
2 tablespoons olive oil

FOR THE FARRO
2 cups farro, soaked in cold water for 30 minutes
    and drained
2½ cups Chicken Stock (page 241) or water
1 thyme sprig
1 bay leaf
½ teaspoon salt, or to taste
½ teaspoon freshly ground black pepper, or to taste
3 tablespoons unsalted butter
½ cup canned chickpeas, rinsed and drained
1 tablespoon olive oil

FOR THE PARSLEY SALAD
2 cups flat-leaf parsley leaves
1 shallot, very thinly sliced
2 tablespoons L'Estornell Spanish garnacha vinegar
    (see Sources, page 00) or other good-quality red wine
    vinegar
¼ cup olive oil
Kosher salt and freshly ground black pepper

1 pomegranate, quartered and seeds removed

Trim the venison of any sinew and pat the meat dry with a paper towel.

To make the marinade, combine the parsley and rosemary sprigs, juniper berries, and oil in a large mixing bowl. Add the venison, turning to coat with oil, cover, and marinate for at least 2 to 3 hours, or up to 1 day, in the refrigerator.

Put the soaked farro in a large saucepan and add the chicken stock or water, thyme sprig, bay leaf, salt, pepper, and 2 tablespoons of the butter. Bring to a simmer and cook for 20 to 30 minutes, uncovered, or until most of the liquid is absorbed and the farro has begun to swell. Taste a few grains to check for tenderness—they should be very tender. Adjust the seasoning (you could serve the unadorned farro at this point), then add the chickpeas. Finish with the remaining tablespoon of butter and the olive oil. (You can make this well in advance of serving: Spread the farro in an even layer on a large baking sheet to cool, then reheat before serving in a little hot stock or water.)

Meanwhile, prepare a hot fire in an outdoor grill. Oil the grill rack. Pat the venison dry and put on the oiled grill rack. Cook for 4 minutes per side, for rare to medium-rare; an instant-read thermometer should read 125°F. Transfer the meat to a rack to rest for 5 minutes to allow the juices to settle.

While the meat rests, make the parsley salad: Toss together the parsley, shallot, vinegar, and olive oil in a small bowl. Season with salt and pepper and toss again.

To serve, slice the venison ¼ inch thick. Spoon the farro onto serving plates, lay the slices of venison over the farro, and garnish with the parsley salad and pomegranate seeds.

To Drink: Barolo (Bruno Giacosa or Luciano Sandrone)

OVERLEAF LEFT: *Jumbo Asparagus with Shaved Parmigiano (page 191);*
OPPOSITE: *Chef Stitt preparing jumbo asparagus*

ZUCCHINI RIBBON SAUTÉ

Serves 4

Living in North Beach in San Francisco during the 1970s, I frequented many of the little Italian restaurants that had been there for years. They had long counters with banks of stools facing the cooks, who were busy sautéing, grilling, and finishing pastas, and I loved to watch these old-timers in action. One dish that was on most menus was this zucchini sauté. A cook would heat up olive oil in a huge sauté pan until it was almost smoking, add a few garlic cloves to brown them, and then drop in ribbons of zucchini, creating an explosion of bubbles as it hit the hot oil. After a mere 45 seconds of theatrics—tossing the zucchini high in the air—he'd add a big pinch of salt and pepper and immediately toss the vegetable onto a waiting platter. The whole place would smell of zucchini, garlic, and olive oil.

5 small to medium zucchini, ends trimmed
1½ tablespoons olive oil
2 garlic cloves, crushed
2 dried red chiles
1 thyme sprig
Kosher salt and freshly ground black pepper

Slice the zucchini lengthwise on a mandoline or a vegetable slicer. You want thin ribbons (about ⅟₁₆ inch thick). Alternatively, use a sharp vegetable peeler to cut the zucchini into strips.

Heat a large sauté pan over medium-high heat. Add the olive oil and garlic and sauté until the garlic is toasted and golden. Add the chile peppers and thyme sprig, and watch for the thyme to sizzle and crackle in the oil. Once it does, add the zucchini, turning carefully so that the entire surface area gets coated with the oil. Cook for 2 to 3 minutes, carefully turning the zucchini, until softened.

Season with salt and pepper and serve.

ROASTED BUTTERNUT SQUASH AND BALSAMICO

Serves 4 to 6

In cool weather, when you want a taste of the season, butternut squash lends an old-time country rusticity to dishes. Roast it until tender and season with sweet-tart balsamic vinegar and fruity olive oil for a slightly exotic, savory change of pace.

1 butternut squash, cut lengthwise in half,
    seeds and membranes removed
Kosher salt and freshly ground black pepper
2 tablespoons fruity extra virgin olive oil
1 tablespoon good-quality balsamic vinegar

Preheat the oven to 350°F.

Season the cut surfaces of the butternut squash with salt and pepper and drizzle with 1 tablespoon of the olive oil. Place cut side down on a baking sheet and bake for 45 minutes to 1 hour, or until just soft.

Remove from the oven and let cool slightly. When the squash is cool enough to handle, remove the skin, then cut the flesh into 2-inch chunks. Toss with the balsamic vinegar and the remaining 1 tablespoon olive oil and serve.

JUMBO ASPARAGUS WITH SHAVED PARMIGIANO

Serves 4 • Pictured on page 186

Big fat green asparagus are one of the most prized spring vegetables. Italians have the right idea, serving the spears simply with shaved Parmigiano and a little butter in the north or a delicate fruity olive oil in the south. We peel the stalks because we love the look and the assured tenderness.

Perfectly blanched in-season asparagus need minimal embellishment. Here is a delightful way to celebrate spring's arrival.

24 jumbo asparagus spears (about 2 pounds),
    tough ends cut away and stalks peeled
3 tablespoons unsalted butter
½ lemon
Kosher salt and freshly ground black pepper
Scant 1 cup shaved Parmigiano-Reggiano

Bring a large pot of generously salted water to a rolling boil. Prepare an ice bath in a large bowl. Add the asparagus to the boiling water and cook until tender, 4 to 6 minutes—the spears should just begin to give when bent. Remove and immediately immerse in the ice water to halt the cooking. Remove them as soon as they are cool, or you risk water-logged spears. Lift out, drain on a kitchen towel, and pat dry.

Heat the butter in a large sauté pan over medium heat until foamy. Squeeze the juice of the lemon half into the pan and add the asparagus and salt and pepper to taste. Toss over medium-high heat until the spears are coated with the lemon butter and heated through.

Arrange the spears on serving plates and garnish with the shaved Parmigiano.

VARIATION: Here is another way to enjoy these spring stalks, one I learned from Richard Olney: Put a little kosher salt and freshly ground black pepper in a bowl, add a splash of good vinegar—red wine, sherry, or balsamic—and stir with a fork as you drizzle in some olive oil. Dip the warm blanched asparagus in this quickly made vinaigrette and eat with your fingers.

VENETIAN SPINACH

Serves 4 • Pictured on page 164

You may never see this dish anywhere in Venice, but the combination of garlicky spinach and sweet golden raisins is reminiscent of the glory days of the sixteenth century, when Venetian ships ruled the spice routes and savory dishes often had a sweet element as well. We often serve this with our roast pork chops (see page 165). You could skip the blanching step and just wilt the spinach in the hot oil, but the preliminary blanching and chilling locks in the vibrant green color of the vegetable. It's also handy when you want to prepare a large batch of spinach ahead of time for a dinner party.

1 pound spinach, trimmed and washed
1 tablespoon olive oil
1 garlic clove, smashed
1 dried red chile
2 tablespoons pine nuts, toasted (see page 255)
2 tablespoons golden raisins, plumped in a few
    tablespoons of white wine or water for 10 minutes
    and drained
1 tablespoon unsalted butter (optional)
Kosher salt and freshly ground black pepper
¼ lemon

Bring a pot of salted water to a boil. Meanwhile, prepare an ice bath.

Using a colander or strainer, immerse the spinach in the boiling water for 1 minute. Transfer the spinach to the ice bath to stop the cooking and to lock in its vibrant color. Leave it just until it is cool, then drain thoroughly.

Heat a medium saucepan over medium heat. Add the olive oil, garlic, and chile and cook until the garlic is golden and fragrant, about 3 minutes. Add the spinach, pine nuts, and drained raisins and sauté for about 3 minutes, until thoroughly hot and well combined. Add the butter, if using, and salt and pepper to taste. Squeeze the lemon wedge over the spinach, remove the chile, and serve.

the jones valley urban farm

Edwin Marty, visionary, farmer, educator, and friend is changing the way Alabama thinks about food. Along the lines of Michael Pollan and Joel Salatin, Edwin is devoted to the locally grown and sustainably raised, and his Jones Valley Urban Farm—in the middle of downtown Birmingham—introduces organic farming to the youth of the inner city. After studying at UC Santa Cruz, Edwin returned to his home in Birmingham and is now turning the tide—reclaiming and rejuvenating tired land, inspiring the young to appreciate just-picked vegetables and fruit, and, along with my wife, Pardis, is leading the way in the Slow Food movement here in Alabama.

Jones Valley offers a role model for other cities. They have programs ("Seed 2 Plant" is the name of one) that teach composting and give children an opportunity to plant, nurture, and grow and harvest vegetables. They also recycle the fryer oil from restaurants to fuel their diesel tractors. Their crops are sold at the local farmer's market and their fields of sunflowers beautify our city. All communities need an Edwin Marty—someone devoted to urban farming, to the stewardship of the land, and to sharing its wisdom.

BOTTEGA CAPONATA

Serves 4 to 6

Caponata is one of my favorite Sicilian dishes. It's a bit like Provençal ratatouille, but the Moorish influence on Sicily gives it its slightly sweet-and-sour edge. This recipe, a combination of soft sweet peppers, tomatoes, onions, and eggplant, perked up with a bit of vinegar and crunchy green celery, is beautiful to behold.

About ½ cup olive oil

2 large globe eggplants or 8 small Japanese eggplants, cut into 1-inch cubes

2 garlic cloves, crushed

1 dried red chile pepper

4 thyme sprigs

½ cup loosely packed basil leaves, chopped (reserve 2 basil stems)

1 large red onion, cut into 1-inch dice

Kosher salt and freshly ground black pepper

2 tablespoons L'Estornell Spanish garnacha vinegar (see Sources, page 260) or other good-quality red wine vinegar or sherry vinegar, or to taste

2 red bell peppers, cored, seeded, and cut into 1-inch squares

1 yellow bell pepper, cored, seeded, and cut into 1-inch squares

1 green bell pepper, cored, seeded, and cut into 1-inch squares

2 cups crushed seeded canned San Marzano tomatoes

3 celery stalks, cut into 1-inch pieces, blanched in boiling water until just tender, cooled in ice water, and drained

3 tablespoons capers

½ cup Picholine or large green Greek or Sicilian olives, halved and pitted

1 tablespoon sugar, or to taste

Heat a large cast-iron skillet over high heat for about 3 minutes. Add 1 tablespoon of the olive oil to coat the bottom of the pan. Working in batches, add the eggplant in a single layer and cook, undisturbed, until deep brown on the first side. Turn and cook, turning occasionally, until well browned on all sides and tender. Transfer the eggplant to a paper-towel-lined plate to cool. Add more oil to the pan as needed as you cook the remaining batches.

Heat 1 tablespoon of the olive oil in a large sauté pan over medium heat. Toss in 1 garlic clove, the dried chile, 1 thyme sprig, and a basil stem. Add the onion, and cook for 5 minutes. Season with a pinch of salt and a few grinds of pepper, and add 1 tablespoon of the vinegar. Cook for another 5 minutes, or until the onion is translucent and tender but has not taken on any color. Transfer the onion to a large bowl; set aside.

Wipe out the pan, add 1 more tablespoon olive oil, and heat over medium-high heat. Add the remaining garlic clove, 1 thyme sprig, and a basil stem, then add the bell peppers and cook for 5 minutes. Add a pinch of salt, pepper, and the remaining tablespoon of vinegar and cook for 6 to 7 minutes, or until the peppers are tender; be careful not to let them brown. Transfer the peppers to the bowl with the onions.

Add the eggplant, tomatoes, celery, capers, and olives to the onion and peppers, mix well, and taste. Adjust the seasonings by adding sugar, vinegar, and salt and pepper as necessary. The caponata should have a subtle sweet-and-sour flavor. Sprinkle with the chopped basil, remaining thyme leaves, and a few tablespoons of olive oil and stir to incorporate.

Serve warm or at room temperature.

COOKED SHELL BEANS

Makes 8½ cups

I share the Italians' love of shell beans—cannellini, borlotti, and their close cousin, cranberry beans, as well as huge fat *gigandes,* which are like big white limas or butter beans. In late summer, Alabama markets are full of fresh beans, which are shelled in huge wooden barrel-shaped contraptions—green and speckled butter beans, pink-eyes, black-eyed peas, crowders, lady peas, and zipper peas, to name a few. Fresh beans, of course, require much less cooking time than dried.

When cooking dried beans, I prefer to soak the beans overnight if time allows, though there are occasions when we don't respect this rule and get right on with the cooking, with little ill effect. Larger older beans benefit most from a prolonged soak, as this allows them to slowly swell and makes them less likely to split when cooked.

3 cups dried beans, such as cannellini, borlotti,
    or cranberry, picked over and soaked overnight
    in water to cover
1 leek, split and washed
1 onion, peeled and quartered
1 carrot, peeled and quartered
3 garlic cloves, smashed
Several thyme, marjoram, and savory sprigs plus 2 bay
    leaves, tied together with kitchen twine or wrapped in
    a leek green and tied to form a bouquet garni
Kosher salt
Fruity extra virgin olive oil
Sea salt and freshly ground black pepper

Drain the beans, place in a large pot, and cover by 3 to 4 inches with cold water. Add the leek, onion, carrot, garlic, and herb bouquet and bring to a simmer. Reduce the heat slightly, partially cover and cook at a gentle simmer for 30 to 45 minutes.

Add a scant tablespoon of kosher salt and continue cooking until the beans are very tender, 30 to 45 minutes more, depending on the beans.

You may need to add water from time to time to keep the beans submerged by 2 inches; this allows you the bonus of having some delicious bean broth.

Drain the beans, reserving the broth for another use, if desired; discard the aromatic vegetables and bouquet garni. Serve the beans drizzled with a generous amount of olive oil, and sprinkled with sea salt and freshly ground black pepper.

CANNELLINI BEAN PUREE WITH
ROASTED GARLIC

Makes 2½ cups

Pureed cannellini beans produce a creamy spread that at a glance appears dangerously rich. This spread is really a healthy dose of protein and fiber made smoother by the tiniest touch of cream. Try it whenever you have some left-over beans—it makes a great crostini topping or use as a base for grilled fish, shellfish, pork, veal, or lamb. The roasted garlic adds a mellower, sweeter flavor than minced raw garlic.

> 2 cups Cooked Shell Beans (page 195),
>   drained and broth reserved
> 2 teaspoons roasted garlic puree (see page 254)
> 1 Yukon Gold potato, boiled until tender, drained,
>   and peeled
> 2 tablespoons heavy cream
> Kosher salt and freshly ground white pepper
> Flat-leaf parsley or tender celery leaves for garnish

Set aside a few of the cannellini beans for garnish, and transfer the rest to a food processor. Add the roasted garlic, potato, and cream, and process to a puree, adding some of the reserved bean broth as needed to facilitate pureeing. Season to taste with salt and pepper.

Serve the puree garnished with the reserved cannellini beans and parsley or celery leaves.

ROASTED FINGERLING POTATOES
WITH HERBS

Serves 6

These roasted potatoes, so simple and so good, are a staple in all of our restaurants—and at home too. Use a handful of whole garlic cloves and more bay leaves than you've probably ever used and toss it all with good olive oil and a sprinkling of sea salt to make these humble roots grand.

> 2 cups halved fingerling potatoes (1 pound)
> 1 garlic bulb, cloves separated but not peeled
> 6 to 10 bay leaves
> 1 teaspoon thyme leaves
> 1 teaspoon finely chopped rosemary leaves
> Sea salt and freshly ground black pepper
> 2 to 3 tablespoons fruity extra virgin olive oil

Set an oven rack in the highest position and preheat the oven to 400°F.

Put the potatoes in a medium bowl, add the garlic, herbs, sea salt and pepper to taste, and oil, and toss to coat. Transfer to a baking sheet and roast for 20 to 25 minutes, giving the pan a shake halfway through cooking. The potatoes are done when slightly charred and tender when pierced.

Serve with all the garlic cloves, so your guests can squeeze out the delicious roasted pulp.

MASHED POTATOES

Serves 4

Just-dug potatoes have a fresh earthiness that makes me look forward to our late spring and early summer harvests. Tune Farm in Falkville, a local organic potato farm, provides us with the best potatoes ever.

    10 medium new-crop red or Yukon Gold potatoes
        (about 1½ pounds), peeled in stripes, to leave some
        skin, or peeled completely
    8 tablespoons (1 stick) unsalted butter, cut into pieces
        and softened
    ⅓ to ½ cup milk, at room temperature
    1½ teaspoons kosher salt
    Pinch of freshly ground white pepper, or more to taste
    2 tablespoons extra virgin olive oil

Cover the potatoes by several inches with generously salted water in a medium pot and bring to a boil over high heat. Reduce the heat to medium so that the water boils very gently, skim off the starchy foam that has risen to the surface, and cook until the potatoes are very tender (and easily crushed with tongs), 25 to 35 minutes.

Drain, then return to the pot and dry over low heat for 2 to 3 minutes. Using a potato masher, mash in the butter and enough milk to achieve a fluffy consistency. Season the potatoes with the salt, white pepper, and olive oil. Serve hot.

POTATO AND FONTINA GRATIN

Serves 4 to 6

Made with just a few simple ingredients—potatoes, cream, and cheese—a classic potato gratin is a rich and comforting dish, with an inviting golden brown topping. The Fontina adds a grassy "fresh-cut hay" aroma.

    1 garlic clove, crushed
    1 tablespoon unsalted butter, softened
    4 pounds Idaho (russet) potatoes, peeled and ends
        trimmed
    2 cups heavy cream
    1 cup freshly grated Parmigiano-Reggiano
    Kosher salt and freshly ground white pepper
    ½ cup grated Fontina

Preheat the oven to 275°F.

Rub the bottom and sides of a 2-quart gratin dish or 3-inch-deep casserole with the crushed garlic clove. Let the dish stand for several minutes so that the oil from the garlic becomes tacky to the touch, then rub the bottom and sides of the dish with the softened butter. Set aside.

Using a mandoline or vegetable slicer, or a very sharp chef's knife, slice the potatoes lengthwise into slices about ⅛ inch thick. Place the slices in a bowl with the cream. Layer one-third of the slices in the baking dish in a slightly overlapping fashion. Top with ⅓ cup of the grated Parmigiano, a drizzle of cream from the bowl, and a pinch each of salt and white pepper. Continue layering so that you have three layers total, finishing with Parmigiano and salt and pepper.

Cover the dish with foil and bake for 2 hours.

Uncover the potatoes, top with the grated Fontina, and bake for 45 minutes to 1 hour more, until the potatoes are very tender and the top is brown and bubbly.

back to the land

Our local Jefferson County Farmers' Market is one of the busiest wholesale markets from Atlanta to New Orleans and New Orleans to Nashville. Every fruit and vegetable stand in this regional triangle draws inventory from this bustling epicenter (open 24 hours a day, 365 days a year).

My Cullman connection has served me well in my dealings with the truck farmers who bring their just-picked goods to sell. My granddad and father were the primary physicians of Cullman— Granddaddy delivered half of Cullman County in his day, and Dad operated on the other half. So when I walk through the aisles formed by pickups and flatbed trucks loaded with produce, the farmers interrupt their marketing to say hello. One might share a story with me about how my dad sewed his finger back on, or another about how Granddad diagnosed a loved one with scarlet fever and saved a life.

These hardworking truck farmers are the backbone of Alabama, and I look forward to our exchanges. Most of these are about crop-growing conditions—how the potatoes are faring in the drought, why the peaches are small (but oh so sweet), or why, when you buy greener tomatoes, you're buying time. These interactions ground me and connect me to my home and to the people who provide sustenance to us all.

The Stitt farm's resident goat, Turnip (his girlfriend, Butterbean, is off chilling in the shade)

RISOTTO FOR ALL SEASONS

Risotto is perhaps the most enduring culinary tradition from Italy after pasta. I adore it and regularly prepare it for late-night dinners at home.

Some purists insist that risotto is made only "to order" and that your guests need to be ready to have the dish delivered the instant it's finished. I admit I enjoy the drama and pageantry of this timing, but in the restaurant, we are more likely to prepare risotto to about 90 percent completion, then transfer it to a baking sheet and spread it out to stop the cooking; it can be refrigerated until ready to finish and serve. We reheat it at the last moment with more steaming broth and then stir in butter, cheese, and herbs.

We make risottos for every season. Start with your favorite ingredients and sauté each vegetable separately until tender, then season, and add to the prepared risotto. Loosen the mixture with a bit of butter and a splash of hot stock. Finish with some chopped fresh herbs. Some combos worth trying:

Summer—corn, cherry tomatoes, zucchini, butter beans, and basil
Fall—pumpkin, carrots, chanterelles, and hearty greens
Winter—leeks, celery, and black truffles
Spring—asparagus, peas, artichokes, spring onions, and mint

A few hints for making risotto:

- Have the stock simmering on a nearby burner for easy additions.

- Use a wooden spoon. With all the stirring required, it's gentler on the pan and your hand than a metal one.

- After sautéing the aromatics—onions, leeks, etc.—toast the rice in the fat remaining in the pan, stirring until it's well coated with the oil, a matter of a minute or two.

- Add about ½ cup stock at a time. Allow each addition to be almost completely absorbed before you add the next one.

- Finish the risotto by tasting for doneness and flavor, then add a generous portion of cheese and butter at the very last moment to enrich.

- Never add cream. Some "super-fancy" Italian restaurants and the French do this, but it makes for an overly rich, heavy, and gluey consistency.

BASIC RISOTTO

Serves 4

In addition to aromatics, consider seasonal vegetables, shrimp, scallops, chicken, quail, guinea hen, or even lamb to make this a one-pot meal. Stir the cooked shellfish or meat in at the last minute, or arrange it on top of the pan of risotto, and bring it to the table to serve family-style.

5 cups Chicken Stock (page 241)
1 tablespoon olive oil
2 tablespoons unsalted butter
½ cup finely chopped onion
1 celery stalk, thinly sliced
1 garlic clove, thinly sliced
2 cups Arborio rice or other Italian short-grain rice,
    such as Carnaroli
½ cup dry white wine or dry vermouth
Kosher salt and freshly ground black pepper
Scant ½ cup freshly grated Parmigiano-Reggiano or
    grana padano

Bring the stock to a boil in a medium saucepan, then reduce the heat to keep it at a bare simmer.

Heat the oil and 1 tablespoon of the butter in a large sauté pan over medium-high heat until foamy. Add the onion and sauté for 5 minutes or until softened. Add the celery and garlic and cook for 5 minutes, or until softened. Add the rice and cook, stirring with a wooden spoon to coat the grains with oil and lightly toast, for about 1 minute. Add the wine or vermouth and cook, stirring, until it evaporates. Reduce the heat to medium, add about ½ cup stock and a little salt and pepper, and stir until the liquid is absorbed; adjust the heat if necessary to keep the stock at a simmer. Continue adding stock ½ cup at a time once each addition is absorbed. After 15 to 18 minutes, taste to test the grains for tenderness: the rice should be al dente, tender but not mushy. If necessary, continue stirring and adding stock, then test again. (You may not need all the stock.)

Stir in the cheese and the remaining 1 tablespoon butter. Taste and season with more salt and pepper as necessary. Then beat briskly with the wooden spoon; the risotto should be creamy. Serve immediately.

To Drink: Tocai (Schiopetto)

RISOTTO WITH SHRIMP AND CLAMS

Serves 4

I prefer this risotto with very small shrimp and clams. Smaller shrimp are a little more work to peel, but their delicate taste and beauty is too often overlooked. Clams provide their own briny broth when steamed, so be sure to include all of their juices when adding them to the rice.

FOR THE SEAFOOD

1 tablespoon olive oil

1 garlic clove, crushed

24 littleneck clams (the smaller, the better), scrubbed

½ cup dry white wine

24 medium (31–35 count) shrimp, peeled and deveined if necessary

FOR THE RISOTTO

2 cups Chicken Stock (page 241) or seafood broth

2 tablespoons olive oil

1 onion, quartered and thinly sliced

1 small leek, cleaned and thinly sliced

1 cup Arborio rice or other Italian short-grain rice, such as Carnaroli

¼ cup dry white wine

1 bay leaf

1 thyme sprig

Kosher salt

2 tablespoons butter, softened

Freshly ground black pepper

Pinch of finely grated lemon zest

To prepare the seafood, heat the olive oil in a medium sauté pan over medium heat. Add the garlic and toast until golden, 2 to 3 minutes. Add the clams and wine, cover the pan and cook, shaking the pan from time to time, for 3 minutes. Add the shrimp to the pan, cover, and cook for 3 to 4 minutes more, until the shrimp are just opaque throughout and the clams have opened. Remove the pan from the heat. If you like, take half of the clams out of the shell, and leave the remaining clams in the shell for presentation, or shell them all. Set the pan aside, covered to keep warm.

To prepare the risotto, bring the stock to a boil in a medium saucepan, then reduce the heat to keep it at a bare simmer.

Heat a large sauté pan over medium-high heat. Add the olive oil, onion, and leek and cook until the vegetables soften, about 5 minutes. Add the rice and toast for 1 minute, stirring with a wooden spoon, until glistening and golden. Add the wine, bay leaf, thyme sprig, and a pinch of salt and cook, stirring, until all the liquid has evaporated. Reduce the heat to medium, add about ½ cup stock, and cook, stirring, until it is absorbed. Continue adding stock ½ cup at a time, allowing the liquid to be absorbed before each new addition. Adjust the heat as necessary so that there is just a perceptible bubbling of liquid. After 15 to 18 minutes test the grains for doneness; the rice should be al dente, cooked through but not mushy.

Remove the pan from the heat, stir in the butter, and taste for seasoning, adding salt if necessary and pepper. Beat the risotto briskly, then gently fold in the seafood until warmed through. Serve garnished with the grated lemon zest and a sprinkling of pepper.

To Drink: Soave (Gini)

RICE PILAF
Serves 4

This is a good basic recipe for cooking rice. Build on it by adding vegetables or topping with grilled meat as you would risotto. We like basmati rice for our pilaf because of its perfumed aroma; use brown or white, whichever you prefer.

1¾ cups Chicken Stock (page 239) or water
½ onion, chopped
Several thyme and parsley sprigs plus 2 bay leaves tied
   together with kitchen twine to form a bouquet garni
Kosher salt
1 cup basmati rice
1 tablespoon unsalted butter

Combine the stock or water, onion, bouquet garni, and a pinch of salt in a medium saucepan and bring to a boil. Add the rice and butter, stir, and bring back to a simmer. Cover and cook over low heat for 16 to 18 minutes or until the grains are tender.

Remove from the heat and fluff with a fork (discard the herb bundle). Season with salt if necessary, and transfer to a warm serving bowl.

RICE In the Low Country of the Carolinas and Georgia, no lunch or dinner is complete without a pilaf or mound of simply steamed rice. I've witnessed some folks get downright angry when faced with a buffet minus the rice. This passion is rooted in the late eighteenth century, when rice was the cash crop of the region.

Southwestern Louisiana and southeastern Arkansas are now our major rice-growing areas. The grain is the bedrock of these regions' cuisines—jambalayas and gumbos and other spicy meat, seafood, and vegetable stews and, in the Low Country, pirlaus and traditional rice stews made with prized local Carolina Gold rice.

Leftover rice is great too. I've come to love *arancini,* the Sicilian snack created by shaping leftover risotto or cooked Arborio rice into balls, stuffing each one with a tiny cube of mozzarella or Fontina, dipping them in egg and bread crumbs, then frying until a golden crust forms over a molten center.

BUTTER BEAN AND MINT PILAF
Serves 4 to 6

When rice and tiny baby butter beans are combined with a little mirepoix, savory broth, and lots of fresh mint, these two humble ingredients make a vegetable dish that's a standout. This is especially terrific with the Pistachio-Crusted Lamb Loin (page 174).

1¾ cups Chicken Stock (page 241)
3 tablespoons unsalted butter
1 small onion, finely diced
1 carrot, peeled and finely diced
1 celery stalk, finely diced
2 thyme sprigs
1 mint sprig
1 bay leaf
1 cup basmati rice
½ cup fresh or frozen shell beans, like small butter beans
   or favas, cooked in boiling salted water until tender
   (see Note, page 59) and drained, cooking liquid reserved
½ cup mint leaves
Kosher salt and freshly ground black pepper
Mint Oil (page 250) for drizzling (optional)

Bring the stock to a simmer in a saucepan over medium-high heat.

Meanwhile, melt 2 tablespoons of the butter in a large sauté pan over medium heat. Add the onion, carrot, and celery and sauté for 3 to 4 minutes, until slightly softened. Add the herbs and rice and stir to coat the rice with the melted butter.

Pour the simmering stock into the rice and stir. Cover, reduce the heat to low, and cook until the rice is tender, 16 to 18 minutes. Transfer the pilaf to a large bowl and cover loosely to keep warm.

Warm the beans in a small saucepan with the remaining 1 tablespoon butter and a little of the reserved cooking broth—they should be rather moist. Meanwhile, chop the mint (if you chop it ahead, it will oxidize and darken). Add the mint to the beans, taste, and season with salt and pepper.

Fold the beans into the cooked rice and serve, drizzled with a little mint oil, if desired.

RISI BISI

Serves 4 to 6

This is a Venetian classic made with their local rice and sweet green peas. At Bottega, we use basmati, a long-grain rice, as opposed to the traditional short-grain Arborio, because it is so aromatic. And when fresh peas aren't in season, we turn to frozen peas, which are often sweeter than fresh because their natural sugars haven't turned to starch.

2 tablespoons unsalted butter

1 yellow onion, quartered and thinly sliced

1 cup basmati rice

1¾ cups Chicken Stock (page 00) or water

1 thyme sprig

1 bay leaf

2 large bulb onions or leeks, thinly sliced,
     or 1 medium onion, thinly sliced

1 cup fresh or frozen sweet peas

1 heaping tablespoon chopped mint

1 tablespoon thinly sliced chives

¼ cup freshly grated Parmigiano-Reggiano

Melt 1 tablespoon of the butter in a medium saucepan over medium heat. Add the onion and cook until softened, about 10 minutes. Add the basmati, stock or water, thyme, and bay leaf and bring to a simmer. Cover the pan tightly and cook for 15 to 18 minutes, until the rice is tender and all the liquid is absorbed. Transfer to a warm serving bowl and cover to keep warm.

Melt the remaining tablespoon of butter in a medium sauté pan over low heat and sauté the bulb onions or leeks until soft, 6 to 8 minutes.

Meanwhile, blanch the peas in a small saucepan of generously salted boiling water for 1 to 2 minutes, until tender; drain the peas, reserving ¼ cup of the cooking liquid.

Add the peas, sautéed onions or leeks, chopped mint, chives, and grated Parmesan to the rice and toss very gently with two forks until just combined, adding some of the reserved cooking liquid as needed to loosen the mixture. Serve immediately.

FARRO WITH BUTTER BEANS

Serves 4 to 6

Along with quinoa, barley, and hominy, farro is one of those grains that we are rediscovering and including on our menus. This ancient grain fueled the Roman Army, and it's one of the most protein-rich plants out there. Its nutty flavor and resilient texture make it an excellent alternative to rice or pasta.

1½ cups farro

1½ cups Chicken Stock (page 241) or water

1 tablespoon unsalted butter

Kosher salt and freshly ground black pepper

1 bay leaf

1 thyme sprig

1 cup fresh or frozen butter beans

A few thyme sprigs, a small celery stalk, and a bay leaf,
     tied together with kitchen twine to form a bouquet
     garni

Extra virgin olive oil for drizzling

Rinse the farro in a strainer under cold running water for a minute to remove any bitter residue. Pour the chicken stock or water into a medium saucepan, add the butter, salt and pepper to taste, bay leaf, and thyme sprig, and bring to a boil over high heat. Add the farro, reduce the heat to a simmer, and cook for 20 minutes, until the farro is tender and most of the liquid has been absorbed.

While the farro simmers, cook the butter beans with the bouquet garni, in a saucepan of generously seasoned boiling water until tender, 20 to 25 minutes. Drain the beans, reserving ¼ cup of the cooking liquid.

Gently fold the beans into the cooked farro and moisten with some of the reserved bean broth. Season with salt and pepper to taste, and finish with a drizzle of extra virgin olive oil.

VARIATION FARRO, RISOTTO-STYLE: Begin by sautéeing a chopped onion in a few tablespoons of olive oil in a saucepan, then add the farro and cook for a few minutes. Add the chicken stock or water and herbs and cook until tender, about 30 minutes. Fold in the butter beans.

CREAMY POLENTA
Serves 6 to 8

Polenta is a hearty side dish, a perfect stand-in for the more usual starches. It's critical to season this creamy version assertively in order to balance the richness of the butter and Parmigiano-Reggiano.

Both yellow and white corn are used for polenta—the white is preferred in the Veneto when the polenta accompanies seafood, but otherwise they're used interchangeably. The white grain yields a slightly more delicate polenta. Our polenta comes from McEwen & Sons in Wilsonville, Alabama or Anson Mills in Columbia, South Carolina (see Sources, page 260).

8 cups spring water

2 teaspoons kosher salt

2 cups polenta

¼ cup heavy cream (optional)

½ cup freshly grated Parmigiano-Reggiano or grana padano

8 tablespoons (1 stick) unsalted butter, cut into pieces

Freshly ground black pepper to taste

Tabasco sauce or Cholula to taste (optional)

Bring the water to a boil in a large pot or heavy saucepan over high heat. Add the salt and reduce the heat to medium. Slowly pour in the polenta, whisking constantly. Turn the heat to medium-low and continue to cook, stirring with a wooden spoon, for 30 to 40 minutes, until the polenta has thickened and pulls away from the sides of the pot but is still pourable.

Remove the pot from the heat and whisk in the cream, if using, the cheese, butter, pepper, and pepper sauce, if desired. Taste and adjust the seasonings to your liking. Serve hot.

VARIATION FIRM POLENTA: Pour the just-cooked polenta onto a baking sheet, spreading it with a rubber spatula to an even 1-inch thickness. Let cool, then place the pan in the refrigerator to chill. When the polenta is cold and firm, cut it into squares, rectangles, circles, or other shapes. Brush the cutouts with butter or olive oil and broil or grill to serve as a rustic accompaniment. When we are making polenta for grilling or broiling, we usually omit the butter.

GRITS AND POLENTA It's odd that over the last twenty years, polenta's star has risen on the menus of the choicest restaurants in Manhattan, Paris, London, and Tokyo, yet the South's humble grits are still underappreciated. Don't get me wrong—there's been a boom in the popularity of organic stone-ground grits, but they do not have the cachet of their Italian cousin. Perhaps because in contrast to coarse Italian polenta, from the 1960s on, most American grits were the insipid processed, "quick-cooking" variety—not the stone-ground grits of yore.

Polenta is dried ground corn that has been passed through a slightly smaller screen than is used for traditional grits, yielding a finer grain. As a result, it cooks up a little smoother than grits (not as "gritty"), but this is the only difference, and it's quite subtle. In Birmingham, we liberally butter and add Parmesan to our grits, just as we do when we prepare polenta, and the result is almost identical.

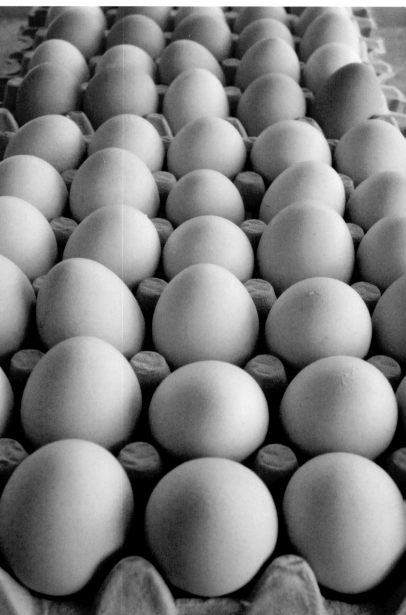

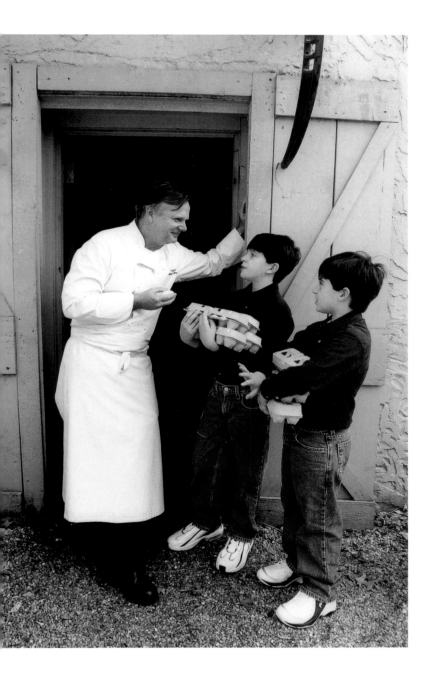

mcewen & sons—a family affair from farm to table

Our dear friends and one of our favorite purveyors, the McEwen family, bring us both eggs and the incomparable stone-ground organic white and yellow corn grits and polenta that are mainstays on our menu. The McEwen sons, thirteen-year-old Frank Jr. and twelve-year-old Luke, keep us supplied with all-natural free-range farm eggs. Their granddad, Ralph, tends some three hundred birds, and he swears that allowing the chickens to roam across the horse paddocks decimates the fly population, creating a healthier farm environment and yielding tastier eggs. The boys work hard gathering the mass of multihued eggs that their prolific hens produce. The eggs are sold to locals at the family's Saturday morning farm stand at the Pepper Place Farmers' Market near downtown Birmingham. These industrious young boys put half of all their earnings in a college fund. Their dad, Frank Sr., gives them a good deal on the price of chicken feed—it's free!

Frank Sr. followed in his father's footsteps and runs Coosa Valley Milling & Hardware in the agricultural community of Wilsonville, just south of Birmingham. A number of years ago his lovely wife, Helen, pressured him into expanding their grist mill's offerings to include organic grains, making it possible for us to get most of our grits and polenta, in addition to those rich farm eggs. The "seed and feed" store also sells young chicks, guinea hens, and ducks, and Frank has provided all of the birds (about forty so far) for my farm just a few miles down the road. At Coosa Valley Milling, you can buy just about anything a working farm might require—from fencing and gate hardware to farmers' hats and even custom-blended livestock feed. It's the bustling place to be most mornings down in the idyllic countryside south of Birmingham and, even if you're not so close, it's well worth the trip.

Tiramisù

Panna Cotta

Lemon Semifreddo

Gelato Conflict

Strawberry Ice Cream Parfait

Warm Cream Cheese Tart with Cinnamon and Almonds

Aurora Tart

Almond Dacquoise

In Lieu of Dessert

Apple Crostata

Zabaglione Meringue Cake

Polenta Pound Cake

Zabaglione with Summer Fruit and Vanilla Ice Cream

Coconut Pecan Cake

Biscotti

OVERLEAF LEFT: *Zabaglione Meringue Cake (a Chef Stitt favorite)*
(page 229); OPPOSITE: *Dol (Bottega's adored pastry chef) with the Almond*
Dacquoise (page 224)

TIRAMISÙ

Serves 8 to 10

Slices of polenta pound cake take the place of delicate lady-fingers in Bottega's version of this Italian classic. The result is decidedly rustic, and the cake holds up well to the bold, rich espresso. Make this the day before you plan to serve it to allow the flavors to meld. Substitute store-bought pound cake slices or more classic ladyfingers if you like.

9 large eggs, separated
2½ cups sugar
2 cups (two 250-gram containers) mascarpone,
    at room temperature
½ Polenta Pound Cake (page 230), cut into ½-inch-thick
    slices
2 shots (½ cup) espresso
1 cup strong black coffee
½ cup (about 1½ ounces) shaved bittersweet chocolate

Beat the egg yolks in a mixing bowl with a whisk to break them up. Add the sugar and whisk until thick and creamy. Fold in the mascarpone just until incorporated.

Whisk the egg whites in a separate bowl until they form soft peaks. Fold the egg whites into the mascarpone mixture.

Arrange a single layer of pound cake slices in the bottom of a 13-by-9-inch baking dish. Combine the espresso and coffee in a small bowl, and ladle or pour half the liquid over the cake slices to moisten. Spread a layer of half the mascarpone custard on top of the cake. Top with an even layer of half the chocolate shavings. Follow with another layer of pound cake and moisten with the remaining espresso mixture. Top with another layer of custard and a final layer of chocolate shavings. Cover and chill overnight to allow the flavors to come together before serving. (This dessert keeps well for 4 or 5 days in the refrigerator.)

To Drink: Torcolato (Maculan)

PANNA COTTA

Serves 8

Not long ago, crème brulée or crème caramel was the requisite dessert offering on American restaurant menus. Now many chefs and diners realize the delicate beauty of subtly flavored panna cotta, at once lighter than custard but every bit as satisfyingly creamy and jiggly. This is our basic panna cotta, a mainstay, but we've also served versions flavored with grappa, calvados, lemon verbena, and even scented geranium.

2 cups whole milk
2 envelopes unflavored gelatin
4 cups heavy cream
1 cup sugar
Grated zest of 1 lemon (see Note)
1 cinnamon stick
Raspberries, blueberries, or strawberries for garnish
    (optional)
Biscotti (page 233) or other crisp cookies

Pour the milk into a bowl and sprinkle the gelatin over the surface. Let stand for 5 minutes, or until the gelatin has softened.

Combine the cream, sugar, lemon zest, and cinnamon stick in a large heavy saucepan and bring to a simmer. Remove the pan from the heat, cover, and let stand for 5 minutes to infuse the cream with the lemon and cinnamon, then strain into a medium bowl.

Stir the gelatin mixture into the infused cream until incorporated. Divide the mixture among eight 6-ounce ramekins, then transfer them to a baking sheet. Place the pan in the refrigerator and let chill and set overnight.

To serve, run a knife around the sides of each ramekin, place into a shallow pan of warm water for a few seconds to loosen the panna cotta, and then invert a plate over the ramekin and shake to release the pudding from the mold. Garnish with berries, if desired, and a few cookies.

To Drink: Vin Santo or Moscato d'Asti (Marcarini)

LEMON SEMIFREDDO

Serves 8

This frozen layered terrine is an ideal dessert to make ahead and so easy to pull out, slice, and serve when an elegant finish is called for. Keep it in mind when the weather turns warm. Wrapped in plastic, it holds well for 2 weeks in the freezer.

The lemon zest garnish must be made at least 1 day ahead. At Bottega, we serve the semifreddo on top of a basic génoise sponge (as pictured opposite).

FOR THE CANDIED LEMON ZEST
4 lemons, scrubbed
2 cups sugar
1 cup cold water

FOR THE LEMON CURD
1 cup fresh lemon juice (you can use the lemons
    you zested; you'll need a couple more)
2 cups sugar
2 large eggs
8 large egg yolks
½ pound (2 sticks) unsalted butter, cut into pieces

2½ cups chilled heavy cream
Juice of 1 lemon

To prepare the candied zest, remove the zest from the lemons with a zester, making sure not to remove any of the bitter white pith. Place the zest in a small bowl, cover with boiling water, and let stand for 30 minutes. Drain.

Bring the sugar and cold water to a boil in a small saucepan over medium-high heat, stirring to dissolve the sugar. Add the drained zest, reduce the heat to medium-low, and cook for 10 minutes. Transfer the zest and syrup to a bowl, cover, and let stand overnight.

The next day, transfer the zest and syrup to an airtight container. (The zest can be stored in the refrigerator for up to 2 weeks.)

To make the lemon curd, prepare an ice bath and set aside. Whisk together the lemon juice, sugar, eggs, egg yolks, and butter in a large heavy saucepan and cook over medium heat, whisking constantly (do not walk away), until it begins to boil and becomes thick and puddinglike, 10 to 15 minutes.

Strain the curd through a fine-mesh strainer into a bowl, and set the bowl in the ice bath. Stir the curd periodically until it is cool, then remove the bowl from the ice bath and place a sheet of plastic wrap directly on the surface of the lemon curd. Refrigerate for at least 1 hour. (The curd can be refrigerated for up to 3 days.)

Whip 1½ cups of the chilled heavy cream in a large mixing bowl with a wire whisk or electric mixer until soft peaks form. Remove the chilled lemon curd from the refrigerator, and set aside ½ cup for the sauce. Gently fold the remaining lemon curd into the whipped cream until well combined. Refrigerate the reserved lemon curd. (It can be refrigerated, tightly covered, for up to 1 week.)

Arrange eight 3-inch ring molds or 6-ounce ramekins on a parchment-lined baking sheet. Spoon the lemon mousse into the molds, filling each with about ¾ cup. Cover and transfer to the freezer to firm up for at least 4 hours. (The mousse can be frozen for up to 1 week.)

Drain the candied lemon zest, reserving the syrup for the sauce, and set the zest aside on a plate or sheet of parchment. Whisk ⅓ cup of the lemon syrup with the remaining ½ cup lemon curd and the lemon juice in a small bowl; set the sauce aside.

To serve, remove the ring molds or ramekins from the freezer and let them warm up for 4 to 5 minutes. (If using ramekins, you can dip each one briefly in hot water to release the semifreddo.)

Meanwhile, whisk the remaining 1 cup chilled cream in a medium bowl until soft peaks form. Unmold the mousse onto individual dessert plates. Spoon the lemon sauce around the mousse, top with the whipped cream, and finish with a garnish of candied lemon zest.

To Drink: Moscato d'Asti (Marcarini)

gelato conflict

When we were students, my brother and I traveled through Italy, and we spent several days in Florence, where a particular gelato stand was one of my favorite indulgences. The two of us didn't have many fights on our journey, so it is somewhat surprising that our biggest come-apart would occur over gelato, or ice cream.

I must admit that even in my youth I had a knack for tracking down fascinating places for food and drink. Thus, when we came across a little gelateria off the beaten path, I knew we had discovered a sweet-tooth's mecca: the line that had formed outside the place, filled with visitors and locals alike, young and old, snaked around the corner. I studied everyone's cones and cups with the concentration of an archaeologist examining ancient ruins. David was getting a little tired of me at this point, but I wouldn't believe that he was oblivious to the magnitude of our find. And although I couldn't possibly try every flavor, I simply would not leave without tasting as many as I could. And so, cup after cup, tangerine and melon, pistachio and hazelnut, I tasted and tasted. Eventually my brother could no longer endure my obsession, and he left me there, standing on the curb with just one more *coppa* of the best ice cream I had ever tasted.

STRAWBERRY ICE CREAM PARFAIT

Serves 4

Timeless and simple: lush strawberries three ways, layered in tall glasses soda-fountain-style. Make the strawberry sauce only when local strawberries are at their sweet prime in springtime, and then make it often, because this dessert is a crowd pleaser.

FOR THE STRAWBERRY SAUCE

1 pint strawberries, stemmed
¼ cup sugar, or to taste
Juice of ½ lemon, or to taste

1½ cups strawberries, stemmed and sliced
2 to 3 tablespoons sugar
2 pints best-quality strawberry ice cream
¼ cup heavy cream, lightly whipped
Mint sprigs for garnish (optional)

To make the sauce, combine all the ingredients in a blender and blend for 1 minute, or until very smooth. Taste and adjust the sugar or lemon juice to sweeten or brighten. (The sauce can be refrigerated, tightly covered, for up to 3 days.)

Toss the sliced strawberries with the sugar; let macerate briefly to bring out the juices.

Place a scoop of ice cream in the bottom of each of four parfait, pilsner, or wineglasses and top with 2 tablespoons of the strawberry sauce and a heaping tablespoon of the strawberries. Repeat the layering (reserve any extra sauce for another dessert). Place a spoonful of whipped cream on top of each parfait, garnish with a sprig of mint, if desired, and serve.

WARM CREAM CHEESE TART WITH CINNAMON AND ALMONDS

Serves 10 to 12

Our pastry chef, Dol, and I often shake our heads about this dessert—how can anything so simple and easy be so good? This tart has just the right balance of buttery crust, creamy filling, and sweet and spicy topping, with a bit of almond crunch. Even when it appears in a lineup of much fancier, more complex, and more exotic desserts, it always stands out.

FOR THE FILLING

8 ounces cream cheese, softened
8 tablespoons (1 stick) unsalted butter, softened
⅓ cup sugar
2 large eggs
2 teaspoons vanilla extract

1 baked Sweet Pastry Tart Shell (page 243), cooled

FOR THE GLAZE

½ cup confectioners' sugar
¼ teaspoon ground cinnamon
2 tablespoons hot water

1 cup sliced almonds
Whipped cream (optional)

Preheat the oven to 350°F.

To make the filling, combine the cream cheese, butter, and sugar in a food processor and process until light and creamy. Add the eggs and vanilla extract and process until smooth. Spread the filling evenly in the prepared tart shell.

Bake for 20 to 25 minutes, until the center is set and the edges are light golden. Remove the pan from the oven and allow the tart to stand for 2 to 3 minutes, while you prepare the glaze.

Whisk the confectioners' sugar, cinnamon, and hot water together in a small bowl until smooth.

Spread the glaze over the top of the tart. Garnish the top with the sliced almonds. Serve warm, with whipped cream, if you like.

To Drink: Moscato d'Asti (Marcarini)

AURORA TART

Serves 10

Even my grown-up willpower is no match for this incredible caramel tart topped with praline-flecked whipped cream. You have to cook the caramel long enough so that it becomes dark and flavorful, but pay close attention—go too dark, and it becomes bitter.

FOR THE CARAMEL CUSTARD FILLING

3 cups heavy cream

1¾ cups sugar

3 tablespoons unsalted butter, cut into cubes

1 large egg

4 large egg yolks

1 baked Basic Tart Shell (page 243), cooled

FOR THE CHOCOLATE GLAZE

1 ounce bittersweet chocolate, chopped

2 tablespoons heavy cream

1 teaspoon vanilla extract

FOR THE PRALINE CREAM

2 tablespoons unsalted butter for the pan
   (unless using a silicone pan liner), softened

1 cup sugar

½ cup almonds or pecans, lightly toasted (see page 255)

1 cup heavy cream

Preheat the oven to 300°F.

To make the caramel custard, bring the heavy cream to a boil in a large saucepan over medium-high heat, then reduce the heat to low and keep the cream warm while you caramelize the sugar.

Put the sugar in a 2-quart saucepan and cook it over medium-high heat, stirring continuously, until it dissolves and the caramel syrup turns dark amber, 8 minutes. Remove from the heat and slowly whisk in the warm cream to combine—be careful, the mixture will bubble up. If it seizes and hardens, stir it over low heat to liquefy the lumps of caramel, then remove from the heat. Stir in the butter, and let the caramel cool for about 5 minutes so that it will not cook the eggs when added to them.

Whisk together the egg and egg yolks in a heatproof bowl. Slowly at first, then in a steady stream, add the warm caramel to the eggs, whisking constantly until incorporated. Strain the custard through a fine-mesh sieve, then pour it into the prebaked crust in the springform pan.

Bake the tart, rotating the pan occasionally, for 20 to 25 minutes, until the filling is just set—it should still jiggle slightly in the center when the pan is shaken. Transfer the pan to a rack to cool to room temperature, then transfer it to the refrigerator to chill for at least 2 hours, or overnight.

To make the chocolate glaze, melt the chocolate with the cream in the top of a double boiler over barely simmering water. Add the vanilla and stir to blend.

Spread the warm glaze over the chilled custard in a thin layer, then chill the tart again for at least 1 hour.

To make the praline cream, line a 12-by-17-inch jelly-roll pan or baking sheet with parchment paper and grease with the butter, or line it with a silicone liner.

Put the sugar in a small heavy saucepan and cook over medium-high heat, stirring with a wooden spoon, until it dissolves and the caramel turns light amber, about 6 minutes. Add the nuts and continue stirring over the heat, being very watchful, just until the sugar syrup turns dark amber, 1 minute more. Carefully pour the hot praline onto the lined pan, spreading it evening into a thin layer. Let it cool completely.

Break the praline into pieces and grind into a coarse powder in a food processor. (The praline powder can be made ahead and stored in a jar for several weeks at room temperature or frozen in an airtight container for 1 to 2 months.)

Whip the cream in a medium bowl until stiff peaks form. Fold in ½ cup of the praline powder.

Pipe or spread the praline cream over the chilled tart. Sprinkle the remaining praline powder over the top, and refrigerate the tart for at least 8 hours, or overnight. (The tart can be refrigerated for up to 2 days.) Serve chilled.

ALMOND DACQUOISE

Serves 15 • Pictured on page 213

People go crazy over this sweet, crunchy almond extravagance. There are quite a few steps involved, but much of the work can be done in stages: Both the buttercream and the baked meringue can be made up to a week in advance. And you can bake the génoise a day before you're planning to assemble the dessert. The finished cake is worth the effort—very dramatic and, quite possibly, one of the best desserts ever! It's even better the second and third day after it's made, and it will keep for several days in the freezer.

The cake is baked in a half sheet pan, sometimes called a jelly-roll pan; it measures 17 by 12 inches and is 1 inch deep. We build the cake in long narrow loaf pans (15 by 5 by 4 inches deep); a Pullman loaf pan or terrine mold works well.

FOR THE GÉNOISE

Nonstick cooking spray for the pan

2¾ cups cake flour

1½ cups granulated sugar

1 tablespoon plus ¾ teaspoon baking powder

¾ teaspoon salt

12 tablespoons (1½ sticks) unsalted butter,
    cut into pieces, softened

¾ cup whole or low-fat milk, at room temperature

1½ teaspoons vanilla extract

4 large eggs, at room temperature

FOR THE ALMOND BUTTERCREAM

¾ cup water

2¼ cups sugar

1 tablespoon corn syrup

2 large eggs

2 large egg whites

1¼ pounds (5 sticks) unsalted butter,
    cut into pieces, softened

Pinch of salt

1 tablespoon amaretto

FOR THE ALMOND MERINGUE

10 ounces (3 cups) sliced almonds, toasted
    (see page 255)

1 cup sugar

2 tablespoons all-purpose flour

7 large egg whites

Pinch of salt

FOR THE AMARETTO SYRUP

½ cup sugar

⅓ cup water

2 tablespoons amaretto

1½ cups sliced almonds, toasted (see page 255)

To make the génoise, position a rack in the center of the oven and preheat the oven to 350°F. Line a 17-by-12-inch baking sheet with parchment and lightly coat the paper with cooking spray.

Sift the cake flour, sugar, baking powder, and salt into the bowl of a stand mixer fitted with the paddle attachment. Mix on low speed until the ingredients are well combined. Add the softened butter and mix on low speed for 20 to 30 seconds to incorporate the butter into the dry ingredients. The mixture should look a little lumpy, with the largest lumps being about the size of a hazelnut. Add the milk and vanilla extract. Mix on medium speed for 1 minute to thoroughly blend the ingredients and lighten the batter. Scrape down the sides of the bowl with a spatula. Add the eggs one at a time, mixing on medium speed for about 15 seconds after each addition. Scrape down the bowl after the second egg, and then again at the end.

Use an offset spatula or the back of a spoon to spread the batter evenly in the prepared pan. Bake for 12 to 15 minutes, until it is golden brown and the top feels firm but springs back a little when pressed lightly with a finger. A skewer inserted into the center of the cake should come out clean. Put the pan on a rack, run a table knife around the edges of the cake to release it, and let it cool in the pan for 30 minutes.

Invert the cake onto the rack, lift off the pan, peel off the parchment, and let the cake cool completely. (The cake can be baked up to a day ahead. Wrap it tightly in plastic once cool and store at room temperature.)

To make the buttercream, combine the water, sugar, and corn syrup in a medium heavy saucepan and bring to a boil over medium heat, stirring to dissolve the sugar. Attach a candy thermometer to the side of the pan and cook until the syrup reaches 240°F.

Meanwhile, in the bowl of an electric mixer fitted with the whisk attachment, beat the eggs and egg whites at high speed until tripled in volume. While beating, gradually add the hot syrup, then continue beating until the mixture is cool—this will take approximately 15 minutes. When the bowl is cool to the touch, begin adding the butter bit by bit, beating until smooth, then add the salt and amaretto and mix until thoroughly combined. (The buttercream can be made ahead and refrigerated for up to a week. Let stand at room temperature to soften a bit before proceeding.)

To make the almond meringue, preheat the oven to 200°F.

Pulse the almonds with ⅔ cup of the sugar and the flour until finely ground in a food processor.

In the bowl of an electric mixer fitted with the whisk attachment, beat the egg whites and salt on high speed until just foamy, then gradually add the remaining ⅓ cup sugar and whisk until you have stiff peaks. Fold in the nut mixture.

You will be assembling the cake in a 15-by-5-inch loaf pan that is 4 inches deep. Place the pan on a sheet of parchment paper and trace the shape of the bottom of the pan onto the paper, then repeat, to use as guides for piping out the 2 layers of meringue. Line a baking sheet with the parchment.

Spoon the meringue mixture into a pastry bag without a tip and pipe a ½-inch-thick layer of meringue inside each template. Transfer the pan to the oven and bake for 4 hours to dry out the meringues. Transfer the pan to a rack and let the meringues cool. (You can wrap the meringues tightly in plastic and freeze in large freezer bags for up to 1 week. There is no need to thaw the meringues before layering in the finished dessert.)

To prepare the amaretto syrup, combine the sugar and water in a small saucepan and heat over medium heat, stirring, until the sugar dissolves. Let cool, then add the amaretto.

To assemble the cake, cut 2 rectangles from the génoise that will fit inside your loaf pan (see headnote). Split one of the layers horizontally in half to make 2 layers. Place the unsplit layer of cake in the bottom of the ungreased pan and brush it with 2 tablespoons of the amaretto syrup, then spread 1 cup of the buttercream on top. Sprinkle with toasted almonds. Place a meringue layer on top, then repeat with a layer of cake, syrup, almonds, another layer of buttercream, and the remaining layer of meringue. Finish with a layer of cake. Cover the pan with plastic wrap and freeze the cake for at least 1 hour to firm up before unmolding. Cover the remaining buttercream and refrigerate; let stand briefly at room temperature to soften before finishing the cake.

Run a thin knife around the sides of the cake to release it, and unmold it onto a cake plate or cardboard cake rectangle. Cover the top and sides with the remaining buttercream. Garnish with the toasted almonds. (The cake can be kept for a few days in the freezer.) When ready to serve, let the cake stand at room temperature for about 10 minutes, then cut into ¾-inch slices.

IN LIEU OF DESSERT Fruit and cheese are a wonderful alternative. Instead of offering a plate of many different Italian cheeses, I have gotten into the habit of choosing just one type—a wedge of Gorgonzola *piccante,* say, served with sliced peaches, a few leaves of arugula *selvetica,* and a drizzle of Smoky Mountain sourwood honey. This is a fabulous and simple way to end a meal and an opportunity to try a rare Picolit sweet wine or to just continue with a big red like Amarone or Barbaresco.

APPLE CROSTATA

Serves 6

A crostata is a rustic, free-form pastry made with a buttery, flaky crust surrounding a flavorful fruit filling. It can be filled in as many ways as a savory crostini might be topped. We make numerous versions—peach, blueberry, strawberry, raspberry, and pear, but it's our apple and almond filling that I like best.

You can prepare the dough well in advance and refrigerate or even freeze it with no loss in quality. Just remember that it's crucial to keep it thoroughly chilled right up until baking time to ensure a flaky crust. This recipe makes twice as much frangipane as you will need, but it also freezes well. Use it later for another crostata—or perhaps a pear tart.

FOR THE CRUST
1 cup all-purpose flour
2 teaspoons sugar
¼ teaspoon salt
6 tablespoons unsalted butter, cut into 1-inch cubes
   and chilled
3 to 4 tablespoons ice water

FOR THE FRANGIPANE
⅔ cup sugar
1 cup slivered almonds
Tiny pinch of salt
9 tablespoons (1 stick plus 1 tablespoon) unsalted
   butter, softened
1 large egg
1 large egg yolk
1½ teaspoons all-purpose flour

4 Granny Smith apples, peeled, cored,
   and sliced into ½-inch-thick wedges
2 tablespoons unsalted butter, melted
3 tablespoons light brown sugar
Rum Crème Anglaise (optional; page 242)

To prepare the crust, combine the flour, sugar, and salt in the bowl of a mixer fitted with the paddle attachment. Add the chilled butter cubes and mix until the butter is partially broken up but still very chunky. Add 3 tablespoons ice water and mix until the dough just comes together. If needed, add additional ice water in very small increments.

Gather the dough together, shape it into a disk, and wrap in plastic. Chill for at least 30 minutes. (The dough can be refrigerated for up to 2 days or frozen for up to 2 months.)

While the dough chills, prepare the frangipane: Place ¼ cup of the sugar, the almonds, and salt in the bowl of a food processor and process until the almonds are finely ground, about 1 minute. Set aside.

Wipe out the bowl of the mixer, add the softened butter and the remaining sugar, and beat on high speed with the paddle attachment until well combined, about 1 minute. Add the pulverized almond mixture and mix on low speed until well combined. Add the egg and then the egg yolk, beating well after each addition. Continue beating the mixture on medium-high speed until light and fluffy, about 3 minutes. Mix in the flour until just combined. Set the frangipane aside.

Position a rack in the center of the oven and preheat the oven to 375°F.

Lightly flour your work surface, and roll the chilled dough out into a circle 15 inches in diameter. Transfer the dough to a baking sheet lined with parchment paper. (It's okay if the dough hangs over the edges for the moment.)

Spread half (1 cup) of the frangipane evenly over the dough, leaving a 2-inch border around the perimeter. (Freeze the remaining frangipane for up to 2 months to use later.) Arrange the apples in an even layer over the frangipane. Fold the border of the crust over toward the center of the circle, partially covering the apples.

Brush the crust with the melted butter. Sprinkle 2 tablespoons of the brown sugar over the crust, and the remaining tablespoon of sugar over the apples.

Bake the crostata for 45 minutes to 1 hour, until the apples are tender and the crust is golden brown. Slide the tart off the pan onto a wire rack, remove the parchment paper, and let cool before slicing into wedges. Serve with a ladle of the crème anglaise, if using.

To Drink: Vin Santo

ZABAGLIONE MERINGUE CAKE
Serves 8 to 10

A snowy mountain of meringue layered with a creamy filling bound with tender vanilla cakes. The cake is easier to slice and serve if made at least two to three days ahead, so the filling has a chance to firm up in the refrigerator.

FOR THE ZABAGLIONE FILLING
3 large egg yolks
½ cup sugar
3 tablespoons all-purpose flour
½ cup dry white wine
½ cup dry sherry
1½ cups heavy cream

FOR THE HOT MILK SPONGE CAKE
1 cup sifted cake flour
¼ teaspoon salt
4 large eggs
1 cup sugar
¼ cup plus 2 tablespoons milk
1 vanilla bean, split lengthwise

FOR THE MERINGUE
4 large egg whites, at room temperature
Juice of ½ lemon
1 teaspoon vanilla extract
1 cup sugar, plus 1 to 2 tablespoons for sprinkling

To make the zabaglione filling, whisk the egg yolks in the bowl of a stand mixer (or use a large bowl and a handheld mixer) for 1 minute. Add the sugar and beat until the mixture is pale yellow and thick. Add the flour 1 tablespoon at a time, beating thoroughly after each addition. Beat in the white wine and sherry.

Transfer the mixture to a saucepan and heat it over medium heat, stirring constantly, until it is just about to boil. Transfer the custard to a bowl and let it cool; give it a whisk from time to time to keep a skin from forming on the surface. Once cool, place a piece of plastic wrap directly on the surface of the custard and refrigerate for at least 2 hours, or up to 24 hours.

To make the cake, preheat the oven to 350°F. Grease and flour a 9-by-2-inch round cake pan. Line the bottom with parchment paper.

Sift the cake flour and salt together into a mixing bowl. Repeat two more times; set aside. Bring a medium saucepan of water to a gentle simmer. Meanwhile, in the bowl of a stand mixer fitted with the whisk attachment, whisk the eggs and sugar until pale and thick, about 3 minutes. Place the mixer bowl over the pan of gently simmering water and whisk until the sugar is dissolved and the mixture reaches 110°F on an instant-read thermometer, about 6 minutes.

Return the bowl to the stand mixer. Using the whisk attachment, beat the mixture on high until thickened and pale, about 6 minutes.

Meanwhile, heat the milk and split vanilla bean in a small saucepan over medium heat until hot but not boiling. Remove the pan from the heat and scrape the tiny seeds from the vanilla bean into the hot milk; discard the pod.

While beating, pour the hot infused milk into the egg mixture in a slow, steady stream, beating until incorporated. Fold in the sifted flour.

Pour the batter into the prepared cake pan. Bake for 30 minutes, or until a tester inserted into the center comes out clean and the cake springs back when lightly pressed in the middle. Transfer the pan to a wire rack to cool for 15 minutes.

Carefully invert the cake onto the rack, remove the parchment, and let cool completely. (The cake will be easier to cut into layers if you let it stand overnight, well wrapped, at room temperature before slicing. And it's best to assemble the cake 2 to 3 days ahead; keep refrigerated.)

When you are ready to assemble the cake, finish the filling: Whip the cream until stiff peaks form. Gently but thoroughly fold it into the zabaglione.

To assemble the cake, using a long serrated knife, slice the cake horizontally into 3 layers. Place a layer of cake onto a cookie sheet and spread half of the zabaglione filling over it. Top with a second layer of cake and, using a cutting board or cake pan, press gently on the cake to compress it a bit. It is okay if a little filling oozes out, you will use it to frost the sides of the cake. Spread all but ½ cup of the remaining filling over it, then top with the third layer. Again, gently compress. Using a spatula, spread the remaining filling evenly over the sides of the cake. Cover and refrigerate until ready to make the meringue.

(continued)

Preheat the broiler and adjust an oven rack so it is about 10 inches from the heat source. Alternatively, you can use a household propane torch (see below) to brown the meringue peaks.

Whip the egg whites in the bowl of a stand mixer (or use a large bowl and a handheld mixer) until they are frothy. Beat in the lemon juice and vanilla extract, then gradually add the 1 cup sugar and continue to beat the meringue until it is very thick and glossy and forms stiff peaks.

Spread a thick layer of the meringue over the top of the cake with an icing spatula. To form decorative peaks, gently press the spatula down on the meringue and lift it straight up. Sprinkle with the 2 tablespoons sugar.

Put the cake under the broiler to brown the peaks of the meringue a bit; this will take just a few minutes, so watch it carefully and remove the cake from the oven as soon as the meringue peaks begin to brown. Alternatively, fire up the propane torch and, holding it 10 to 12 inches from the surface of the cake, carefully brown the peaks of meringue. Slide the cake onto a cake plate and chill until serving time, up to 6 to 8 hours.

To Drink: Moscato d'Asti (Saracco)

POLENTA POUND CAKE
Serves 12

This cake is a component of our Tiramisù (page 215), but it's also wonderful served like any other pound cake—toasted, with a little butter and orange marmalade—for nibbling with a morning cappuccino. It's crucial to use the right size pan for this recipe—a 9½-inch round cake pan that is 3 inches deep.

- 2 cups all-purpose flour
- ½ teaspoon baking soda
- 6 large eggs, separated
- ½ pound (2 sticks) unsalted butter, softened
- 2 cups sugar
- 1 teaspoon finely grated lemon zest
- 1 cup yellow cornmeal, plus more for dusting the pan
- ¼ teaspoon vanilla extract
- 1 cup sour cream

Preheat the oven to 350°F. Grease a 9½-by-3-inch round cake pan, then dust with a little cornmeal. Set aside.

Sift the flour and baking soda together into a bowl. Set aside.

In the bowl of a stand mixer fitted with the whisk attachment, beat the egg whites until they form stiff peaks. Transfer to another bowl and wipe out the mixer bowl.

Add the butter, sugar, and lemon zest to the mixer bowl and beat at medium speed until light and fluffy, approximately 10 minutes. Add the egg yolks one at a time, beating until incorporated after each addition. Add the cornmeal and beat until incorporated, scraping down the sides of the bowl as necessary. Beat in the vanilla extract. Add the flour mixture in 3 batches, alternating with the sour cream, starting and ending with flour. Fold in the beaten egg whites. Pour the batter into the prepared cake pan.

Bake for 1½ hours, or until a skewer stuck into the center comes out clean. Cool on a rack for 15 minutes, then carefully remove the cake from the pan and cool completely on the rack.

To Drink: Vin Santo

ZABAGLIONE WITH SUMMER FRUIT AND VANILLA ICE CREAM

Serves 6

While exploring the upper Veneto, to the northwest of Venice, my wife and I ran into Primo Franco, a winemaker and friend, who insisted we dine with him under a tent at his favorite local restaurant. The patroness greeted Primo as if he were a long lost son; he proposed that she send out a sampling for us—three hours later the food was still being presented. All was incredible, the veal chops, the pasta, and yet, as full as we were, the dessert was the showstopper! A huge platter featured a (unlikely to my mind) concoction of zabaglione, ice cream, fresh peaches, strawberries, and raspberries. I love them all separately but would have never made the combination—it was so good! For an unequivocal dessert success, try this one. And the supreme graciousness of our hostess is not a bad attribute to emulate—her charm made everything taste all the better. Thanks Primo!

12 large egg yolks
¼ cup sugar
¾ cup white wine or prosecco
¾ cup dry Marsala

6 large scoops vanilla ice cream
2 large ripe yet firm peaches, peeled and sliced
1 cup blueberries
1 cup raspberries
1 cup strawberries, sliced
1 cup cherries, pitted (optional)
1 cup nectarines, sliced (optional)

In a large stainless steel bowl over a direct flame or (for a safer version) over a pan of simmering water, whisk the egg yolks with the sugar until they are foamy and well combined. Add the prosecco and Marsala over a medium heat and whip vigorously until the zabaglione thickens (this takes patience, determination, and muscle). The mixture will increase in volume and become warm, but do not let it boil.

Transfer the custard to a bowl and let it cool; give it a whisk from time to time to keep a skin from forming on the surface. Once cool, place a piece of plastic wrap directly on the surface of the custard and refrigerate for at least 2 hours, or up to 24 hours.

Place a large scoop of vanilla ice cream in the center of a shallow bowl and surround with the peaches, blueberries, raspberries, strawberries, and extra fruit if using. Ladle the zabaglione over all. Serve immediately.

COCONUT PECAN CAKE

Serves 12 to 14

Old-fashioned, sinfully rich, incredibly moist, and absolutely irresistible—there is nothing light and dainty about this cake. It's for indulgent occasions.

FOR THE CAKE

1 cup firmly packed sweetened shredded coconut

¾ cup pecan halves, toasted (see page 255)

2 cups sugar

2¼ cups all-purpose flour

1 tablespoon baking powder

¾ teaspoon salt

12 tablespoons (1½ sticks) unsalted butter, softened

¼ cup cream of coconut (such as Coco Lopez)

4 large eggs

1 teaspoon coconut extract

1 cup plus 2 tablespoons unsweetened coconut milk

FOR THE FILLING

2 large yolks, lightly beaten

¾ cup sweetened condensed milk

4 tablespoons unsalted butter

1 tablespoon cream of coconut

1 cup sweetened shredded coconut

1 cup Simple Syrup (page 251)

FOR THE ICING

1 cup heavy cream

¼ cup confectioners' sugar

1 teaspoon coconut extract

2 cups sweetened coconut, toasted (see Note)

To make the cake, preheat the oven to 350°F. Grease two 9-inch round cake pans and line the bottom of each with a circle of parchment paper. Grease the parchment paper, then dust with flour, tapping out any excess. Set the pans aside.

Finely grind the coconut in a food processor, then transfer it to a bowl. Add the pecans to the processor, along with 2 tablespoons of the sugar, and finely grind them. Set aside. Sift together the flour, baking powder, and salt into a large bowl. Stir in the ground coconut and pecans; set aside.

In the bowl of an electric mixer fitted with the paddle attachment (or use a large bowl and a handheld mixer), beat the butter, cream of coconut, and the remaining 1¾ cups plus 2 tablespoons sugar on high speed until light and fluffy, about 4 minutes. Beat in the eggs one at a time, beating well after each addition, then beat in the coconut extract. Add the flour mixture in 3 batches, alternating with the coconut milk, starting and ending with flour mixture.

Divide the batter between the prepared pans and smooth the top of each with a spatula. Bake until the cakes are golden and a tester comes out clean, 30 to 35 minutes. Let the cakes cool in the pan on a rack for 30 minutes. Run a knife around the edge of each cake, invert onto a wire rack, and remove the parchment. Let cool completely.

While the cakes are cooling, prepare the filling: Place the egg yolks in a small heatproof bowl. Combine the condensed milk, butter, and cream of coconut in a small saucepan and cook over medium-low heat for 3 to 4 minutes, stirring constantly, until hot. Whisk one-third of the hot milk mixture into the egg yolks. Transfer the egg mixture to the saucepan of milk and whisk constantly over medium-low heat until the consistency of pudding, about 4 minutes. Do not allow the custard to become too thick, or it will be difficult to spread on the cake.

Transfer the custard to a bowl and stir in the shredded coconut. Let cool completely. (The filling can be refrigerated in an airtight container for up to 3 days; let it stand at room temperature until it is soft enough to spread before assembling the cake.)

To assemble the cake, cut each cake horizontally in half. Build the layer cake in a cake pan: Place one layer in the bottom of a 9-inch cake pan. Moisten the top with some of the simple syrup. Spread ½ cup of the coconut filling in a thin, even layer with an offset spatula. Repeat to make 2 more layers of cake and filling, then place the last layer on top. Refrigerate the cake for about 1 hour.

To unmold, run a spatula around the edges of the chilled cake, invert a cake plate over the top, and flip the cake over onto the plate.

To make the icing, whip the cream with the confectioners' sugar and coconut extract until stiff peaks form. Spread the whipped cream on the top and sides of the cake and sprinkle with the toasted coconut. Refrigerate until ready to serve.

NOTE: To toast coconut, preheat the oven to 300°F. Spread out the coconut on a baking sheet and toast in the oven, shaking the pan every 5 minutes or so, until aromatic and golden brown, 10 to 15 minutes. Let cool completely.

To Drink: Bual or Malmsey Madeira

BISCOTTI

Makes about 2½ dozen.

Crunchy almond cookies with a hint of vanilla—these are dunkin' cookies par excellence. Dip them into a sweet dessert wine such as Vin Santo as the Tuscans do, or dunk them into a morning cappuccino as I do. My kids have been known to immerse them in glasses of ice-cold milk. These slightly eggy, not-too-sweet Bottega standards have been baked every week since we opened in 1988. As a variation, substitute pistachios or pecans for the almonds, or dip the twice-baked cookies in melted chocolate.

3¼ cups all-purpose flour, or as needed

2½ cups sugar

1 teaspoon baking powder

Pinch of salt

3 large eggs, at room temperature

2 large egg yolks, at room temperature

1 teaspoon vanilla extract

1⅔ cups raw almonds or pecans, toasted (see page 255) and roughly chopped

1 egg, beaten for egg wash

Preheat the oven to 350°F. Line a 12-by-17-inch baking sheet with parchment paper. Butter and lightly flour the parchment paper. Set aside.

Combine the dry ingredients in the bowl of a stand mixer fitted with the paddle attachment (or use a large bowl and a handheld mixer). Add the eggs, egg yolks, and vanilla, and beat on low speed until just incorporated. Transfer the dough to a floured work surface and knead until smooth. Work in the nuts thoroughly, sprinkling with additional flour as needed. Continue kneading for 4 to 5 minutes.

Form the dough into a 2½-by-15-inch log on the prepared baking sheet. Brush with the egg wash.

Bake for 40 to 45 minutes until golden and crunchy. Remove the pan from the oven and reduce the oven temperature to 325°F.

Cut the log into ½-inch-thick slices and lay them on their sides on the baking sheet. Return the pan to the oven and bake for another 15 minutes, or until very dry. Transfer the biscotti to a cooling rack to cool completely. Store in an airtight container.

BOTTEGA BASICS

INTEGRAL INGREDIENTS

Braised Artichokes

Oven-Roasted Tomatoes

Charred Red Onion

Wilted Greens

Bread Crumbs

Greens Are Good For You

Sautéed Mushrooms

Mushrooms

Chicken Stock

Béchamel Sauce

Rum Crème Anglaise

Basic Tart Shell

Sweet Pastry Tart Shell

EMBELLISHMENTS

White Wine Butter Sauce

Brown Butter

Homemade Mayonnaise

Aïoli

Horseradish Sauce

Marinara Sauce

Bottega Tartar Sauce

Romesco Sauce

Salsa Verde

Pesto

Parsley and Orange Zest Gremolata

Fig Relish for Fish

Tapenade

Mint Oil

Rosemary Sauce

Simple Syrup

OVERLEAF LEFT: *Braised Artichokes (page 238)*

BRAISED ARTICHOKES

Serves 4 • Pictured on page 234

We often serve braised artichokes at our restaurants, as a side or part of another dish (see Lamb Ragù with Artichokes, Oven-Roasted Tomatoes, and Basil, page 178). Braised in wine and olive oil with aromatic vegetables and herbs, these artichoke bottoms—or trimmed baby artichokes—emerge tender and succulent.

2 large or 8 baby artichokes, trimmed (see page 252)
1 celery stalk, thinly sliced on the diagonal
1 carrot, peeled and thinly sliced on the diagonal
1 garlic clove, smashed
1 mint sprig
1 large thyme sprig
1 bay leaf
½ cup dry white wine
½ cup water
⅓ cup olive oil
4 lemon slices
Kosher salt

Put the artichokes in a pan large enough to hold them in a single layer. Add the celery, carrot, garlic, mint, thyme, bay leaf, wine, water, olive oil, lemon, and salt to taste. Bring to a simmer, cover, and cook until tender, about 20 minutes for baby artichokes, 30 minutes for large artichoke bottoms. Drain and serve.

OVEN-ROASTED TOMATOES

Makes 20 tomato halves

Just a little concentration of tomato flavor goes a long way in many dishes. These simply roasted tomatoes are reminiscent of traditional Italian sun-dried tomatoes, but we rely on the convenience of our oven instead of a rooftop. Use on pizzas and crostini, and add to pasta dishes for robust tomato flavor.

10 plum tomatoes
2 tablespoons extra virgin olive oil
1 teaspoon sugar
1 teaspoon red wine vinegar
Kosher salt and freshly ground black pepper

Preheat the oven to 250°F. Line a baking sheet with parchment paper.

Halve the tomatoes lengthwise and place them in a large bowl. Season with the olive oil, sugar, vinegar, and salt and pepper to taste, then place cut side up on the baking sheet.

Roast for 2 hours, until the tomatoes are collapsed but not dried out and the flavor is slightly concentrated. Let cool, then refrigerate, tightly covered, until ready to use.

CHARRED RED ONION

Something wonderful happens when thick-sliced onion rings are given a dark char on the grill or in a cast-iron skillet. Sweetness overtakes their sharp bite and subtle burn marks add a flavorful smoky dimension. We toss these charred onions in salads, and put them on pizzas and in sandwiches. They are the stars of our Charred Onion Dip (page 23).

Olive oil
Red onions, sliced ½ to ¾ inch thick

Prepare a hot fire in a grill or heat a cast-iron grill pan over medium-high heat until hot.

Rub the grill grate or brush the grill pan with olive oil. Add the onion slices and cook, turning once, until charred and just tender, about 6 minutes per side. Transfer to a plate to cool.

WILTED GREENS

Makes about ½ cup

This is an easy way to wilt and flavor any variety of leafy greens. We fold them into pasta dishes, spread them on pizzas, and mound them in bowls before ladling in soups. We use the dried whole red chiles found in jars in the spice aisle of any supermarket; no soaking, seeding, or other handling required.

2 to 3 tablespoons extra virgin olive oil
1 garlic clove, crushed
1 dried red chile
2 cups coarsely chopped greens, such as escarole,
    mustard, or spinach, rinsed
Kosher salt and freshly ground black pepper
¼ lemon

Heat 2 tablespoons of the oil in a large sauté pan over medium-low heat. Add the garlic clove and cook until it is golden, about 3 minutes. Add the chile and toast for 20 seconds, or until aromatic. Add the still-damp greens and toss them over medium heat for 1 minute. Add about ¼ cup water if the pan seems dry, and continue tossing until the greens have just wilted. Season the greens with salt and pepper, a squeeze of lemon, and another tablespoon of olive oil, if desired.

GREENS ARE GOOD FOR YOU When the northwest wind blows, our local field greens—sturdy mustard, turnip, and beet greens; chard and collards; and upland cress—acquire an intensified flavor. During the cold days of late autumn and winter, we look forward to the slightly bitter, unique twang of these greens. When heaps of these bundled hearty leaves appear at the market, Southerners know the time has arrived to celebrate the glory of greens.

I take a special pride in our Southern greens. The mess of canned leaves served up by mediocre restaurants can't compete with a carefully selected bunch of greens harvested just after the first frost. Imagine collard greens sidling up to some sautéed onions, garlic, and hot chile with, oh yes, a little bit of the pig thrown in—a ham hock, a slice of belly, or a rasher of hickory-smoked bacon. You know you're living high on the hog when you're given a plate of such greens, along with a wedge of corn bread hot from the oven, and there's nothing left to do but dig in. Pass the pepper sauce, please!

BREAD CRUMBS

Makes about 2 cups

Forget the pulverized versions in a supermarket canister—perfect crumbs are not uniform in size. To get truly crunchy toppings or crisp crusts, you need a mixture of fine, medium, and coarse crumbs. Making them at home is best, and it's as easy as pulsing day-old bread in a food processor. The bread shouldn't be either too dry or too fresh and moist. Just leave leftover bread on the counter overnight, then whirl into crumbs the next day. Keep the crumbs in a zip-top bag in the freezer and pull out as needed. Make whenever leftover bread is on hand, and you'll always have a steady supply.

8 slices baguette or other crusty bread,
    preferably a day old (see Note)

Remove the crust from the bread and cut it into chunks. Pulse the bread in a food processor until you have an amalgam of fine, medium, and coarse crumbs ranging in size from that of a lentil to a juniper berry.

NOTE: If you do not have any day-old bread, remove the crusts from a baguette and cube the bread. Arrange the cubes in a single layer on a sheet pan and toast in a 300°F oven for 10 minutes. Remove and cool, then process to crumbs.

SAUTÉED MUSHROOMS

Makes about 1 cup

Plan and simple mushrooms are transformed with the addition of shallot and fresh thyme. Use these on pizza, in pasta dishes, with grilled meats, or as a crostini topper.

2 scant cups thick-sliced (⅓-inch) button mushrooms or cremini

1 tablespoon olive oil or unsalted butter

½ shallot, finely minced

1 large thyme sprig, leaves only

Kosher salt and freshly ground black pepper

Heat a sauté pan large enough to accommodate the mushrooms in more or less a single layer over medium-high heat. Add the oil or butter and heat until hot. Add the mushrooms and shallots and sauté for 3 minutes, or until they just begin to soften. Season with thyme and the salt and pepper and toss well. Remove from the heat. The mushrooms can be refrigerated, covered, for up to 1 day.

MUSHROOMS Button mushrooms, cremini, and portobellos (which are just "grown-up" cremini mushrooms) are underappreciated today. They give dishes unique texture and flavor that can be expanded upon now that the beautiful brown beech (honshimeji) are also readily available. Oyster, maitake, and shiitake are other varieties that are worth experimenting with in your kitchen.

It wasn't that long ago that plain old button mushrooms seemed rather exotic in the small towns of America. When my mother encouraged our local grocer, Bruno's, to stock mushrooms in the '60s, few customers had any interest in them. Not until I left to explore the food and cooking of Italy and France did I encounter the glories of truly wild mushrooms.

There is a cultlike fascination in Italy with the discovery and gathering of wild mushrooms, a pleasure in which I hope to indulge one day. Until then, I rely on our purveyors to bring us a variety of both wild and cultivated mushrooms. Porcini are highly prized in Italy, and foraging for wild mushrooms is like prospecting for gold. The frenzy begins in autumn as the weather turns cooler and rainy. Baskets in hand, people sneak into the woods to keep others from discovering the prime mushrooming spots. I encourage you to celebrate wild mushrooms such as morels, porcini, and exquisite golden chanterelles when in season—treat them reverentially and share them with those you love.

Wild mushrooms must be inspected carefully. Black trumpets need to be split and quickly rinsed (they always harbor some forest grit). Hedgehogs should be picked free of pine needles and given a quick rinse to remove excess loam—this is true for most wild mushrooms. A quick spray of cold water is much preferred to taking a gritty bite at the table. Cultivated mushrooms can be wiped clean with a damp towel. I like to trim about one-eighth inch off the stems just to freshen up button or cremini mushrooms. When sautéing these mushrooms, sliced or quartered, depending on size, be careful not to overcook. But some wild mushrooms, such as chanterelles, need to be sautéed until they give up their moisture, then cooked further until that moisture has evaporated. We use sautéed mushrooms on our pizzas, crostini, and in pasta dishes.

CHICKEN STOCK

Makes about 6 quarts

If you do buy commercially prepared chicken stock, choose a variety that is organic and low in sodium. When time allows, however, nothing beats homemade stock. You can freeze it in batches and pull out just what you need, plus you can adapt the recipe to your taste by changing the herbs or aromatics used.

A few tips to keep in mind when making homemade stock: Bones with some meat left on them will give the stock more flavor. All the pieces should be trimmed of skin and excess fat. Proper caramelization of the bones and vegetables concentrates color and flavor. And careful skimming and slow simmering will result in a clear, unclouded stock. You might try including some beef bones in a chicken broth to add depth of flavor.

4 pounds chicken bones (backs, wings, and/or necks), rinsed and excess fat removed

1 tablespoon canola or grapeseed oil

2 onions, quartered

5 carrots, peeled and cut into 2-inch pieces

3 celery stalks, cut into 2-inch pieces

1 cup mushroom stems (optional)

½ head unpeeled garlic (halve the head horizontally)

10 quarts cold water

A couple of thyme and parsley sprigs and 2 or 3 bay leaves, tied with kitchen string to form a bouquet garni

1 teaspoon kosher salt

A few black peppercorns

Preheat the oven to 400°F.

Place the chicken bones in a roasting pan, drizzle with the oil, and toss to coat (the oil helps the chicken brown). Roast for 15 to 20 minutes, until lightly colored.

Add the onions, carrots, celery, mushrooms, if using, and garlic and roast, turning the chicken and vegetables occasionally, until the bones are golden brown, about 30 minutes longer.

Transfer the bones and vegetables to a tall stockpot and add the cold water. Pour off any excess fat from the roasting pan, then add a splash of water, scrape up the browned bits from the bottom of the pan, and add this to the stockpot. Bring the stock just to a simmer over medium-high heat. Skim the fat that has risen to the surface, then reduce the heat to low and add the bouquet garni, salt, and peppercorns. Simmer gently for 2 to 3 hours (monitor the heat so that the stock does not boil), skimming from time to time and adding more water as necessary to keep the bones covered.

Strain the stock through a colander into a large container; let the bones and vegetables drain thoroughly before discarding them. Strain the stock again through a fine-mesh or a cheesecloth-lined strainer into a container. Set the container in an ice bath and let cool, stirring occasionally.

When it is cool, cover the stock and refrigerate. Once it has chilled, remove any fat from the surface. The stock will keep for 3 to 4 days in the refrigerator; if not ready to use it by then, bring it to a boil and simmer for 3 minutes, then refrigerate for up to 3 days. Or freeze in small batches for up to 2 to 3 months.

BÉCHAMEL SAUCE

Makes about 2 cups

This old-fashioned sauce is still essential for making the best lasagna and mac and cheese.

    2 cups whole milk
    ¼ cup chopped yellow onion
    1 bay leaf
    ½ teaspoon salt
    ¼ teaspoon freshly ground white pepper
    4 tablespoons unsalted butter
    ¼ cup all-purpose flour
    Pinch of freshly grated nutmeg
    Pinch of cayenne

Combine the milk, onion, bay leaf, salt, and pepper in a medium saucepan and bring to a simmer over medium-low heat. Continue to cook, stirring occasionally, until reduced by one-quarter, about 15 minutes. Strain the milk and set aside.

Melt the butter in a medium saucepan over medium heat. Whisk in the flour, reduce the heat to low, and cook, whisking constantly, for about 3 minutes, until the roux is bubbling. Vigorously whisk in the infused milk and cook, stirring often, for 20 to 25 minutes. Remove the heat and add the nutmeg and cayenne. Taste and adjust the seasoning with more salt and/or white pepper to suit your taste.

RUM CRÈME ANGLAISE

Makes 2 cups

Crème anglaise is the greatest all-purpose dessert sauce. It's perfect for enriching almost any dessert and is the foundation for countless others—including ice cream. In this recipe, we flavor the English pouring sauce with aromatic aged rum. Try to find artisanal rums of the Caribbean like Flor de Caña Centenario 21—it's super! Serve this with the Apple Crostata (page 226).

    1½ cups half-and-half
    4 large egg yolks
    ¼ cup sugar
    ¼ vanilla bean, split
    2 to 3 tablespoons dark rum, to taste

Bring the half-and-half to a boil in a medium saucepan.

Meanwhile, whisk the egg yolks and sugar in a medium bowl until smooth and pale yellow. Gradually add about ½ cup of the hot half-and-half to the egg yolks, whisking constantly, to temper them. Transfer the egg mixture to the saucepan and cook, stirring constantly, until the sauce coats the back of a spoon, 2 to 3 minutes; it should register 175°F on an instant-read thermometer.

Strain into a bowl and add the vanilla bean and rum. Let cool to room temperature, then refrigerate until chilled. The crème anglaise can be kept refrigerated for up to 3 days.

BASIC TART SHELL

Makes one 10½-inch tart shell

We use this for the Aurora Tart (page 223). It's sturdier than the sweet pastry at right, and it works better with the generous amount of caramel filling.

> 1¾ cups all purpose flour
> ⅓ cup sugar
> Pinch of salt
> 12 tablespoons (1½ sticks) unsalted butter,
>   cut into cubes and chilled
> 2 large egg yolks
> 1 tablespoon heavy cream
> ½ teaspoon vanilla extract

Combine the flour, sugar, and salt in a food processor and pulse to mix. Add the butter and pulse until the mixture resembles coarse cornmeal. Whisk together the yolks, cream, and vanilla in a small bowl, add to the butter mixture, and pulse until the dough comes together. Gather the dough into a ball, flatten into a disk, and wrap in plastic. Refrigerate for at least 45 minutes, or overnight.

Roll out the dough on a lightly floured surface into a 14-inch circle, turning the dough with each roll to prevent it from sticking. Carefully drape the dough over the rolling pin and ease into a 10½-inch springform pan, pressing it evenly over the bottom and up the sides. Chill the tart shell in the freezer for at least 1 hour, or overnight.

Preheat the oven to 375°F.

Line the tart shell with foil and weight with dried beans or pie weights. Bake until the pastry is set and cooked through, 20 to 30 minutes. Remove the foil and weights and bake for about 5 minutes longer, just to brown lightly. Cool on a rack before filling.

SWEET PASTRY TART SHELL

Makes two 10½- to 11-inch tart shells

This versatile dough is the base for our Warm Cream Cheese Tart with Cinnamon and Almonds (page 221).

> 2½ cups all-purpose flour
> Pinch of salt
> ½ pound (2 sticks) unsalted butter,
>   cut into cubes and chilled
> Scant 1 cup confectioners' sugar
> 3 large egg yolks

Combine the flour and salt in a food processor and pulse to mix. Add the butter and pulse until the mixture resembles coarse bread crumbs. Add the sugar and egg yolks and pulse again, just until the mixture comes together and pulls away from the sides of the bowl. Transfer the dough to a sheet of plastic wrap, divide in half equally, shape into 2 disks, and wrap in plastic. Chill for at least 1 hour, or overnight.

Preheat the oven to 350°F.

Roll the pastry rounds out on a lightly floured surface into two 12-inch circles. Fit the dough into two 10½- to 11-inch loose-bottomed tart pans with fluted sides, pressing it evenly over the bottom and up the sides. Line the tarts with foil and fill with dried beans or pie weights.

Bake the tart shells for 20 minutes, or until the edges are very light brown. Remove the parchment paper and weights and bake until lightly golden, 5 to 10 minutes more. Cool on a rack before filling.

WHITE WINE BUTTER SAUCE
Makes about 2¼ cups

This all-purpose sauce is essential for Parmesan Soufflés (page 40) and Bottega Chicken Scaloppine (page 155) and it is the classic sauce for poached, sautéed, or grilled fish and shellfish.

¾ cup dry white wine

¾ cup white wine vinegar (or 6 tablespoons each sherry vinegar and white wine vinegar), or more to taste

1 shallot, finely minced

1 thyme sprig

1½ teaspoons heavy cream

½ pound (2 sticks) unsalted butter, softened

Kosher salt and freshly ground white pepper

Fresh lemon juice to taste

Hot sauce, such as Tabasco or Cholula

Combine the wine, vinegar, shallot, and thyme in a small heavy nonreactive saucepan, bring to a boil over high heat, and reduce to a syrupy glaze, about 12 minutes.

Remove the saucepan from the heat and stir in the cream. Bring to a simmer and simmer for about 1 minute. Reduce the heat to low and whisk in the butter bit by bit, adding more only after each previous addition has been incorporated. Regulate the heat so the sauce is warm—not too hot, or it will separate. Add salt and pepper, lemon juice, and hot sauce. Taste and add a little more vinegar and/or lemon juice as needed. Strain and serve, or cover to keep warm and use as soon as possible.

BROWN BUTTER
Makes a generous ½ cup

Butter that's cooked until the milk solids turn deep amber becomes a rich, nutty sauce for fish and pasta, such as the Tortelloni with Crabmeat, Ricotta, and Brown Butter (page 113). It's also the basis for a vinaigrette, which we serve with monkfish (see page 137). The key to its success is attentiveness. You have to remove the pan from the heat just as the butter goes from golden to chestnut, but before it gets too dark; it moves from perfection to burned and bitter quickly. But it's equally important to let it get dark enough, or it will lack flavor. As soon as you smell a pronounced nutty aroma, remove the pan from the heat and strain the butter. Make a batch and keep it in a jar in the refrigerator. It's great for sautés and for some desserts too.

12 tablespoons (1½ sticks) unsalted butter

Melt the butter in a small saucepan over low heat. Continue to cook, whisking occasionally, until the butter turns brown and smells nutty, 15 to 20 minutes. Immediately strain the butter through a fine-mesh strainer into a bowl, leaving the solids behind. Brown butter will keep in a jar in the refrigerator for 5 days.

VARIATION BROWN BUTTER VINAIGRETTE: Combine 1 shallot, finely minced, with a pinch of salt, ½ teaspoon thyme leaves, and 1 tablespoon balsamic vinegar in a small bowl. Set aside to macerate for 15 minutes while you prepare the brown butter. Whisk a scant ¼ cup strained brown butter into the vinegar mixture. If using the vinaigrette on fish, you may wish to bump up the acid a bit with a squeeze of lemon juice; or, to enrich it further, whisk 1 tablespoon unsalted butter into the warm vinaigrette. Vary the vinegar—sherry vinegar, Banyuls, garnacha, or other red wine—to suit your taste and the tartness of the finished sauce.

HOMEMADE MAYONNAISE

Makes 1¾ cups

Homemade mayonnaise is one of the most versatile sauces there is. During my first book tour, a Southern grande dame exclaimed, "Southern ladies do not serve store-bought mayonnaise!" At the restaurant, we make mayo by hand with a balloon whisk and elbow grease, but the food processor does a good job. In a pinch, good store-bought mayonnaise (I like Hellman's, called Best Food out West) is a fine stand-in.

1 large egg
1 egg yolk
½ teaspoon salt, or to taste
Juice of ½ lemon
1 teaspoon Dijon mustard
Pinch of cayenne
1½ cups canola or grapeseed oil
1 to 2 tablespoons warm water, if needed

Combine the egg, egg yolk, and salt in a food processor and process for 30 seconds. Add the lemon juice, mustard, and cayenne and process for 15 seconds with the machine running. Slowly pour the oil through the feed tube until the mayonnaise is thick and emulsified. If the mixture becomes too dense, stop pouring in the oil and add warm water, a little at a time, until the mayonnaise loosens, then slowly incorporate the remaining oil. Taste and adjust the seasoning. The mayonnaise can be stored, covered, in the refrigerator for up to 1 week.

AÏOLI

Makes 1½ cups

We call this aïoli but veer from the traditional Provençal rendition infused with raw garlic by tempering our homemade mayonnaise with roasted garlic puree. This all-purpose sauce has become a component of countless Bottega Café classics, from zesty Tomato Chutney Aïoli (below) to variations on Caesar salad, tartar sauce, and sauce gribiche.

2 large egg yolks
Pinch of kosher salt
Pinch of freshly ground white pepper
Dash of Tabasco sauce
1 teaspoon roasted garlic puree (see page 254)
1 cup canola or grapeseed oil
¼ cup extra virgin olive oil
1 to 2 tablespoons warm water or juice of ¼ lemon,
    if necessary

Combine the egg yolks, salt, pepper, and Tabasco in a food processor and process for 30 seconds. Add the roasted garlic and process for 15 seconds. With the machine running, pour in the oils in a very slow, steady stream until the mayonnaise is thick and emulsified. Thin the aïoli with warm water or lemon juice, if necessary, to achieve the desired consistency. Taste and adjust the seasonings. Aïoli can be kept, covered, for up to 5 days in the refrigerator; after that, the flavor of the garlic becomes harsh.

VARIATION TOMATO CHUTNEY AÏOLI: add 1 heaping tablespoon Alecia's Tomato Chutney (see Sources, page 260) to ½ cup aïoli.

HORSERADISH SAUCE
Makes a generous 2 cups

Perfect for beef carpaccio, this simple sauce makes a great sandwich condiment or dip for boiled shrimp.

1 cup grated fresh horseradish
2 tablespoons Homemade Mayonnaise (page 245) or
    store-bought mayonnaise
1 cup sour cream
1 tablespoon fresh lemon juice, or more to taste
Kosher salt and freshly ground black pepper to taste

Combine all the ingredients in a bowl and mix until thoroughly combined. Adjust the seasonings by adding more salt, pepper, or lemon juice if necessary. The sauce keeps in the refrigerator for 3 to 5 days.

BOTTEGA TARTAR SAUCE
Makes about 1½ cups

Obviously, a homemade tartar sauce can start with your homemade mayo. But the mayonnaise also can come from a jar. The capers, tart cornichons, diced potato, eggs, and herbs make this as irresistible a dip as it is a sauce for fish.

1 cup Homemade Mayonnaise (page 245) or store-
    bought mayonnaise
1 tablespoon capers, rinsed
1 tablespoon chopped cornichons
1 red potato, boiled until tender, peeled, and finely diced
1 tablespoon thinly sliced chives or chopped scallions
¼ teaspoon dried tarragon
Juice of ½ lemon
⅛ teaspoon cayenne
1 teaspoon L'Estornell Spanish garnacha vinegar
    (see Sources, page 260) or other good-quality
    red wine vinegar
2 large hard-boiled eggs, finely chopped

Combine all the ingredients in a medium bowl, stirring well to blend. Tarter Sauce can be refrigerated for 3 to 5 days.

MARINARA SAUCE
Makes 4 cups

This is our standard tomato sauce, the base for most of our pizzas and a staple we always have on hand. Use it for baked feta as well as for pasta.

¼ cup olive oil
1 large white onion, cut into 1-inch dice
3 garlic cloves, finely chopped
2 carrots, peeled and cut into 1-inch dice
2 celery stalks, cut into 1-inch dice
2 cups dry white wine
One 28-ounce can San Marzano tomatoes,
    with their juice
Bouquet garni: 4 or 5 sprigs each thyme, basil,
    and parsley; 4 bay leaves; 2 dried red chiles; and
    optional Parmesan rind wrapped in cheesecloth
1 tablespoon dried oregano
Pinch of red pepper flakes
Kosher salt and freshly ground black pepper

Pour the oil into a large saucepan and heat over high heat. When the oil begins to shimmer, add the onion, garlic, carrots, and celery and sauté, stirring frequently, until the vegetables have softened considerably, about 15 minutes.

Add the white wine, bring to a simmer, and simmer until reduced by half. Pour in the tomatoes with their juice and stir well. Push the bouquet garni down into the middle of the mixture. Reduce the heat to medium and simmer until the vegetables break apart when pressed gently against the side of the pan with a spoon, about 30 minutes.

Remove the bouquet garni and add the oregano and pepper flakes. Blend with a hand-held immersion blender, or in a food processor or regular blender, until smooth. Taste the sauce and season with salt and pepper to your liking. This keeps for several days in the refrigerator and freezes well.

ROMESCO SAUCE

Makes 2 cups

From Greece, we get skordalia and tzatziki; from North Africa, harissa; and from Turkey, baba ghanoush—all distinctive sauces of their regions. This romesco sauce is borrowed from Catalonian Spain. It's one of the great sauces of the Mediterranean Basin—rustic, hearty, not shy of flavor, and with every element combining to make the whole much greater than the sum of its parts. The charred flavor of the grilled bread adds an open-fire aroma, as does the smokiness of grilled peppers. Almonds lend their richness, while the paprika and hot peppers add piquant spice. Olive oil binds it all together. We use more roasted sweet pepper in our version than most.

Serve with grilled fish or any meat—pork, lamb, or beef.

Two ½-inch-thick slices of bread, such as yeasty
    sourdough, or two 4-by-2-inch rectangles
    Focaccia (page 82)
1 red bell pepper or pimento pepper
2 tomatoes
3 garlic cloves
Maldon sea salt
20 unblanched whole almonds, toasted (see page 255)
2 teaspoons paprika, preferably Spanish
1 teaspoon pimentón (smoked Spanish paprika,
    hot or sweet; see Sources, page 260)
2 tablespoons red wine vinegar
1 tablespoon sherry vinegar
1 dried ancho chile, softened in warm water for
    20 minutes, then drained and chopped
Pinch of hot red pepper flakes
1 cup extra virgin olive oil

Prepare a hot fire in a grill or preheat the broiler.

Grill or toast the bread until slightly blackened on the edges on both sides. Coarsely chop.

Roast the pepper over the fire or over a gas flame on your stovetop (or under the broiler) until charred all over, and then transfer to a bowl and cover with plastic wrap to steam for 20 minutes. Peel the charred skin away, without rinsing the pepper, and remove the core and seeds. Coarsely chop the pepper.

Meanwhile, roast the tomatoes over the fire or under the broiler until the skin blackens. Let cool, then remove the skin, cut the tomatoes in half, and give them a squeeze to expel the seeds. Coarsely chop the flesh.

Place the garlic in a large mortar or a food processor and pound or pulse with a pinch of sea salt to create a paste. Add the almonds and continue pounding (if using a mortar, you may want to coarsely chop the almonds or pulse them in a food processor first) or processing to a coarse paste. Add the paprikas and vinegars and pound or pulse to blend. If you have used a mortar up to this point, transfer the mixture to the bowl of a food processor.

Add the bread, roasted pepper, tomato, chile, and pepper flakes and pulse until just combined. With the machine running, slowly add the olive oil through the feed tube. Do not overprocess; the sauce should be a coarse puree. Taste and adjust the seasonings. The romesco should be spicy, salty, and rich with olive oil, with just a hint of the vinegar's sharpness. The sauce keeps in the refrigerator for 2 to 3 days.

SALSA VERDE

Makes 1 cup

Vibrant green and so fresh tasting, this sauce appears in many different cuisines in many variations. We serve this versatile blend with grilled meats and seafood, or use it as a condiment for sandwiches or to garnish scrambled eggs. This is the sort of preparation that deserves your very best olive oil. For variation, add a chopped anchovy, fold in a diced hard-boiled egg, and/or add a little minced tarragon or marjoram.

½ cup loosely packed flat-leaf parsley leaves
⅓ cup loosely packed basil leaves
¼ cup loosely packed mint leaves
2 tablespoons finely sliced chives
½ garlic clove
1 tablespoon drained capers
1 tablespoon minced shallot
½ cup extra virgin olive oil
1½ teaspoons champagne vinegar
Kosher salt and freshly ground black pepper

Combine the herbs, garlic, 1½ teaspoons of the capers, 1½ teaspoons of the minced shallot, and the olive oil in a food processor and pulse to achieve a chunky blend.

Transfer to a bowl and fold in the remaining capers and shallots and the vinegar. Season the salsa verde to taste with salt and pepper. The sauce keeps for 1 to 2 days in the refrigerator.

PESTO

Makes 1 cup

In Liguria, basil is grown commercially but sold when still young and tender, to be turned into the region's most famous sauce—jade green pesto, loose with pounded basil, pine nuts, and cheese. Be conservative with the garlic—you want to taste the other ingredients.

A Mexican molcajete is a relatively inexpensive mortar and pestle made of lava rock and is as formidable a tool for pesto as for guacamole. Find one at your local Latin market. Its wonderful rough texture facilitates the grinding of ingredients, keeping the pesto coarse, as it should be. Pulsing the ingredients in your food processor is a secondary option.

2 plump garlic cloves
Kosher or sea salt
2½ cups loosely packed basil leaves
2 tablespoons pine nuts, lightly toasted (see page 255)
1 cup olive oil
⅓ cup grated Parmigiano-Reggiano

Place the garlic in a large mortar with a pinch of salt and pound with the pestle until reduced to a paste. Give the basil a rough chop, add it to the mortar, and pound until thoroughly broken down, about 2 minutes. Add the pine nuts and pound until crushed. Add about a tablespoon of the olive oil and stir and pound to incorporate, then add a little cheese and stir and pound to incorporate. Proceed in this manner until you've added all of the oil and cheese and the pesto is thick. Pesto can be refrigerated for 1 to 2 days.

PARSLEY AND ORANGE ZEST GREMOLATA

Makes about ¼ cup

Traditionally gremolata is a mixture of chopped parsley, garlic, and lemon zest—here we make a very small variation and add orange zest. Be careful not to let the garlic dominate—this should be more about the citrus aroma and green parsley, with a hint of garlic.

The aromatic oils are more intense if you combine the ingredients just before serving. It is the just-prepared flavor and aroma of the fresh zest and chopped herbs that make this preparation so wonderful. Gremolata is classic with osso buco and adds bright flavor to other rich, meaty braises like our Short Ribs and Oxtail with Gremolata and Green Olives (page 184).

½ cup flat-leaf parsley leaves, finely chopped
Zest of ½ orange—removed with a zester and chopped
Zest of 1 lemon—removed with a zester and chopped
1 small garlic clove, crushed and very finely chopped

Combine the parsley, zests, and garlic on a cutting board and finely chop them together. Scrape into a small bowl. Use as soon as possible.

FIG RELISH FOR FISH

Makes about 1½ cups

A relish with grilled onion, herbs, olive oil, and vinegar makes an excellent all-purpose sauce for grilled fish—here we add fresh figs and mint for a distinctive late-summer variation.

1 Charred Red Onion (page 238), cut into medium dice
2 kirby cucumbers, peeled, seeded, and diced
1 heaping cup thickly sliced fresh figs (purple or green, or a combination)
¼ cup walnuts, toasted (see page 255) and coarsely chopped
¼ shallot, finely diced
Grated zest and juice of ½ lemon
1 tablespoon red wine vinegar or sherry vinegar
¼ cup extra virgin olive oil
¼ cup finely chopped mint
Kosher salt and freshly ground black pepper

Combine the onion, cucumbers, figs, walnuts, shallot, lemon zest and juice, vinegar, olive oil, and mint in a large bowl and toss gently to mix. Season with salt and pepper and serve. The relish can be made a few hours in advance, but in that case, chop and add the mint leaves just before serving.

TAPENADE

Makes a generous 1 cup

This olive mixture is superb as a topping for crostini, a pungent sauce for grilled tuna, or as an addition to deviled eggs. Try it with Farm Eggs with Tapenade (page 31). Even if you think you dislike anchovies, please give them a try—they are a distinctive but not at all overpowering seasoning here.

8 ounces pitted black Greek or Niçoise olives
  (about 1½ cups)
2 small anchovy fillets, rinsed and patted dry
3 tablespoons capers, rinsed
½ small garlic clove, pounded to a paste in a mortar or
  very finely chopped and then mashed
Pinch of cayenne
1 scant tablespoon chopped flat-leaf parsley
½ cup extra virgin olive oil
1 tablespoon brandy or grappa (optional)

Combine the olives, anchovies, capers, garlic, cayenne, and parsley in a food processor and pulse until the olives are coarsely chopped. Add the olive oil and pulse until just combined. Add the brandy or grappa, if desired, and pulse to mix.

MINT OIL

Makes ½ cup

Other tender-leaved herbs can be prepared in the same way to make flavored oil; see the variation below. We use this mint oil on our Pistachio-Crusted Lamb Loin (page 174) and Butter Bean and Mint Pilaf (page 204). It's delicious drizzled on meat hot off the grill or used as a garnish for beef or tuna carpaccio or other *crudi* of fish. Use only the smallest amount, as it is intense.

¼ cup kosher salt
4 cups loosely packed mint leaves
¾ cup grapeseed or canola oil

Prepare an ice bath. Bring 4 cups water and the salt to a rolling boil in a saucepan. Add the mint leaves and blanch for 10 to 15 seconds. Transfer them to the ice bath to stop the cooking and preserve the green color. When cool, remove the mint and squeeze dry.

Combine half the leaves with enough grapeseed or canola oil just to cover in a blender and blend for 2 minutes. Add the remaining leaves and oil and blend for 2 minutes more.

Transfer to a jar and let stand in the refrigerator for 1 day to intensify the flavor of the oil, then strain it through cheesecloth; discard the solids. The oil can be refrigerated for up to 5 days.

VARIATION BASIL OIL: substitute basil leaves for the mint.

ROSEMARY SAUCE

Makes a scant ½ cup

This woodsy sauce goes beautifully with pan-sautéed wild striped bass or other meaty white fish, and it is also a great match for grilled meats. Salt-packed Sicilian anchovies are the best, but you can use oil-packed anchovy fillets in a pinch.

Two 5-inch sprigs rosemary, leaves removed and finely chopped (about 2 tablespoons)
2 garlic cloves
1 salt-packed anchovy, filleted, rinsed, and patted dry, or 2 oil-packed anchovy fillets, rinsed and patted dry
Kosher salt and freshly ground black pepper
¼ cup olive oil
1 tablespoon fresh lemon juice

Combine the rosemary, garlic, and anchovies with a pinch each of salt and pepper in a mortar and pound to a paste with the pestle. Alternatively, combine in a food processor and pulse to a paste. Gradually whisk in the olive oil, or, with the machine running, pour it through the feed tube of the processor. Add the lemon juice, and use immediately.

SIMPLE SYRUP

Makes 2 cups

Keep simple syrup on hand for mixing cocktails or sweetening your tea or fresh-squeezed lemonade.

2 cups sugar
2 cups water

Combine the sugar and water in a small heavy saucepan and bring to a simmer over medium heat, stirring and swirling to dissolve the sugar. Dip a pastry brush in hot water and wipe down the sides of the pan to dissolve any sugar crystals that cling to the sides. Simmer for 2 minutes, then remove from the heat and let cool.

Simple syrup keeps for weeks in a tightly sealed jar in the refrigerator.

VARIATION MINT SIMPLE SYRUP: Add a large bunch of mint to the hot syrup. Once cool, let the syrup infuse for at least 2 hours, or overnight, in the refrigerator, then strain the syrup. Try other herbs too, such as lemon thyme, basil, or lemon verbena.

Bottega Pantry

OLIVE OIL You will want a minimum of two good olive oils for your pantry. Choose an all-purpose extra virgin olive oil for sautéing, frying, and other uses. Then select a more special extra virgin oil to use for finishing a dish and in some vinaigrettes. I like the fruity green olive flavor of oils from Sicily and southern Italy, such as Apulia and Abruzzo. The oils from Liguria and the region around Lake Garda are delicate and graceful, while those of Tuscany have a potent, almost peppery, finish. Sample them all to hone in on your favored variety. Lighter olive oils are well suited to fish and most vegetables; use stronger oils for more substantial offerings.

Many cooks make the mistake of being too stingy with prized olive oils, thus keeping them much too long. Olive oil will begin to deteriorate once opened and should be used within a couple of months. Go ahead and enjoy your investment while the fresh olive aroma and flavor are at their prime.

OTHER OILS Not essential, but certainly delectable are the citrus-infused olive oils that Manicaretti imports from Apulia (see Sources, page 260). Fresh lemons or tangerines are tossed in with the olives as they are crushed, and the resulting oil has an absolutely pure and beautiful aroma. These are wonderful for adding a final punch of flavor to a dish. Truffle oil is often of poor quality, so choose carefully; I like Urbani, available in gourmet shops and online (see Sources, page 260). I prefer black truffle oil over the white. Walnut and hazelnut oils add a powerfully perfumed flavor to salads, marinated meats, vegetables, and other dishes. They must be used soon after being opened as they quickly turn rancid, so buy them in small quantities and keep them in the refrigerator. Porcini oil adds the unmistakably earthy and sublime aroma of Italy's favorite mushroom—use it to enhance any mushroom dish.

VINEGARS Good white and red wine vinegar, sherry vinegar, and balsamic and aged balsamic should be in every cook's arsenal. For red wine vinegar, I love the Spanish garnacha vinegar from L'Estornell, made from the grenache grape (see Sources, page 260). There are also many excellent French and California red wine vinegars. Sherry vinegar from Jerez, Spain, where sherry is produced, is one of a chef's greatest tools for vinaigrettes, sauces, reductions, mayonnaises, and more. Have both a balsamic vinegar from the less expensive "condimento" level and one that is aged—around three years produces a nice depth of flavor. For a big splurge, seek out older barrel-aged balsamicos.

NUTS Pine nuts, walnuts, almonds, and hazelnuts are Italian standards and loved by Southern cooks too. Nuts are perishable, and the oils in the nutmeats can turn bitter and rancid. Buy nuts in small amounts and freeze if planning to keep for more than a month.

CHILE PEPPERS Jars of inch-long dried whole red chiles can be found in the spice section of most supermarkets. But keep in mind that no Southern kitchen is without a hot chile sauce like Tabasco.

SUN-DRIED TOMATOES We primarily use sun-dried tomatoes sold in bulk, rather than the commercial oil-packed version. Reconstitute in warm water for 15 minutes, then drain and pat dry. Use right away, or marinate in olive oil to preserve for a bit longer.

MOSTARDAS A wonderful and unique condiment most commonly from northern Italy—Lombardia, Emilia-Romagna, and Piemonte. Fruits, vegetables, and/or nuts, cooked with vinegar, sugar, and spices such as ginger and clove, mostardas are traditionally served with roasted meats. Modern Italians have discovered how good they are with cheeses. We currently serve a green tomato mostarda with pecorino toscano. Mostarda Mantovana di Pomodori Verdi is imported by Forever Cheese (see Sources, page 260), one of our suppliers, who also provides us with a number of high-quality cheeses from Italy, Spain, and Portugal. Made with green tomato, sugar, lemon, and mustard essence, this mostarda is wonderful with Taleggio or other semisoft cheeses, such as cacio de Roma.

OLIVES Keep on hand a selection of both oil-cured and brine-cured olives. There are many olives to choose from: our pantry usually includes Ligurian black olives, Taggiasche, Cerignola, Niçoise, Picholine, and Kalamata.

CAPERS AND CAPER BERRIES The best capers are packed in salt, which preserves the flavor well, but brined ones work as long as they are rinsed, not just drained. Salt-packed anchovies must also be rinsed before using. Capers are the tiny unopened flower buds of the caper bush; caper berries are the considerably larger fruit of the bush, filled with tiny edible seeds. Capers add their distinctive flavor to many dishes; caper berries are generally used as a garnish.

ROASTED RED PEPPERS Good-quality jarred roasted peppers are handy when there is no time to roast and peel your own. Pat them dry before using. Look for piquillo peppers from Spain, which are roasted over a wood fire. They give a nice bit of heat and sweetness to dishes.

CANNED SAN MARZANO TOMATOES Canned tomatoes are a better option when vine-ripened local tomatoes are not in season. Look for the brightly acidic San Marzano variety of canned tomatoes, which have truly robust flavor (and make sure they are real San Marzano tomatoes, imported from Italy).

CANNED BEANS We buy good-quality canned chickpeas, cannellini, and borlotti beans. Drain and rinse before using.

CANNED FISH The best-quality canned fish products are packed in olive oil, which preserves the flavor and texture of the fish. We use tuna, sardines, and anchovies packed in olive oil.

SALT We use both coarse sea salt and kosher salt. I really like Maldon sea salt from England, with its pleasant crunch and large flake. Use your fingers, not a salt shaker, to season food.

RICE Arborio and Carnaroli are short-grain Italian rices traditionally used for risotto. With the addition of stock, they plump up and have a dense, toothsome texture. I like basmati, a fragrant longer-grain rice for pilafs and simple boiled rice dishes.

DRIED PASTA Some of the dried pastas we commonly use are penne, bucatini, capellini, linguine, garganelli, macaroni, lasagne noodles, and shells.

POLENTA Look for organically grown polenta (like those from McEwen & Sons or Anson Mills; see Sources, page 260) for pure sweet corn taste; never use quick-cooking polenta. The white varieties tend to be a bit more delicately flavored than the yellow grains. Store in airtight containers in the refrigerator.

ESPRESSO POWDER Use espresso powder in desserts and sauces and sometimes in a rub for meat. Medaglia d'Oro instant espresso is available in most supermarkets.

Techniques

TRIMMING ARTICHOKES I recommend wearing latex gloves when working with artichokes so the strong tannins don't stain your hands. Fill a bowl with water and add a generous squeeze of lemon juice (the acidulated water will keep the trimmed artichokes from turning brown). Work with one artichoke at a time: Trim off the stem so the bottom is flat. Pull off the tough outer leaves until you reach the cone of pale inner leaves, and cut off the cone of leaves. You can scrape out the hairy choke with a sharp spoon now (a grapefruit spoon works well), or remove it after cooking the artichoke. As you work, rub the cut surfaces with a lemon half to keep them from darkening. Using a paring knife, trim away the dark green skin, working around the artichoke, until you reach the pale green meat of the artichoke bottom. Drop the trimmed artichoke into the acidulated water and continue with the remaining artichokes.

To trim baby artichokes, cut away the top third and trim the sides and bottom until the dark green color changes to a paler shade.

ROASTING GARLIC Roasted garlic has a sweet, caramelized flavor that is all the goodness of garlic without the pungency. We roast the whole heads, then use the roasted cloves whole or puree them for use in vinaigrettes, on pizzas, and in sauces. Roasted garlic puree makes a more gentle Caesar Dressing (page 72), and it is a great addition to mashed potatoes and bean purees. **To prepare roasted garlic cloves,** cut off the top ¼ inch of one or more bulbs of garlic, and place each one on a sheet of aluminum foil. Season with salt and pepper, a few thyme sprigs, and a teaspoon of extra virgin olive oil. Wrap tightly in the foil and roast in a 325°F oven for about 45 minutes, or until the cloves are soft but not mushy. Let cool, then squeeze out the soft pulp. **To make roasted garlic puree,** press the pulp from a whole head of roasted garlic through a strainer, and season the puree with a bit of salt and pepper. The roasted garlic and the puree will keep for 2 to 3 days, covered and refrigerated.

ROASTING BELL PEPPERS AND CHILES Roasting bell peppers gives them a luscious texture and sweet smoky flavor; roasting chiles gives them a similar texture and greater depth of flavor. I prefer the smokiness of a wood-fired grill for roasting peppers, but you can use the broiler or a gas burner on your stovetop. Roast the peppers (or chiles), turning occasionally, until the skin is blackened all over. Transfer to a bowl, cover with plastic wrap, and let steam for 20 minutes. Remove the blackened skin with your fingertips (use latex gloves if working with chiles, if you wish), then remove the stem and seeds. It's fine if a bit of skin remains—don't be tempted to rinse the peppers, or you will wash away their flavorful oils. You can store the roasted peppers in a jar, covered with olive oil to keep out air, for up to 5 days in the refrigerator.

PEELING AND SEEDING TOMATOES I confess I do not always peel tomatoes, because the skin rarely bothers me, but we do peel them for certain preparations. **To peel tomatoes,** cut an X in the bottom of each one and blanch in a pot of boiling water just until the skin starts to peel away at the X, about 30 seconds. Transfer them to an ice bath to cool them quickly, then drain and slip off the skin. **To seed tomatoes,** cut them crosswise in half and scoop out the seeds with a little spoon or your finger; or hold each half cut side down over the sink and give it a little squeeze so the seeds fall out.

PEELING VEGETABLES Vegetables oxidize once peeled and cut, so we peel shallots and garlic just before use. And we chop or crush garlic only moments before cooking. Do not buy packaged peeled garlic: it has a lingeringly unpleasant strong taste.

BLANCHING AND SHOCKING VEGETABLES AND HEARTY GREENS Blanching, or briefly cooking, vegetables in boiling water and then shocking them in ice water locks in their vibrant color, removes the bitterness of certain greens, and gets a bit of a jump-start on the cooking process. Bring a large pot of generously salted water to a boil. Meanwhile, prepare an ice bath by filling a large bowl with ice and cold water. Add the vegetables or greens to the boiling water and cook for 2 to 3 minutes, or until they are bright and just al dente or crisp-tender. Drain the vegetables and shock in the ice bath to stop the cooking and set the color. Remove the vegetables as soon as they are cool to the touch so that they do not get waterlogged, then drain and pat dry.

BLANCHING SPINACH AND OTHER TENDER GREENS Blanch spinach or delicate greens in the same way as described above, but blanch for only 30 seconds. Shock, drain, and squeeze out excess moisture.

GLAZING VEGETABLES We often glaze vegetables, such as spring onions, carrots, and tiny roots. To glaze vegetables, place them in a pan large enough to hold them snugly in a single layer, then cover by a third to a half with water. Season with kosher salt, freshly ground black pepper, and a pinch of sugar and dot with a tablespoon or so of butter. Cook over medium heat until the vegetables are tender and lightly colored and the liquid is reduced to a syrupy glaze. Add a little more water if the vegetables are not tender by the time the liquid has reduced.

PREPARING A BOUQUET GARNI A classic bouquet garni is composed of thyme sprigs, parsley sprigs, and a bay leaf, but any combination of herbs and spices you like can be used. Simply tie a few herb sprigs and a bay leaf together with kitchen twine; we sometimes tie the herbs inside a leek green. The bouquet garni allows you to easily remove the herbs from the finished dish. If using whole spices too, such as peppercorns or juniper berries, wrap the herbs and spices in a square of cheesecloth and tie with kitchen twine to create a sachet.

SOAKING DRIED MUSHROOMS Soak dried mushrooms, such as porcini, in warm water to cover for 20 to 30 minutes, then lift out, leaving any grit behind. Strain the flavorful broth and use the liquid as part of your dish, or reserve for another use.

TOASTING NUTS Toasting nuts brings out their flavor and gives them added crunch. Spread the nuts on a baking sheet and bake in a preheated 325°F oven, shaking the pan from time to time, until the nuts are aromatic and lightly browned, 10 to 15 minutes. Monitor them carefully, as they can burn quickly. If you need only a small quantity of toasted nuts, you can toast them in a dry skillet over medium heat, shaking the pan occasionally, until fragrant. We usually toast pine nuts in a skillet, so we can keep an eye on them; they tend to scorch easily because of their high oil content. Blanching hazelnuts or other nuts means removing their skins. **To toast and blanch hazelnuts, walnuts, or almonds,** toast as above, then wrap the warm nuts in a kitchen towel and rub together to remove the skins (don't worry about removing every last bit of skin).

TOASTING SPICES AND SEEDS Toasting spices, such as allspice or juniper berries, and seeds like fennel and cumin, draws out their flavorful oils and fills the air with their aroma. Toast the whole spices or seeds in a small dry heavy skillet over medium heat, shaking the skillet from time to time, until they are fragrant, usually a few minutes. Remove from the skillet, so they don't burn, and let cool.

PREPARING CITRUS SUPRÊMES Suprêmes are cleaned citrus segments, free of any peel, pith, or membrane. Using a sharp knife or serrated knife, cut a ½-inch slice off the top and bottom of the citrus fruit. Stand the fruit on a cutting board and cut away the skin and pith in strips by slicing from top to bottom, working your way around the fruit. Then gently pick up the fruit, holding it over a bowl to collect the juices, and slice along each membrane to separate the segments and release each beautiful suprême. Remove any seeds.

BRAISING To ensure a moist braise, cut a piece of parchment paper the size of your braising pan and place it on top of the just barely simmering meat or poultry, then cover the pan tightly with the lid or aluminum foil. The paper helps keep the top of the braise from drying out, so the finished dish remains moist and succulent. To test the meat for doneness, insert a knife into the meat toward the end of the cooking time (resist the temptation to check too early, or you will lose the buildup of moist heat): you should feel no resistance whatsoever and the meat should be practically falling apart.

Once your braise is tender, allow the meat to rest in the pan for 10 minutes, then transfer it to a rack set over a platter or baking sheet and cover loosely with foil to keep warm. Strain the braising liquid through a fine-mesh strainer into a saucepan, gently pushing down on the vegetables with the back of a ladle or a wooden spoon to extract all the liquid. (Discard the vegetables, as they will have released their flavors into the broth.)

To skim the braising liquid, place the pan half on and half off a burner, over medium heat, and bring to a simmer. The fat will accumulate on the cool side, making it easy to skim off. Continue simmering and reducing the broth to concentrate the flavor, skimming from time to time, until every trace of fat has been removed. When the broth is sufficiently flavorful, generally reducing it by one-half to three-quarters, we usually finish the sauce by whisking in a couple of tablespoons of cool butter. This gives the sauce a rich, silky texture and mellow flavor.

CUTTING UP A CHICKEN Place the chicken breast side up on a cutting board, pull one leg away, and cut through the skin between the body and the thigh. Next bend the leg away from the body until the ball-and-socket joint is exposed and cut through it; the leg and thigh will come away. Repeat with the other leg and thigh. Separate each whole leg into two pieces by holding the leg at the ankle joint and slicing through the joint between the thigh and the drumstick. Remove the wings by pulling each wing away from the body and slicing through the joint. Separate the backbone from the breast by cutting through the rib bones from the tail end all the way up and through the shoulder joint. Reserve the back and wings for stock. Place the breast skin side up and, with a strong hand, slice through the center of the breast: Use both hands, with one steadying the knife and the other pushing down with the heel of your hand, forcing the knife through the breastbone. Cut the two breasts crosswise to make four pieces. This leaves you with eight pieces. This technique also applies to guinea hen and other birds.

POUNDING MEAT FOR SCALOPPINE To pound meat for scaloppine, place the trimmed piece of meat on a sheet of plastic wrap and cover with a second sheet. Pound with a meat pounder until thin and of even thickness.

REMOVING SILVERSKIN To remove the silverskin, the tough membrane that looks like a shiny sheet of tendon, from meat, insert the tip of a sharp boning knife or other thin knife just under the taut membrane and create a "tab" at one end that you can hold with your other hand. Angle the knife underneath the silverskin up toward the tough membrane and slide the knife along the length of the meat to remove the membrane. Continue removing the membrane in strips until none remains.

WARMING PLATES No matter how organized you are, or how simple the menu, by the time you've arranged the food carefully on serving plates, the temperature will have dropped. To avoid this problem, warm the plates beforehand by placing them in a 200°F oven for 5 to 10 minutes.

Tools

Cooking should be fun, and I enjoy cooking all the more with certain "tools of the trade." For example, enameled ironware, like Le Creuset gratin dishes, is simply beautiful to me. I love using these for many different purposes—for marinating meats, storing roasted vegetables until ready to serve, and arranging my *mise en place,* as well as for making crusty golden gratins. The following is a list of my personal favorite kitchen tools and equipment.

CASSEROLES Casseroles are large deep pots, also called Dutch ovens, with tight-fitting lids. I prefer cast-iron pots with an enameled finish—again, Le Creuset is a wonderful choice—but they can be made from tempered glass (Pyrex), stoneware, or earthenware. These latter types are good for the oven but not for use over a direct flame. Flameproof casseroles can be used for sautéing or browning foods on the stovetop before transferring the braise or other dish to a slow oven to finish cooking.

SAUTÉ PANS Sauté pans are heavy pans with sloping shallow sides. I love French black steel for searing meats, fish, and most sautéing. (Previn carries these imported pans; see Sources, page 260.) Once seasoned, these are great for almost everything except reducing high-acid sauces, which will react with the pan and taste metallic. For this, use a nonreactive pan, such as enameled cast iron or stainless steel. For home cooks, 9½- or 10-inch pans are most versatile, but 12-inch pans are great for cooking larger portions of food. I try to avoid lightweight sauté pans, as foods tend to scorch easily.

SAUCEPANS AND POTS When it comes to **saucepans,** I prefer Sitram, French stainless steel pans with a copper layer sandwiched in the bottom. The pans conduct heat uniformly, without scorching, and they have a handy lip for pouring. They are sturdy with a great overall balance and should last a lifetime. Le Creuset saucepans have both charm and excellent functional qualities—heaviness for distributing heat evenly and a nonreactive enamel coating over the cast iron. Another good choice would be the wonderful all-purpose saucepans manufactured by All-Clad. In addition to making stock, a **tall stockpot** is ideal for blanching large amounts of vegetables and for making soup. Stainless-steel stockpots are our first choice, provided they have heavy bottoms. A bonus pan for any kitchen would be a ridged cast-iron **grill pan.**

GRATIN DISHES These are typically shallow oval baking dishes made of ceramic or cast iron coated with enamel, such as those by Le Creuset. Copper versions, generally more expensive, can also be found. The ceramic and enameled cast-iron dishes are also ideal vessels in which to marinate foods. Food baked in gratin dishes will have a large surface area that allows it to develop enough crispy crust for everyone to have a portion. And they look good enough to go straight from the oven to the table.

RAMEKINS Ceramic or glass ramekins are available in a variety of sizes. We use them for baking sweet or savory souffles and custards, as well as for holding ingredients for our *mise en place.*

COOLING RACKS Wire cooling racks are essential equipment in all our restaurant kitchens because letting practically everything rest on a rack—whether seared or cooked meat, poultry, or fish—makes it better. The rack prevents excess moisture—the juices—from escaping: If these items were placed on a platter or board, the cells touching the surface would open and release their juices. A cooling rack minimizes the surface area contact and allows air to circulate around the food so it doesn't steam in its own juices. Typically we will grill a fillet of grouper, for example, to just a bit underdone and transfer it to a cooling rack to let it rest for a couple of minutes. The residual, or carryover, heat allows the fish to finish cooking perfectly, and no juices are lost. Set the cooling rack, of whatever size is most practical, over a baking sheet or platter to catch any drips.

BAKING SHEETS Known professionally as sheet pans, these are the workhorses of the restaurant kitchen. Available as both half sheet pans and full sheet pans, they are sturdy aluminum pans with a 1-inch rim on all four sides. We roast on them and use them to catch spills in the oven. When baking pastries and cookies, we sometimes choose heavy flat French steel pans without sides. These dark heavy-duty pans conduct heat better and allow a little more even cooking. Otherwise, when baking, we use a Silpat, a silicone pan liner, to line our aluminum sheet pans.

MIXING BOWLS I really like using heavy ceramic English mixing bowls, and I have a set of these. A variety of stainless-steel or heatproof glass bowls is also very handy.

ELECTRIC MIXERS We use both a **heavy-duty stand mixer** and a sturdy electric **hand mixer** for many tasks, from beating egg whites and whipping cream to making compound butters to blending batters. For a stand mixer, the dependable standby is the KitchenAid 4¼- or 5-quart mixer.

FOOD PROCESSOR The food processor is great for myriad tasks, from making fresh bread crumbs and grinding nuts to pureeing vegetables and blending tart doughs. Cuisinart set the standard for home use; Robot Coupe is the professional model for restaurants.

FOOD MILL This is essentially a sturdy metal strainer fitted with a hand-crank mechanism and interchangeable (fine, medium, and coarse) screens through which cooked foods are passed to achieve a smooth puree. Any fibrous solids, seeds, and so forth are then discarded. This traditional way of pureeing foods results in a finer texture than most other methods, including the food processor and blender.

PASTA MACHINE A manual pasta machine opens the door to innumerable pasta preparations, from filled ravioli and tortellini to long, tender strands of fettuccine. If you find you make pasta often, a **pasta drying rack** will come in handy.

KNIVES Always keep your knives sharp. Clean them by hand after each use and wipe them dry. (In the restaurant world, knife etiquette is important business. You never use someone else's knife. Our cooks bring in and take home their own each day.) Make sure to use a wooden or soft composite cutting board for chopping or slicing. Some so-called cutting boards (synthetic) are way too hard and may damage your knives.

The workhorse of any kitchen is the **chef's knife,** with an 8- to 10-inch-long blade for chopping, slicing, mincing, dicing, and so forth. Wüsthof brand has been a favorite of mine, but MCA from Japan and Sabatier from France are other good choices. Originally designed for pastry use, an **offset serrated knife** is really a great multipurpose knife, especially useful for slicing tomatoes and citrus fruits. F. Dick and Wüsthof make good ones. A regular **serrated bread knife** is also useful. Keep a 3-inch **paring knife** on hand for everyday tasks. A **boning knife** with a thin flexible blade should be used only for boning. A heavy-duty **meat cleaver** is good for dealing with thick bones, while a **Chinese cleaver** is great for those fearful of nicking their fingers: its wide blade keeps them at a safe distance. Another knife that is a great addition to any kitchen is a **carving knife** for turkey, beef, and other roasts. Typically these have a thin blade about 10 inches long. A **diamond steel** is important for keeping your knives sharp, but once knives become dull, it won't sharpen them. Have your knives professionally sharpened when necessary.

Oyster knives and **clam knives** are short, sturdy specialty knives. Buy an oyster knife with a tip that is tilted up. Clam knives are a little thinner and sharper.

SHEARS AND SCISSORS Heavy-duty kitchen shears are fantastic for cutting through poultry bones and the like. A small pair of all-purpose scissors for clipping herbs, cutting parchment paper, and the like is equally essential.

MANDOLINE An inexpensive plastic vegetable slicer is all you really need—although the expensive classic French mandoline, now made of stainless steel, may be tempting. Both types are super for slicing quantities of vegetables such as radishes, cucumbers, and cabbage. Very handy, but mind the fingers and knuckles: most of them come with hand guards—for a reason.

MICROPLANE GRATERS These rasp-type graters are a breakthrough. Long and narrow, they work wonders at finely grating all sorts of ingredients including cheese, chocolate, and, perhaps best of all, citrus zest. Some people use them for "mincing" (i.e., grating) garlic.

MORTAR AND PESTLE The world of cooks is divided between those who think that using a mortar with a pestle is a bit of archaic self-torture and those who rejoice in that age-old feeling of working with a stone or wooden bowl and gradually transforming ingredients (garlic, basil, spices) into an essence of flavor. For the latter, the whirling violence of mechanical choppers will never provide the same satisfaction. I prefer Mexican mortars and pestles. They are great big, heavy, greenish-black volcanic-rock jobs that are very cheap and, strangely enough, often sold in Asian food stores. I find that marble mortars and pestles have too slick a surface, so they are not abrasive enough to be effective.

WHISKS At home, I have a very small wooden-handled whisk, the overall length of which is about 10 inches. It is perfect for making vinaigrettes. A large **balloon whisk** is helpful for whisking egg whites and cream. Medium-sized whisks are perfect for making mayonnaise.

OTHER FAVORITE HAND TOOLS Many cooks prefer the new-style ergonomic pivoting **vegetable peeler;** the problem is that the design makes it all too easy to remove too much of the vegetable. Old-fashioned inexpensive peelers really do the job best; my favorite has a Teflon-coated blade. A pair of 8-inch **tongs** is essential. I think of these as an extension of my own hand, using them to turn foods on the grill or in the sauté pan, removing hot food from the pan, and many other tasks. A small French **fish spatula** with a slotted blade is great for lifting delicate items. And a wooden-handled **Chinese mesh skimmer,** or "spider," is very handy for lifting vegetables out of a pot of boiling water and for removing deep-fried foods from hot oil.

Ladles are another necessity. Although they are a little more expensive, I prefer the heavy-duty one-piece designs; they last forever and you can really bear down when pressing an essence through a sieve. A **fine-mesh sieve** is invaluable for straining delicate sauces. We use a **stainless steel chinois,** or "china cap," a perforated conical strainer, for soups and sauces. **Wire-mesh strainers,** both coarse and fine, are also important.

KITCHEN TWINE This is essential for trussing birds and tying bundles of herbs into a bouquet garni.

THERMOMETERS Have an **oven thermometer** on hand to check your oven periodically to see if it needs calibrating. An **instant-read thermometer** is necessary for testing the temperature of roasted meats. A **deep-frying** or **candy thermometer** is handy for those certain occasions. I also keep a thermometer inside my refrigerator to make sure it keeps foods at the proper temperature.

Sources

ALECIA'S SPECIALTY FOODS
2332 Montevallo Road, SW
Leeds, AL 35094
205-699-6777
tomato chutney

ANSON MILLS
1922-C Gervais Street
Columbia, SC 29201
803-467-4122
www.ansonmills.com
polenta

ASHLEY FARMS
4787 Kinnamon Road
Winston Salem, NC 27103
336-766-9900
www.ashleyfarms.com
naturally raised chicken, guinea, and pheasant

BELLE CHÈVRE
800-735-2238
www.bellechevre.com
artisanal goat cheese

BENTON'S SMOKY MOUNTAIN
COUNTRY HAMS
2603 Highway 411
Madisonville, TN 37354
423-442-5003
www.bentonshams.com
prosciutto, bacon, and ham

BROWNE TRADING COMPANY
260 Commercial Street
Portland, ME 04101
800-944-7848
www.browne-trading.com
seafood and caviar

CHEFS COLLABORATIVE
262 Beacon Street
Boston, MA 02116
617-236-5200
www.chefscollaborative.org

COACH FARM
105 Mill Hill Road
Pine Plains, NY 12567
800-999-4628
www.coachfarm.com
artisanal goat cheeses

COLEMAN NATURAL FOODS
1767 Denver West Marriott
Road, Suite 200
Golden, CO 80401
800-442-8666
www.colemannatural.com
sustainably raised meats and poultry

CORTI BROTHERS
5810 Folsom Boulevard
Sacramento, CA 95819
916-736-3800
www.cortibros.biz
a wide variety of imported and domestic specialty food, including high-quality canned seafood

DEAN & DELUCA
560 Broadway
New York, NY 10012
212-226-6800
www.deananddeluca.com
imported and domestic gourmet foods, including Spanish piquillo peppers

D'ARTAGNAN
280 Wilson Avenue
Newark, NJ 07105
800-327-8246
www.dartagnan.com
game, poultry, cured meats, truffles, and mushrooms

FOREVER CHEESE
36-36 33rd Street, Suite 200
Long Island City, NY 11106
718-777-0722
www.forevercheese.com
imported cheeses

FRESH & WILD
P.O. Box 2981
Vancouver, WA 98668
360-737-3652
wild mushrooms

GREG ABRAMS SEAFOOD, INC.
P.O. Box 1030
Panama City, FL 32402
850-769-4658
gaseafood@aol.com
fresh oysters, shrimp, and pristine Gulf Coast fish

HONOLULU FISH COMPANY
824 Gulick Avenue
Honolulu, HI 96819
888-475-MAHI
www.honolulufish.com
fine Pacific fish

JAMISON FARM
171 Jamison Lane
Latrobe, PA 15650
800.237.5262
www.jamisonfarm.com
naturally raised lamb

LEFISH COMPANY
(owned by Lee Carry)
6920 Hurricane Road
Gilbertown, AL 36908
877-981-8282
Bayou LaBatre shrimp, crab, oysters, redfish, speckled trout

MANICARETTI
5332 College Avenue, Suite 200
Oakland, CA 94618
800-799-9830
www.manicaretti.com
Agrumato oil, pastas

MARCHE AUX DELICES
P.O. Box 1164
New York, NY 10028
888-547-5471
www.auxdelices.com
mushrooms

McEWEN & SONS
Coosa Valley Milling
30620 Highway 25 South
Wilsonville, AL 35186
205-669-6605
www.coosavalleymilling.com
stone-ground yellow, white, and blue corn grits and polenta

MEYER RANCH
300 Red Angus Lane
Helmville, MT 59853
406-793-5653
www.meyerbeef.com
sustainably raised meats

NIMAN RANCH
P.O. Box 90460
San Jose, CA 95109
510-808-0330
www.nimanranch.com
naturally raised pork and beef

PENZEYS SPICES
P.O. Box 933
Muskego, WI 53150
800-741-7787
www.penzeys.com
spices, dried herbs, dried chiles

PREVIN INC.
2044 Rittenhouse Square
Philadelphia, PA 19103
888-285-9947
www.previninc.com
specialty kitchen equipment

SLOW FOOD USA
434 Broadway, 6th Floor
New York, NY 10013
212-965-5640
www.slowfoodusa.org

SNAPPER GRABBERS SEAFOOD
MARKET
(also owned by Lee Carry)
521 Montgomery Highway
Birmingham, AL 35216
205-824-9799
Gulf Coast seafood (see LeFish, above)

SWEET GRASS DAIRY
19635 U.S. Highway 19N
Thomasville, GA 31792
229-227-0752
www.sweetgrassdairy.com
artisanal cheeses

ZINGERMAN'S
620 Phoenix Drive
Ann Arbor, MI 48108
888-636-8162
www.zingermans.com
olive oils from across the globe, and many other specialty foods

Acknowledgments

Pardis, my wife, came into Bottega's life about eighteen years ago, and she has restored it, nursed it, prodded it, and inspired it. The same could be said for her effect upon me and this book. By her smile and hypercritical dark-brown eyes she entices us, and without her sprinkling of fairy dust, none of this would be possible.

Our staff is too vast to mention all, but Bob North has been with us since day one, a veteran of the highest order; our chef, John Rolen, Dolester Miles, Jeff Mincey, Cliff Lawler, Clarence Young, Pat Thompson, Mary Ann Saylor, and Geri Crenshaw all deserve to be recognized for their loyalty and honor.

Christopher Hirsheimer, her vision, her photographs, and her friendship are a blessing and I cherish our time together (along the back roads of Alabama or the hills of Barbaresco).

Katherine Cobbs has worked tirelessly to pull these stories out of me, her determined spirit pushed me time and time again to dig deeper to expose the kernels of truth that explain the glorious magic of the Bottega story and its food. Katherine has been with me every step of the way, and her creative intelligence has helped shape this book in the most profound way. She organized a legion of home cooks who tested and retested these recipes whenever necessary—thanks to them all.

The farmers: Margaret Ann Toohuy and David Snow, Michael Dean, Edwin Marty, and Jason Powell.

The fishermen: Greg Abrams and Lee Fish; our hog farmer, Henry Fudge; John and Sukey Jamison for their lamb; Ron Joyce for his guinea fowl, chickens, and pheasant—thank you for caring for the land and providing us with ingredients that are respected.

Thanks to Wendell Berry for being the greatest spokesperson for small farms, and thanks to Michael Pollan for his common sense. Thanks to my fellow Southern chefs who inspire and push me, especially Ben Barker, Hugh Acheson, Linton Hopkins, and Mike Latta. Thanks to Mario Battali for being chef "in full" and for his brilliant restaurants; to Daniel Boulud for his pursuit of excellence; and to the spirit of my mentor, Richard Olney, for his obsession with food and wine.

Thanks to the Cipriani family for all the dreamlike moments, lingering lunches, and decadent dinners at Harry's Bar in Venice; and thanks to La Fontellina on Capri for the most perfect summer lunches on earth.

Thanks to our patrons who enter our doors and support what we love doing.

Thanks to Ann Bramson and her team at Artisan for their patience, belief, and guidance.

Finally thanks to my long-gone parents, Marie and Dr. Frank Stitt Jr., for molding me and bringing us together at our kitchen table; and to my children, Marie and Weston, who I love more than all the stars in the sky.

Index